Nursing and Informatics for the 21st Century – Embracing a Digital World, 3rd Edition, Book 2

Nursing and Informatics for the 21st Century – Embracing a Digital World, 3rd Edition is comprised of four books which can be purchased individually at www.routledge.com:

Book 1: Realizing Digital Health – Bold Challenges and Opportunities for Nursing – ISBN: 9780367516888

Book 2: Nursing Education and Digital Health Strategies – ISBN: 9781032249728

Book 3: Innovation, Technology, and Applied Informatics for Nurses – ISBN: 9781032249803

Book 4: Nursing in an Integrated Digital World that Supports People, Systems, and the Planet – ISBN: 9781032249827

Nursing and Informatics for the 21st Century – Embracing a Digital World, 3rd Edition, Book 2

Nursing Education and Digital Health Strategies

Edited by
Connie White Delaney, PhD, RN, FAAN, FACMI, FNAP
Charlotte A. Weaver, PhD, MSPH, RN, FHIMSS, FAAN
Joyce Sensmeier, MS, RN-BC, FHIMSS, FAAN
Lisiane Pruinelli, PhD, MS, RN, FAMIA
Patrick Weber, MA, RN, FIAHSI, FGBHI

Foreword by Deborah Trautman, PhD, RN, FAAN
President and Chief Executive Officer,
American Association of Colleges of Nursing

Foreword by Kedar Mate, MD
President and CEO,
Institute for Healthcare Improvement

Foreword by Howard Catton
Chief Executive Officer,
International Council of Nurses

A PRODUCTIVITY PRESS BOOK

First published 2022
by Routledge
605 Third Avenue, New York, NY 10158

and by Routledge
2 Park Square, Milton Park, Abingdon, Oxon, OX14 4RN

Routledge is an imprint of the Taylor & Francis Group, an informa business

© 2022 selection and editorial matter, Connie White Delaney, Charlotte A. Weaver, Joyce Sensmeier, Lisiane Pruinelli & Patrick Weber; individual chapters, the contributors

The right of Connie White Delaney, Charlotte A. Weaver, Joyce Sensmeier, Lisiane Pruinelli & Patrick Weber to be identified as the authors of the editorial material, and of the authors for their individual chapters, has been asserted in accordance with sections 77 and 78 of the Copyright, Designs and Patents Act 1988.

All rights reserved. No part of this book may be reprinted or reproduced or utilised in any form or by any electronic, mechanical, or other means, now known or hereafter invented, including photocopying and recording, or in any information storage or retrieval system, without permission in writing from the publishers.

Trademark notice: Product or corporate names may be trademarks or registered trademarks, and are used only for identification and explanation without intent to infringe.

ISBN: 9781032249780 (hbk)
ISBN: 9781032249728 (pbk)
ISBN: 9781003281009 (ebk)

DOI: 10.4324/9781003281009

Typeset in Garamond
by Deanta Global Publishing Services, Chennai, India

Dedication for Connie White Delaney

Responding to the urgent and powerful invitation for community, partnership and collaboration, this *Nursing and Informatics for the 21st Century—Embracing a Digital World*, 3rd Edition is dedicated to all individuals, organizations and informaticians who are co-creating futures, health and healthcare. May these co-created informatics-anchored futures radiate the brain of intellect and wisdom, the brain of heart and compassion, and the action brain of impact, voice, caring and awakening.

Dedication for Charlotte A. Weaver

Reflecting these painful times, this dedication goes out to all our frontline nurses and fellow healthcare workers who have taken care of us all around the globe at the risk of their own lives and well-being. We owe you.

Dedication for Joyce Sensmeier

To my husband and life partner, who has faithfully supported my informatics journey, encouraging me to take risks along the way and congratulating me on every success. Thank you for believing in me.

Dedication for Lisiane Pruinelli

To those who battle every day for a better world … 'I don't write a book so that it will be the final word; I write a book so that other books are possible, not necessarily written by me.'—Michel Foucault

Dedication for Patrick Weber

For the sake of the population, the empowerment of nurses worldwide is the best effort to improve disease prevention and promote good health. Thank you to my co-editors and all the authors for their work on this book series.

Contents

Foreword by Deborah Trautman ix
Foreword by Kedar Mate xi
Foreword by Howard Catton xiii
Preface xv
Acknowledgement xxi
Editors xxiii
Contributors xxvii
Introduction xxxi

1 Nursing Informatics Educational Programs in Academia and in Practice 1
   BRENDA KULHANEK AND PATRICIA SENGSTACK

2 International Health and Healthcare Education Current State 19
   POLUN CHANG, JOHN MANTAS, CHIAO-LING CHELSEY HSU,
   I-CHING EVITA HOU, YUAN CHEN, QIAN XIAO, MEIHUA JI,
   JIWEN SUN, CUIHONG LIU

3 Health and Healthcare Education Current State 47
   JANE MARIE KIRSCHLING AND MARY ETTA MILLS

4 Using Digital as a Tool, Not Being the Tool of the Technology Giants 63
   PETER KLEIN, BOB BARKER, KEVIN BRYANT AND
   ALEXANDER M.K. MACKENZIE

5 Learning from Clients/Patients to Advance Education and Scholarship 81
   JENNIE C. DE GAGNE, KATRINA GREEN AND
   MARGARET H. STURDIVANT

6 Cultivating a Workforce of Nurse Disruptors: An Academic–Practice Innovation Hub 95
LINDA MCCAULEY, SHARON PAPPAS AND ROSE HAYES

7 Nursing Education and Digital Health Strategies 113
MARISA L. WILSON

8 Nursing Informatics Competencies for the Next Decade 131
ERIKA LOZADA PEREZMITRE, SAMIRA ALI AND
LAURA-MARIA PELTONEN

9 Interprofessional Practice and Education: Interrelationship with Knowledge Generation, the IPE Core Data Set and National Information Exchange Infrastructure 149
LAURA PEJSA, CHRISTINE ARENSON, JAMES T. PACALA,
JENNIFER KERTZ AND BARBARA BRANDT

10 The use of the IMIA Education Recommendations and the IMIA Knowledge Base as a Foundation for Competencies in Health Informatics in Africa.. 171
GRAHAM WRIGHT, HELEN J. BETTS, FRANK VERBEKE,
MARTIN C. WERE, FRANCES B. DA-COSTA VROOM AND
KIMUTAI SOME

11 Simulation-Based Learning from across the Globe 183
JUAN ANTONIO MURO SANS, LAURA GONZALEZ AND
VIRGINIA LA ROSA-SALAS

Index 201

Foreword

When the nation's nursing school deans voted to endorse *The Essentials: Core Competencies for Professional Nursing Education* in April 2021, new competency expectations for tomorrow's nurses came into focus. Driven in part by the need to ensure consistency among graduates of entry-level and advanced-level nursing education programs, one area receiving special emphasis across roles is nursing informatics. As we considered how best to prepare professional nurses to thrive in the future, the need for providers to 'use information and communication technologies and informatics processes to deliver safe nursing care to diverse populations in a variety of settings' (Essential 8.3) was affirmed as a key competency expectation.

Over the past 20 years, informatics increasingly has been a focus in nursing education, given the rapid rise in the use of technology to guide healthcare delivery and clinical decision-making and the need to critically consider all available data when engaging in evidence-based practice and precision healthcare. Basic informatics competencies are foundational to all nursing practice.

Reaching this point in the evolution of our understanding of informatics would not have been possible without pioneers in the field. The authors of *Nursing and Informatics for the 21st Century—Embracing a Digital World*, 3rd Edition—Connie White Delaney, Charlotte A. Weaver, Joyce Sensmeier, Lisiane Pruinelli and Patrick Weber—stand among the world's leading authorities on health informatics, data science and digital health. Committed to enhancing the scholarship of discovery, these nurse leaders are known internationally for their trailblazing work that has been recognized by such authorities as the Alliance for Nursing Informatics, American Medical Informatics Association, International Academy of Health Sciences Informatics and the Healthcare Information and Management Systems Society. Their pedigrees are undeniable, their thought leadership profound.

The publication of this expansive resource comes at a time when nursing is once again divining its future into the next decade. In addition to the re-envisioned AACN's *Essentials*, which is setting a new standard for nursing education, recent National Academy of Medicine reports on *The Future of Nursing* and *Implementing High Quality Primary Care* point the way forward for nursing practice, research priorities and interprofessional engagement. All these paths demand a greater understanding and reliance on informatics as a driver of innovation and impact. Further, healthcare's move to address pressing social needs, including a shared desire to achieve health equity, gain insight into the social determinants of health, expand consumer access to data and attend to global health concerns are all considered within the context of digital technologies and applied data science as part of this new book series.

Nursing and Informatics for the 21st Century—Embracing a Digital World, 3rd Edition will be of great interest to nurses and other health professionals in the US and globally who are eager to learn more about leveraging automated systems and emerging science to sustain health and improve healthcare delivery. This book series serves as an important resource for practice leaders, nurse researchers, systems analysts, healthcare consumers and graduate students looking to explore opportunities for innovation that develop at the nexus of nursing science, emerging technologies, critical thinking and patient-centered care.

As we look to a future with nursing education that is more competency-based, informatics will be front and center. For faculty wishing to keep pace with the latest thinking on contemporary nursing education and practice, this essential resource will help to inform your understanding about the value and reach of informatics and may also generate new ideas for developing experiential learning opportunities using artificial intelligence, telehealth, simulation and other leading-edge technologies. These emerging tools and practices are transforming nursing roles as well as the skills and knowledge needed to manage care remotely. This comprehensive work will help lead conversations to inspire future generations of nurses to explore how best to leverage nursing informatics in their research, practice and leadership roles.

Deborah Trautman, PhD, RN, FAAN
President and Chief Executive Officer
American Association of Colleges of Nursing

Foreword

Walk onto any clinical service unit in a modern hospital, and you will realize that clinical practice today is a fully socio-technological phenomenon—entirely reliant both upon a nurse's compassion and upon our technology's capacity to supply information and services just in time. Technologies are no longer working their way into health and healthcare—they are already integral to both. But the promise of these incredibly exciting digital therapeutics, diagnostics and monitoring systems depends on, just as more conventional medicines have for decades, the human systems required to implement them. This interface—between nurses and the digital information that can make care more effective, efficient, and reliable—is at the heart of 21st-century nursing informatics.

Years ago, the field of quality improvement in healthcare started with a simple premise—we could work on those human processes to take the fruits of clinical science—medications, new diagnostic assays, vaccines—and more reliably deliver them to patients to create lasting health effects. It is time for a complementary agenda—quality and reliability sciences must now be applied to improve the delivery of proven digital therapies and diagnostics. Just as we created reliable workflows that delivered antibiotics that would prevent sepsis deaths, so too must we create workflows that will leverage new data sources and technologies to improve the way we care for patients. Digital will change healthcare just as antibiotics have, but neither will achieve impact without implementation methods that ensure that the 'medicine' gets to the patient.

This is crucial because of the incredible potential of technology and data to improve care and outcomes. Consider how good artificial intelligence (AI)-guided diagnosis and triage have become: for some clinical conditions, AI now gets diagnostic and treatment accuracy over 90% right compared to clinicians in urgent care environments. These technologies won't replace the nurse or the physician, but they can radically affect the capacity of a clinician to see patients. If much of the time-consuming fact-finding, differential diagnosis, care plan documentation, and charting can be done by an AI-guided automated assistant, nurses can spend much more time caring for patients.

Realizing technology's transformative potential in nursing requires a comprehensive understanding of how to turn data into information; information into knowledge; knowledge into wisdom; and wisdom into applied practice. This book series is essential to such an understanding. This new edition is a detailed and exhaustive exploration of the myriad contexts, approaches, challenges and success stories of how effective informatics can improve every dimension of health, including the fiercely urgent dimensions of needing to improve access to care and ensuring health equity.

For those new to the field of informatics, this series contains an illuminating history of the rapid and profound changes in digital health over the past decade. And for those with deep experience in the field, there are chapters detailing both what's happening at the cutting-edge and what the future holds. Anyone who wants to improve nursing practice in the modern era needs to read this book series and heed its calls to action.

Kedar Mate, MD
President and CEO
Institute for Healthcare Improvement

Foreword

As the COVID-19 pandemic has so painfully shown us, it is hard to accurately predict the future. While the temptation is to spend time and effort on futurology—it can be hard to resist—our time is probably better spent on trying to prepare flexibly for what is coming next and, in some way, help to shape it.

What seems certain is that digital health will feature in our futures and that nurses are in a prime position to take advantage of the benefits it can bring. In fact, as we have seen, recent developments in digital health are some of the few positives to have come out of the pandemic.

Finding ways to deal with the pandemic brought about a rapid increase in access to digitally enhanced care, whether it be through the use of videoconferencing for consultations and telehealth or through increased access to massive amounts of data that were previously buried and heavily guarded in the depths of healthcare organizations' information technology systems. The issue now is understanding the data and using it meaningfully to improve services and reduce costs.

While only a year or so ago it would have been correct to say the future is digital, we can now say that, in many parts of the world, digital health is already here and that it looks like it's here to stay. We can see it in the development of nurse-led models of care and how the use of data and new equipment is changing the traditional, paternalistic models of care to more responsive ones that are personalized, faster, sustainable and more affordable.

The biggest challenge ahead will be to expand access to nursing informatics to all nurses, wherever they are so that they can provide equitable access to state-of-the-art care to people everywhere.

This is especially important as the world deals with and recovers from the COVID-19 pandemic. Nurse-led models of care, underpinned by access to data, are a big part of the solution as we strengthen our health systems for the post-pandemic world to come.

I am delighted to write this foreword for what is likely to be a very influential book series about nursing and informatics and how nurses can maximize the impact of digital health for the benefit of patients and their families and the health systems that they work in.

In the past, information technology has promised so much but often failed to deliver on its potential. If it is to fulfil its promise, it must be an enabler for people to be empowered, and it must improve access to services, the quality and efficiency of those services, and the patient's care and health outcomes.

For this to happen, the people on the receiving end of care need to be at the centre of the systems that are developed, and nurses must be involved in all stages of their design, development and implementation. In the past, we have seen how the ill-thought-out introduction of some systems has taken nurses away from direct care, to the detriment of their patients and the annoyance of the nurses.

Nurses do not want to spend hours in front of computer screens, as they have been required to in the past. They do not want to spend their time inputting data into counterintuitive systems that do not meet their requirements. What they want is quick and easy access to the information they need at their fingertips, in people's homes, at the nurses' station on wards, at the bedside and in the clinics where they work, in real time while they are interacting with their patients.

We see the power of technology and data-driven change across the globe, from low- to high-income settings, from the use of Apps on mobile phones to the adoption of sophisticated information systems and algorithms. But underlying it all is the continuing need for a highly skilled and educated nursing workforce. Whatever the future holds in terms of information technology, artificial intelligence and robotics, they will always be used in support of the compassion, the relationships and the dynamic human factors that only nurses can provide.

This *Nursing and Informatics for the 21st Century—Embracing a Digital World*, 3rd Edition shows the path ahead for our profession to become fully digitally enabled. I am sure it will prove to be an indispensable guide along the way.

Howard Catton
Chief Executive Officer
International Council of Nurses

Preface

While we commit to living in the 21st century and maintaining our open minds and hearts to the needs, wishes and wisdom that will inform our future, we have found the pace of change to be challenging in preparing this book series. Every day, new technologies and partnerships are in the social news media, and healthcare systems announce new digital health programs that push care out into the hands of patients and into the home. Additionally, these new care modalities and technology changes are occurring simultaneously with national and international policy mandates to address social injustices and inequities, equality in access to care, and planetary health. Tremendous innovation has transpired since the publication of this book's second edition in 2010. In that space of time, medical sensing devices and mobile technologies have become ubiquitous, permeating every aspect of our lives. Concurrently, the synergistic effect of new technologies and tools such as cloud data storage, application programming interfaces, artificial intelligence and machine learning are game changers in advancing digital health. Together with legislation and regulatory changes, the proprietary limitations of electronic health record (EHR) systems have been upended. The voice of the consumer and insistence on patient-centered, connected and readily accessible care have never had greater velocity, urging our unremitting attention.

Thus, in planning this third edition, we abandoned the previous framework of presenting an 'international snapshot of current state' on EHR adoption and nursing. Technology changes and new applications that extract data, apply AI systems, dashboards, and suggest care protocols made a primary EHR framework irrelevant. Increasingly, economics and policy mandates push healthcare systems to embrace a preventative, wellness and population health focus that requires new thinking toward advanced technology applications that extend services into clinics, community and the home. In the United States, reimbursement linked to Alternative Payment Models (APM) and 'value-based purchasing' with dependency on quality metrics require healthcare systems to collaborate with community resources and post-acute care providers. All collaboration, local to world-wide, demands exchanging and sharing information, as well as actively engaging individual patients and their families. A plethora of digital/mobile applications have emerged to fill this evolving 'non-acute care/non-EHR' space. As chapters from geographic areas spanning the globe describe, economic imperatives, mandates to deliver equal access to care in rural as well as metro areas, and the need to incorporate social determinants of health into care delivery have also driven the adoption of digital health solutions. Therefore, this third edition focuses on these new technologies and the care delivery models they make possible: thus, we gave this work the subtitle *'Embracing a Digital World.'*

Kristine Mednansky, Senior Editor from Taylor & Francis Group, LLC, asked us to consider a new edition, based on feedback from the readers of our previous works. Our full gratitude goes to Ms Mednansky for this series' existence. Her voice was the key driver for creating this work, the *Nursing and Informatics for the 21st Century*, 3rd Edition. Ms Mednansky ensured that this current work would meet the needs of readers in a variety of formats: electronic, print, and the option to purchase either an individual chapter or an entire book. Moreover, readers will note another major difference in the look and feel of the previous hardcover book: this work has been converted to a four-book series to deliver a resource that is more easily consumed. Our hope is that with this flexibility in access and usability, the work embodied in this collection of contributing authors will be widely read and extensively shared. We look forward to receiving your feedback on this novel approach.

This work is organized into a series of four books, each with 11 chapters: (1) Realizing Digital Health–Bold Challenges and Opportunities for Nursing; (2) Nursing Education and Digital Health Strategies; (3) Innovation, Technology, and Applied Informatics for Nurses; and (4) Nursing in an Integrated Digital World that Supports People, Systems, and the Planet. Each book in the series includes international contributors with authors from Africa and South Africa, Brazil, Belgium, Canada, China, England, Finland, Germany, Italy, Norway, the Philippines, South Korea, Sri Lanka, Switzerland, Taiwan, and the United States, as well as authors of additional exemplars from China, India and the West Balkan countries. Throughout this series, the wisdom of leading-edge innovators is interwoven with digital health applications, global thought leaders and multinational, cooperative research initiatives, all against the backdrop of health equity and policy-setting bodies, such as the United Nations and the World Health Organization.

We begin Book 1 of the series by introducing the paradigm of digital health, and its underlying technologies, offering examples of its potential use and future impacts. This introduction is followed by an in-depth look at the ethical considerations in digital health that nurses and informaticists need to understand, authored by an international team of nursing informatics leaders from Finland, Canada and England. The growing movement in consumerism and patient engagement is described in a collaborative research initiative between academia–government–industry. This chapter is bolstered by numerous exemplars, all illustrating the importance of the engaged patient enabled by new digital technologies with the goal of making possible comprehensive access to individuals' digital health information, regardless of system or location. Several chapters focus on the underlying need for terminology and data standards to capture the data necessary to enable new science and knowledge discoveries. Subsequent chapters outline the critical and urgent role that nurse executive leaders' play in advancing digital health, as well as the knowledge and skills needed to take advantage of new digital technologies. We follow with chapters on the role(s) of nursing informatics leaders in large, US health systems, as well as a global perspective from Brazil, Italy and the Philippines. To provide a clear understanding of the challenges facing the United Nations and World Health Organizations' goals for health equity and equality, we include a critical examination of South Africa's healthcare delivery system, technologies and nursing's role across these structural segments. We close Book 1 with a look at the information sharing needed to support true team care spanning multiple settings and systems.

Book 2 is dedicated to a deep examination of nursing education's best practices, strategies, and informatics competencies. The chapters included in Book 2 span nursing education and learning for applied critical thinking, including the use of technology, content, skills versus tools, the use of 'smart' systems for care delivery and the role of critical thinking as essential to nursing care delivery. These concepts are understood as a paradigm shift that must be incorporated into nursing and healthcare education. Best practices for workforce and degree-level education are presented in a description of Emory's Academic/Practice partnership focusing on disruption through nurse innovation enabled by all nurses and students having access to big data. This book closes with a review of innovative methodologies being used in simulation labs across the globe, including some uses of virtual and augmented reality simulations.

Book 3 defines the foundations of artificial intelligence (AI), machine learning (ML) and various digital technologies, including social media, the Internet of Things, telehealth and applied data analytics, all with a look toward the future state. The Applied Healthcare Data Science Roadmap is presented as a framework aiming to educate healthcare leaders on the use of data science principles and tools to inform decision-making. We focus particular attention on the cautions, potential for harm, and biases that artificial intelligence technologies and machine learning may pose in healthcare, with the role of advocate and protector from harm falling under the nurse's role. Book 3 concludes by outlining four case studies featuring innovations developed by nurses in response to COVID-19, which highlight the creative use of technologies to support patients, care providers and healthcare systems during the global pandemic.

We continue with a focus on the theme of enabling digital technologies in Book 4 as they are used to address planetary health issues and care equity across developing countries. Throughout the development of this series, the world has struggled with the core issues of equity in access to care, needed medical equipment and supplies and vaccines. Sustainability and global health policy are linked to the new digital technologies in the chapters that illustrate healthcare delivery modalities, which nurse innovators are developing, leading and using to deliver care to hard-to-reach populations for better population health. Social media use in South Korea for health messaging, community initiatives and nursing research are presented with additional references to other Asian countries. A US description of consumer engagement with patient ownership of all their medical records data is presented with the underlying technologies explained in simple, understandable terms. Additionally, we tapped experts to highlight the legal statutes, government regulations and civil rights law in place for patients' rights, privacy and confidentiality, and consents for the United States, the United Kingdom and the European Union. The next chapter in Book 4 is written by two participants of the 'Future of Nursing 2020–2030' task force who deliver an optimistic message. These authors recognize the work that needs to be done around health equity and equality and review nursing's role responsibilities to effect these changes. Their optimism comes from all the opportunities that social policy and enabling digital technologies make possible for nursing. The authors outline how these changes in care delivery models, the patient/provider role and dependence on digital tools all present opportunities for new nursing roles, access to expansive data resources for research with the exponential growth of our science base and for entrepreneurship.

We conclude this book series with a chapter written by the editors in which we envision the near future. We explore the impact that digital technologies will have on: a) how care is delivered, including expanding care settings into community and home; b) virtual monitoring; and c) the type and quantity of patient-generated data and how it is used to advance knowledge and care excellence. Ultimately these changes highlight the numerous ways that nursing roles and skill sets related to digital health are needed to support the global goal of equal access to health and care. We emphasize the necessity for partnering. We send the message that nursing, along with our transdisciplinary partners, is being called to lead and create unparalleled transformation of healthcare to person-centered, connected and accessible care anchored in digital health.

Acknowledgement

We share our deep gratitude with all of the persons, including care providers, researchers, educators, business and corporate leaders, and informatics experts in all settings, for requesting an update to the second edition of *Nursing and Informatics for the 21st Century*. Together, you recognized the value and synergy of nursing and informatics, the core function of informatics in shaping nursing, health and healthcare, and the reciprocal learning that a global perspective offers us. Thank you to Taylor & Francis Group, LLC, and especially Kristine Mednansky, Senior Editor, for giving us the opportunity to produce this third edition as a totally new body of work in this post-EHR era. But most especially, for your creativity and flexibility as we presented a book double our original plan. Thus, this third edition is presented as a four-book series enveloping *Nursing and Informatics for the 21st Century*. We are deeply humbled by the dedication, work and creativity of our contributing authors, many of whom formed teams that expanded across continents to be able to capture the fullest coverage and latest information. The contributors bring state-of-the-art knowledge, coupled with real-world practice and education. It is the integration of nursing and informatics knowledge and practice that will sustain our health, communities and planet. Last, we would be remiss not to say a deep thank you to Midori V. Green, our project manager par excellence, who kept us organized and on track through her diplomacy and hard work and without which we would not have made our deadlines.

In gratitude,

Connie White Delaney
Charlotte A. Weaver
Joyce Sensmeier
Lisiane Pruinelli
Patrick Weber

Editors

Connie White Delaney, PhD, RN, FAAN, FACMI, FNAP serves as Professor and Dean at the University of Minnesota School of Nursing and is the Knowledge Generation Lead for the National Center for Interprofessional Practice and Education. She served as Associate Director of the Clinical Translational Science Institute—Biomedical Informatics, and Acting Director of the Institute for Health Informatics (IHI) in the Academic Health Center from 2010 to 2015. She serves as an adjunct professor in the Faculty of Medicine and Faculty of Nursing at the University of Iceland, where she received the Doctor Scientiae Curationis Honoris Causa (Honorary Doctor of Philosophy in Nursing) in 2011. She is an elected Fellow in the American Academy of Nursing, American College of Medical Informatics, and National Academies of Practice. Delaney is the first Fellow in the College of Medical Informatics to serve as a Dean of Nursing. Delaney was an inaugural appointee to the USA Health Information Technology Policy Committee, Office of the National Coordinator, and Office of the Secretary for the U.S. Department of Health and Human Services (HHS). She is an active researcher in data and information technology standards for nursing, healthcare. Delaney is past president of Friends of the National Institute of Nursing Research (FNINR) and currently serves as Vice-Chair of CGFNS, Inc. She holds a BSN with majors in nursing and mathematics, MA in Nursing, PhD Educational Administration and Computer Applications, postdoctoral study in Nursing & Medical Informatics and a Certificate in Integrative Therapies & Healing Practices.

Charlotte A. Weaver, Ph.D., MSPH, RN, FHIMSS, FAAN is a visionary senior executive, now retired after 40+ years of experience in nursing informatics, patient safety and quality, evidence-based nursing practices and healthcare automation in acute, ambulatory and post-acute care. She created a breakthrough in the nursing educational curricula by introducing learning using an electronic health record (EHR) in virtual environments and pioneered the corporate-level, Chief Nurse Officer role. She also has Board Director experience in the public/non-profit healthcare sectors. With 15+ years of experience at the chief executive level in the corporate HIT industry and healthcare delivery organizations with Board-reporting responsibilities, her fields of specialization include EHR, health IT policy, post-acute care delivery in home health and hospice provider organizations. Dr. Weaver serves on a number of academic, healthcare systems and healthcare technology company Boards. She is a fellow in the American Academy of Nursing and the Health Information Management Systems Society (HIMSS). She is a frequent presenter at national and international conferences and has published extensively as a writer and editor. Dr. Weaver has a PhD in Medical Anthropology from the University of California, Berkeley and San Francisco, an MSPH in Epidemiology and a BA in Anthropology from the University of Washington, and a Nursing diploma from St Elizabeth's School of Nursing. She was a post-doctoral fellow at the University of Hawaii.

Joyce Sensmeier, MS, RN-BC, FHIMSS, FAAN is the Senior Advisor, Informatics for HIMSS, a non-profit organization focused on reforming the global health ecosystem through the power of information and technology. In this role, she provides thought leadership in the areas of clinical informatics, interoperability and standards programs and initiatives. Sensmeier served as Vice President, Informatics at HIMSS from 2005 to 2019. She is president of IHE USA, a non-profit organization whose mission is to improve our nation's healthcare by promoting the adoption and use of IHE and other world-class standards, tools and services for interoperability. An internationally recognized speaker and author of numerous book chapters and articles, Sensmeier achieved fellowship in the American Academy of Nursing in 2010.

Lisiane Pruinelli PhD, MS, RN, FAMIA is an Assistant Professor and co-director of the Center for Nursing Informatics in the School of Nursing and Affiliate Faculty at the Institute for Health Informatics, University of Minnesota. She is a Fellow of the American Medical Informatics Association and a University of Minnesota School of Nursing Global Health Scholar. She serves as the co-chair of the Nursing Knowledge Big Data Science Initiative, co-chair for the Data Science and Clinical Analytics workgroup, and as an advisor board member for the International Medical Informatics Association—Student and Emerging Professional interest group. Previously, she served as a co-chair for the Midwest Nursing Research Society Nursing Informatics workgroup. With more than ten years of clinical experience in both transplant coordination and information systems development and implementation, she is part of a new generation of nursing informaticians focused on applied clinical informatics. Her expertise is in applying innovative nursing informatics tools and cutting-edge data science methods to investigate the trajectory of complex disease conditions suitable for clinical implementations. Her work aims to identify the problems and targeted interventions for better patient outcomes. Dr. Pruinelli grew up in Brazil, moved to USA in 2012 and brings an international and diverse perspective to her everyday work and life. She earned a PhD degree from the University of Minnesota School of Nursing in 2016, and a Master's of Sciences (2008), a Teaching Degree in Nursing (2002) and a Bachelor of Nursing Sciences (2000) degree from the Federal University of Rio Grande do Sul, Porto Alegre, Brazil.

Patrick Weber, MA, RN, FIAHSI, FGBHI is Founder, Director and Principal of Nice Computing, SA in Lausanne, Switzerland. He holds a MA degree in healthcare management and is a Registered Nurse with a diploma degree in nursing. Weber has been an active leader in the European health informatics field for over 30 years, serving as his country's representative to IMIA-Nursing for over a decade and has held numerous board-level positions in IMIA-Nursing as well. Weber is an active member and leader in the European Federation for Medical Informatics (EFMI) and has held numerous leadership positions including treasurer, vice president, president and past president over the past decades. He has served as the vice president of MedInfo 2019 at International Medical Informatics Association (IMIA) and vice president Europe, and is currently the IMIA Liaison Officer to WHO, Geneva. Within his own country, Weber leads the expert group for Swiss DRG quality control for medical coding and is President of the Oliver Moeschler Foundation leading pre-hospitalization healthcare emergencies. He is EFMI Leader of EU H2020 projects such as CrowdHealth, FAIR4Health and HosmartAI. He is the co-editor of *Nursing Informatics for the 21st Century: An International Look at Practice, Trends and Future,* first and second editions; *Nursing Informatics 2016 eHealth for All: Every Level Collaboration – From Project to Realization;* and *Forecasting Informatics Competencies for Nurses in the Future of Connected Health.* Weber is a founding member of the International Academy of Health Sciences Informatics and a member of the Board of the Swiss Medical Coding Association.

Contributors

Samira Ali, DNP, RN, Grand Canyon University

Christine Arenson, MD, Co-Director, National Center for Interprofessional Practice & Education; and Professor, Department of Family Medicine and Community Health, University of Minnesota

Bob Barker, CWO, Advisor, Educated Change LLC

Barbara Brandt, PhD, Founding Director, National Center for Interprofessional Practice & Education, University of Minnesota

Helen J. Betts, EdD, MEd (SEN), BA, PGCEA, SRN, SCM, ADM, MTD, HELINA Education Working Group

Kevin Bryant, Chief Executive Officer, Educated Change LLC

Polun Chang, PhD, National Yang-Ming Chiao-Tung University

Yuan Chen, MS, RN, Xiamen Cardiovascular Hospital Xiamen University

Jennie C. De Gagne, PhD, DNP, RN, NPD-BC, CNE, ANEF, FAAN, Professor, Duke University School of Nursing

Katrina Green, MSN, RN, NPD-BC, Administrative Director, Clinical Education and Professional Development, Duke University Health System

Laura Gonzalez, PhD, APRN, CNE, CHSE-A, ANEF, FAAN, Vice President, Clinical Learning Resources Sentinel U

Rose Hayes, MA, RN, BSN, Emory University Nell Hodgson Woodruff School of Nursing

I-Ching Evita Hou, PhD, RN, National Yang-Ming Chiao-Tung University

Chiao-Ling Chelsey Hsu, MS, RN, National Yang-Ming Chiao-Tung University

Meihua Ji, PhD, RN, School of Nursing, Capital Medical University

Cuihong Liu, MS, RN, Affiliated Eye Hospital of Shandong University of Traditional Chinese Medicine

Jennifer Kertz, MPP, Deputy Director/Chief Operating Officer, National Center for Interprofessional Practice & Education, University of Minnesota

Jane Marie Kirschling, PhD, RN, FAAN, Bill and Joanne Conway Dean of Nursing, Professor, University of Maryland School of Nursing; and Director, Interprofessional Education Center, University of Maryland, Baltimore

Peter Klein, Founder, Educated Change LLC

Brenda Kulhanek, PhD, RN, RN-BC, NPD-BC, NE-BC, Vanderbilt University School of Nursing

Alexander M.K. Mackenzie, MSc, Chief Informatics Strategy Officer & Partner, Educated Change LLC

John Mantas, PhD, FEFMI, FACMI, FIAHSI, National and Kapodistrian University of Athens

Linda McCauley, PhD, RN, FAAN, FAAOHN, Emory University Nell Hodgson Woodruff School of Nursing

Mary Etta Mills, ScD, RN, NEA-BC, FAAN, Professor, University of Maryland School of Nursing

James T. Pacala, MD, MS, Professor and Head, Department of Family Medicine and Community Health; Project Director, Minnesota Northstar Geriatrics Workforce Enhancement Program, University of Minnesota

Sharon Pappas, PhD, RN, NEA-BC, FAAN, Emory Healthcare

Laura Pejsa, PhD, Director of Evaluation and Organizational Learning, National Center for Interprofessional Practice & Education, Minnesota Northstar Geriatrics Workforce Enhancement Program, University of Minnesota

Laura-Maria Peltonen, PhD, Docent, FEANS, Department of Nursing Science, University of Turku

Erika Lozada Perezmitre, MPH, RN, Nursing Faculty, Benemérita Universidad Autónoma de Puebla

Virginia La Rosa-Salas, PhD, BSc, MSc, Head of the Simulation Center Faculty of Nursing, Universidad de Navarra

Juan Antonio Muro Sans, PhDc, PgD, BScHon, RN, Head of Simulation Education Program HESAV

Patricia Sengstack, DNP, RN-BC, FAAN, FACMI, Vanderbilt University School of Nursing

Kimutai Some, PhD, MSc, BSc Eng, School of Engineering, University of Eldoret

Margaret H. Sturdivant, MSN, RN, CPPS, Administrative Director, Clinical Education and Professional Development, Duke University Health System

Jiwen Sun, MS, RN, Shanghai Children's Medical Center

Frank Verbeke, MD, PhD, FIAHSI, Digital Health Sociology Research Unit, School of Public Health, University of Lubumbashi

Frances B. da-Costa Vroom, PhD, MSc, BIS, Department of Biostatistics, School of Public Health, University of Ghana

Martin C. Were, MD, MS, FIAHSI, FAMIA, Department of Biomedical Informatics & Medicine, Vanderbilt University Medical Center

Marisa L. Wilson, DNSc, MHSc, RN-BC, CPHIMS, FAMIA, FIAHSI, FAAN, the University of Alabama at Birmingham School of Nursing

Graham Wright, MPhil, MBA, DN (Lon), Cert Ed, FBCS, FIAHSI, SRN, RMN, RNT, Professor Extraordinarius, University of South Africa; Chair, SAHIA Working Group, HELINA Education Working Group

Qian Xiao, PhD, RN, School of Nursing, Capital Medical University

Introduction

This book explores the current state of health and healthcare education, as well as the current state of nursing informatics education across the globe. The topics cover multiple perspectives on education enabled by technology, which are beneficial to all nurses and interprofessional collaborations. The book spans nursing education and learning for applied critical thinking, including the use of technology, content, skills versus tools, the use of 'smart' systems for care delivery and the role of critical thinking as essential to nursing care delivery. These concepts are understood as a paradigm shift that needs to be incorporated in nursing and healthcare education.

In Chapter 1, Kulhanek and Sengstack describe the current state of nursing and interdisciplinary informatics education, both nationally in the United States and globally. The authors highlight the challenges faced by academia and conclude with a call to action for educators to improve the preparation of nurses to effectively design and use technology in any healthcare setting. Continuing with an international perspective, Chang, et al. in Chapter 2 focus on the development of the Taiwanese model for educating clinical nurses and the progress made in applying it in mainland China. The second part of the chapter describes the experience and benefits of the European scientific body of Biomedical and Health Informatics and the support of cross-national mobility and accreditation processes. In Chapter 3, Kirschling and Mills discuss re-envisioning the US nursing education roadmap, technology and practice innovations, healthcare education beyond nursing and attention to the intangibles. The aim is to address health inequalities within an evolving and complex healthcare system.

Beginning with Chapter 4, Klein, Barker, Bryant, and Mackenzie turn the focus to the use of different technologies to foster education and learning. In this chapter, the authors discuss the effects of technology on human behavior, addressing human–factors interaction, interdependence of human–computer interaction and other effects of technology on well-being. De Gagne, Green, and Sturdivant in Chapter 5 describe how learning from clients/patients shapes and advances nursing education and scholarship. McCauley, Pappas, and Hayes describe academic and clinical practice partnerships for a digital future in Chapter 6, along with the ways teams are working together (clinician/teacher) for better healthcare delivery and applied knowledge, including joint appointments (exchange of academia and applied expertise), academic-applied human resources, and interprofessional learning/development.

With a focus on competencies requirements and recommendations in the United States, in Chapter 7 Wilson argues that nurses need a strong foundation in the building blocks of digital health in order to develop the capabilities to engage and lead this digital movement. Perezmitre, Ali, and Peltonen in Chapter 8 look at an international perspective on nursing informatics competencies requirements and what is needed to bridge the disparity among nations, along with different scenarios to emphasize the challenges and importance of overcoming these challenges. In Chapter 9, Pejsa et al. discuss the value of interprofessional education as the critical success factor to address long-standing issues of poor health and health equity in an increasingly complex healthcare and social environment. Insights into the development of Health Informatics Educational Programs in Africa are provided by Wright et al. in Chapter 10. These insights were gained by utilizing tools and concepts developed by the work of the International Medical Informatics Association (IMIA) Education Task Force and IMIA's Strategy Model, the IMIA Recommendations on Education in Biomedical and Health Informatics and the IMIA Knowledge Base. In the final Chapter 11, Sans, Gonzalez, and Rosa-Salas explain how innovative methodologies in simulation are transforming healthcare education while promoting patient safety and improving outcomes. The chapter closes with a discussion about how nursing practice and education will be increasingly driven by more virtual and augmented reality simulations.

The book is a must read for those involved directly and indirectly in nursing informatics education. It provides overviews, resources and examples of what nurses need to know in the near future to enable nurses to lead and excel in what is an already digital world.

Connie White Delaney
Charlotte A. Weaver
Joyce Sensmeier
Lisiane Pruinelli
Patrick Weber

Chapter 1

Nursing Informatics Educational Programs in Academia and in Practice

Brenda Kulhanek and Patricia Sengstack

Contents

Introduction 1
The Need for Informatics Education 2
What Are Informatics Skills and Competencies? 4
Existing Curricula for Informatics Education 9
The Delivery of Informatics Education in Academia 10
    International Nursing Informatics Education 10
Faculty Informatics Competency 12
Challenges 13
Summary 13
References 14

Introduction

The American Nursing Association's Scope and Standards of Practice for Nursing Informatics (*Nursing Informatics: Scope and Standards of Practice*, 2015) defines the informatics nurse specialist (INS) as a registered nurse with formal graduate-level education in informatics or in an informatics-related field. Over the last three decades, academic institutions across the United States have evolved to provide this graduate education. In 1988, the first graduate program in nursing informatics was established in the United States at the University of Maryland, followed in 1990 by an informatics program at the University of Utah (Ozbolt & Saba, 2008). Over subsequent years, informatics programs have emerged both in-person and online across the nation. At this time, there are over 50 academic institutions offering graduate degrees in nursing or healthcare informatics primarily at the master's level, with several institutions offering post master's certifications. To meet the growing need to train nursing informatics leaders at even higher levels, a few institutions now offer doctoral study in the field of informatics at the doctorate of nursing practice (DNP) or PhD levels. While the primary focus was originally on graduate-level education in the field, undergraduate nursing programs have been challenged with integrating informatics content into baccalaureate-level curricula. With nurses comprising the largest sector of the healthcare workforce, and technology evolving at an almost impossible pace, academe realizes that baccalaureate nurses must be prepared to effectively design, use and evaluate technology they will work with on a daily basis. Similar structures and challenges in informatics education can be seen at the international level as nations across the globe implement electronic health records and other technologies. This chapter will describe the current state of informatics education both nationally and abroad. The challenges that confront academia will be illustrated with a closing call to action for educators to continuously improve how we prepare nurses to effectively design and use technology in all healthcare settings.

The Need for Informatics Education

Health information technology is used to support and deliver healthcare in almost all areas within the United States (Colicchio et al., 2019; McBride et al., 2018). With over four million registered and practical nurses using some form of health information technology in their daily practice, there is a growing need to provide education and informatics competencies for all nurses (Farzandipour et al., 2021; Smiley et al., 2018). Nurses who are competent in their understanding and use of health information technology experience fewer healthcare-associated errors, provide safer care, practice more efficiently, produce reliable data for their organizations, and have higher job satisfaction (Aiken et al., 2018; Al-Rawajfah & Tubaishat, 2019; Billings et al., 2019; Brown et al., 2020; Colicchio et al., 2019; Craswell et al., 2016; De Leeuw et al., 2020; Furukawa, 2020; Lambooij et al., 2017; Muthee et al., 2018).

The use of health information technology is rapidly increasing. In the hospital environment nurses may interact with 15 or more devices during their daily work as more devices are being requested to further enhance care efficiency and patient monitoring (Kang et al., 2019). Additionally, added technology may not be interconnected and may require additional skills and competency to operate the equipment within the patient care ecosystem (Aldrich, 2017).

The 2001 sentinel Institute of Medicine (IOM) report stated that increased and effective use of HIT could provide a solution for reducing healthcare-associated errors (*Crossing the Quality Chasm: A New Health System for the 21st Century*, 2001). The nursing profession has often been excluded from ongoing HIT conversations, delaying progress toward attainment of education and competency in the use of HIT for nurses (Weaver & Skiba, 2006). Improved informatics competencies for all nurses contributes to enhanced nursing wisdom through better access to data, information and knowledge (Nation & Wangia-Anderson, 2019).

The development of enhanced nursing informatics competencies is dependent on academic programs and faculty that can produce nurses and INS that are well educated and competent (Rahman, 2015; Sensmeier et al., 2017). However, in the United States, of the workforce of almost 4 million nurses, almost half attended nursing school prior to the incorporation of HIT into nursing practice (Zhang et al., 2018), resulting in a large segment of the nursing workforce that did not obtain informatics education in their academic programs, creating a knowledge and competency gap (Furst et al., 2013; Kinnunen et al., 2019). In an environment where nurses may not receive informatics education during their pre- or post-licensure education, and where a limited number of nursing informatics specialists are available, the importance of informatics education and competency for all nurses cannot be understated (Kinnunen et al., 2017; O'Connor et al., 2017).

In 2004, the Technology Informatics Guiding Education Reform (TIGER) initiative established an initial mission of raising awareness of the need for health information technology competency among all nurses ('The TIGER Initiative—Informatics Competencies for Every Practicing Nurse: Recommendations from the TIGER Collaborative,' 2006), leading to a call for action to add informatics competencies into nursing school curricula (Sensmeier, 2007). Despite the recommendations of the initial TIGER conference in 2006, just over half of the top 25 online Bachelor of Science in Nursing (BSN) schools included informatics in their curricula, two-thirds of online nurse master's programs contained informatics content and 80% of the online DNP programs contained informatics content. These numbers have changed little since a 2013 report (Bove, 2020). A majority of pre-licensure nursing schools report integrating informatics into the curriculum. However, closer inspection reveals that since faculty can interpret the use of technology for online coursework as nursing informatics, the study results may be questionable (Vottero, 2017). An additional barrier to the continuing expansion of informatics education into academic programs involves faculty knowledge and comfort with the informatics subject matter. The ongoing development of nursing informatics competencies through nursing education has been hindered by gaps in faculty informatics knowledge, experience and support of the importance of nursing informatics concepts (Jeon et al., 2016; McGowan et al., 2020).

What Are Informatics Skills and Competencies?

Competency is the successful and consistent integration of knowledge, skills, ability, personal values, attitudes, critical thinking and clinical decision-making in a real-world setting (Farzandipour et al., 2021). Over the past three decades, multiple nursing informatics competency models have been developed, each using a different lens to identify informatics competencies for different nursing roles (Table 1.1). The first attempt at exploring informatics competencies for nurses resulted in a list of discrete tasks for the practicing nurse, nurse leader, nurse educator and nurse researcher (Grobe, 1989). One of the first attempts at refining nursing informatics competencies resulted in a list of 304 informatics competencies categorized for the beginning nurse, the experienced nurse, the informatics specialist, and the informatics innovator (Staggers et al., 2001). A 2002 Delphi study later reduced the original list to 281 informatics competencies assigned to the same four categories of nursing (Staggers et al., 2002). The development of nursing informatics competencies continued to evolve with the work of the Technology Informatics Guiding Education Reform (TIGER) initiative. Similar to the work of Staggers et al. (2002), a broad range of stakeholders convened to continue earlier work and produce a standard list of informatics competencies. The TIGER initiative grouped the final list of informatics competencies into three functional categories that included basic computer competencies, information literacy competencies and information management competencies. A total of 231 individual competencies were published, grouped within the three informatics-related categories ('The TIGER Initiative—Informatics Competencies

Table 1.1 Informatics Standards and Competencies

Organization	Competency Information
ANA Scope and Standards for Nursing Informatics (2021, unpublished)	17 informatics standards that include competencies for each standard: • 175 nursing informatics (NI) competencies. • 95 additional nursing informatics specialist (NIS) competencies. • 270 total competencies.

AACN Essentials	Domain 8: Information and Healthcare Technologies
	• Information and communication technologies and informatics processes are used to:
	  • Provide care.
	  • Gather data.
	  • Form information to drive decision-making.
	  • Support professionals as they expand knowledge and wisdom for practice.
	  • Manage and improve the delivery of safe, high-quality and efficient healthcare services in accordance with best practice and professional and regulatory standards.

Quality and Safety Education for Nurses (QSEN)	Knowledge • Contrast benefits and limitations of common information technology strategies used in the delivery of patient care. • Evaluate the strengths and weaknesses of information systems used in patient care. • Formulate essential information that must be available in a common database to support patient care in the practice specialty. • Evaluate benefits and limitations of different communication technologies and their impact on safety and quality. • Describe and critique taxonomic and terminology systems used in national efforts to enhance interoperability of information systems and knowledge management systems. Skills • Participate in the selection, design, implementation and evaluation of information systems. • Communicate the integral role of information technology in nurses' work. • Model behaviors that support implementation and appropriate use of electronic health records. • Assist team members to adopt information technology by piloting and evaluating proposed technologies. • Promote access to patient care information for all professionals who provide care to patients. • Serve as a resource for how to document nursing care at basic and advanced levels. • Develop safeguards for protected health information.

(Continued)

Table 1.1 (Continued)   Informatics Standards and Competencies

Organization	Competency Information
	• Champion communication technologies that support clinical decision-making, error prevention, care coordination and protection of patient privacy. • Access and evaluate high-quality electronic sources of healthcare information. • Participate in the design of clinical decision-making supports and alerts. • Search, retrieve and manage data to make decisions using information and knowledge management systems. • Anticipate unintended consequences of new technology. Attitudes • Value the use of information and communication technologies in patient care. • Appreciate the need for consensus and collaboration in developing systems to manage information for patient care. • Value the confidentiality and security of all patient records. • Value the importance of standardized terminologies in conducting searches for patient information. • Appreciate the contribution of technological alert systems. • Appreciate the time, effort and skill required for computers, databases and other technologies to become reliable and effective tools for patient care.
AONL Standards for Leaders	• Basic competency in email, common word processing, spreadsheet and Internet programs. • Recognize the relevance of nursing data for improving practice. • Recognize the limitations of computer applications. • Use telecommunications devices. • Utilize hospital database management, decision support and expert systems programs to access information and analyze data from disparate sources for use in planning patient care processes and systems. • Participate in change management processes and utility analysis. • Participate in the evaluation of information in practice settings. • Evaluate and revise patient care processes and systems. • Use computerized management systems to record administrative data (billing data, quality assurance data, workload data, etc.). • Use applications for structured data entry (classification systems, acuity level, etc.). • Recognize the utility of nursing involvement in planning, design, choice and implementation of information systems in the practice environment. • Demonstrate awareness of societal and technological trends, issues and developments as they relate to nursing. • Demonstrate proficient awareness of legal and ethical issues related to client data, information and confidentiality. • Read and interpret benchmarking, financial and occupancy data.

(Continued)

Table 1.1 (Continued)   Informatics Standards and Competencies

Organization	Competency Information
TIGER	Global List of Standards • Access to information, confidentiality, protected health information and health information management • Administration, principles of management, strategic management and governance of eHealth • Business process design and business workflows • Care coordination • Clinical decision support and pathways • Clinical practice and workflows; evidence-based medicine • Coding and terminologies • Collection of data, knowledge management and library skills (curation and preservation) • Communication, change and stakeholder management • Consumer health informatics, patient access and engagement and patient health records • Data analytics, modeling and reporting • Documentation process • eHealth and mHealth • Ethics in eHealth • Financial and account management in eHealth • General eHealth knowledge, system use and applied computer science • Informatics in active and healthy aging • Informatics process and principles of health informatics • Information and communications technology/information systems/information technology (applications and architecture) • Interoperability, interfaces and integration • Issue management and resolution • Leadership in eHealth • Learning techniques in eHealth training • Legal topics in eHealth • Medical technology, assistive technologies and device integration • Medications and allergies • Order entry • Patient-centered interactions and patient identification • Policies and procedures • Population management and public health informatics • Privacy and data protection/security • Project and program management • Quality and safety • Research and biomedicine • Resource planning and management • Risk and compliance • Standards and protocols • System development and implementation/system lifecycle management • Teaching, training and education in eHealth • Telematics and telehealth

(Continued)

Table 1.1 (Continued)   Informatics Standards and Competencies

Organization	Competency Information
AMIA	Ten Domains of Competency • Health • Information science and technology • Social and behavioral science • Health information science and technology • Human factors and sociotechnical systems • Social and behavioral aspects of health • Social, behavioral and information science and technology applied to health • Professionalism • Interprofessional collaborative practice • Leadership

for Every Practicing Nurse: Recommendations from the TIGER Collaborative,' 2006). Despite the intention of utilizing this list of informatics competencies for all nurses with integration into education and practice, the sheer number of competencies created barriers for progress.

Hebda and Calderone (2010) facilitated the spread of informatics competencies into academia by recategorizing the list of informatics competencies initially published by TIGER to reflect the approach of nursing educators. The reformatted competency list was categorized for learning audiences of all nurses, beginner nurses and experienced nurses, reducing the initial list of 231 competencies to 15 conceptual focus areas. This streamlined list of competencies removed concepts that were outdated as the nursing population technologically matured.

Seeking a better competency fit to meet the needs of all nurses, ongoing competency work has resulted in variations on the established models. The discrete task focus of the initial informatics competency models has evolved into a more conceptual approach to nursing informatics competency (Hübner et al., 2018). Despite the attempts to define and qualify a specific list of informatics competencies for nurses, there appears to be no single model or list of informatics competencies for nurses in practice or education (O'Connor et al., 2017) that meets the needs of all nurses.

The efforts to create a standard list of nursing informatics competencies has been incorporated into the globalization of healthcare and informatics competencies for nurses which are being harmonized throughout many countries. This work is producing a unified reflection of informatics requirements for nurses around the world, along with an updated informatics approach that reflects increasing technical competency in nurses. As the international evolution and alignment of nursing informatics competencies continues, competency themes have emerged as discrete competency tasks have proved to be unwieldy. The top six global informatics competency categories for clinical nurses have been established and consist of nursing documentation, information knowledge management, principles of nursing informatics, data protection and security, ethics and IT, and information communication systems (Sensmeier et al., 2017).

Although global informatics competency themes have been identified, multiple approaches and lists of informatics competencies remain. In the past three decades, there has been a shift from a heavy emphasis on technology skills to the use of technology in practice. Some of the sources for informatics competencies for nurses include the Nursing Informatics Scope and Standards (ANA, 2014), the AONL Informatics competencies for leaders (AONL, 2012), the AACN Essentials for Education (AACN, 2021), QSEN Institute Competencies (QSEN, 2021), the TIGER guidelines (TIGER, 2006), AMIA (AMIA, 2017), and competencies from the National League for Nursing (NLN, 2021). Table 1.1 describes informatics standards and competencies listed by several organizations.

Existing Curricula for Informatics Education

There have been some attempts to provide pre-formatted curricula for nursing informatics education. The Canadian Association of Schools of Nursing (CASN) has developed a nursing informatics teaching toolkit that can be used in any pre-licensure nursing program throughout Canada (Forman et al., 2020). In the United States, nursing informatics courses are offered by Healthcare Information and Management Systems Society (HIMSS) through the TIGER Virtual Learning Environment (VLE) for a fee and can be used by educators, students, adult learners, and clinical educators (*TIGER Virtual Learning Environment*, 2021). The United States Office of the National Coordinator (ONC) has produced Health IT Curriculum Resources for the HIT workforce covering topics that include population health, care coordination and interoperability, value-based care, healthcare data analytics, the history of health IT, maintenance of health IT systems, management and leadership for health IT, the culture of healthcare, patient-centered care and more. The 25 free learning modules include PowerPoint slides and a video with voice-over (*Health IT Curriculum Resources for Educators*, 2020).

In addition to available curriculum, there have been numerous textbooks published to support informatics curriculum. Each textbook provides a unique approach and perspective toward nursing informatics and the role of the informatics nurse and these texts are typically used to support classroom approaches to teaching nursing informatics for graduate-level informatics programs.

The Delivery of Informatics Education in Academia

International Nursing Informatics Education

Across the globe, the movement toward integrating a standardized informatics curriculum into nursing education is progressing slowly. Although most countries recognize the need for inclusion of informatics into nursing education, very few nations have achieved a consistent, reliable, and standardized content or the ability to provide educational content and measure outcomes (Forman et al., 2020).

In North America, Canada has taken the lead on standardizing informatics curriculum for integration into academia. Guided by a 2011 vision from the Canadian Association of Schools of Nursing (CASN), a nursing informatics teaching toolkit was developed and published in 2014 (*Nursing Informatics Teaching Toolkit*, 2014). The contents are utilized by Canadian schools of nursing and are available for use by any other stakeholder. In the United States, the call for including informatics concepts into all nursing school curriculum was communicated by the first Technology Informatics Guiding Educational Reform (TIGER) in a 2006 publication ('The TIGER Initiative—Informatics Competencies for Every Practicing Nurse: Recommendations from the TIGER Collaborative,' 2006). Despite almost two decades of increased awareness of the need for informatics competencies in academia, the United States has not achieved 100% integration of informatics curriculum into education. Progress toward this goal has been hampered by the lack of a standardized curricula or even a list of informatics competencies for nurses, as well as gaps in faculty knowledge and the ability to teach informatics (Bove, 2020).

South America and the Caribbean nations face similar challenges to enhance nursing practice by incorporating informatics curricula in nursing school. Brazil has created a national curriculum for undergraduate nurses that includes informatics as a requirement. However, there remains a lack of clarity around the specific informatics knowledge nurses need to know, which informs the development of curriculum. Moreover, there is a shortage of faculty that are knowledgeable and able to provide informatics education to nursing students (de Fatima Faria Barbosa, 2017). Other Latin American countries struggle with the same issues around clarity of informatics competencies to be included in educational programs as well as a lack of instructors qualified to teach informatics to nursing students (Hullin, 2016).

In European nations, similar challenges are seen related to providing a consistent and reliable informatics curriculum within schools of nursing in Finland, Sweden, Austria, Germany, Switzerland and the United Kingdom. Consistent themes seen in these nations include a failure to fully link informatics competencies to practice to provide care, challenges with faculty knowledge, competency and ability to provide informatics education within schools of nursing, and a lack of national standards for content that should be taught at all schools of nursing (Egbert et al., 2019; Kinnunen et al., 2017; Nygårdh et al., 2017; O'Connor & LaRue, 2021). In the Netherlands, there have been multiple efforts over the years to create and integrate an informatics curriculum into nursing education. Although informatics is now present in many schools of nursing in the Netherlands, only at the bachelor's level of education was a new standardized curriculum utilized. Future partnership with technology businesses is expected to expand the incorporation of informatics into all schools of nursing by 2020 (Koster & van Houwelingen, 2017).

Australia published nursing informatics competency standards in 2015 with the requirement that competencies be integrated into all degree programs. Despite the publication of standards, informatics competencies remain inconsistent and integration into all nursing degree programs in the country remains slow as does the implementation of health information technology throughout the nation (*About the Australasian Institute of Digital Health*, 2021). In New Zealand, a nursing informatics curriculum was developed in the 1990s for all nursing undergraduate programs in the country. However, the competencies outlined in the early document are broad and allow for diverse implementation of the competencies at each of the 17 nursing schools in the country. Additional discussions have emerged that underscore the need for a standardized informatics curriculum for nursing. At this time, not all nursing schools in New Zealand have incorporated a standardized informatics curriculum (Honey et al., 2020).

In Asia, most of the same struggles observed by other nations are seen. India includes computer education in undergraduate nursing programs, enabling solid technical skills which may be offset by minimal informatics skills that are presented in limited fashion in a few upper-level nursing courses such as general nursing. However, students and faculty lack access to resources that could provide for additional practice and exploration of informatics skills that would lead to additional competence. There is a need for additional informatics content to be standardized and added to curriculum, along with the technology resources that would allow for practice (Verma & Gupta, 2019). In Korea, not all nursing schools offer informatics courses in their curriculum, and computer technology was the most frequent informatics-related topic covered in school. Faculty with informatics training are insufficient to meet the needs of informatics training for nurses in Korea, and there are recommendations to develop nursing informatics courses based on the emerging international guidelines (Jeon et al., 2016). China, Hong Kong, Taiwan, India, Japan and Singapore all experience variation in the amount and informatics content in schools of nursing. Additionally, the primary need in these nations is the development of content that reflects knowledge that translates into real-world nursing skills in practice (Ying et al., 2017).

On the continent of Africa, Namibia is increasing awareness of the importance of informatics education for nurses and other healthcare professionals, but has a lack of qualified faculty to teach informatics in the schools (Shaanika & Iyamu, 2019). The nation of Malawi suffers from a lack of resources and has partnered internationally to work on developing informatics educational resources for teaching informatics to nursing students. In a setting where resource challenges are ongoing, Malawi anticipates ongoing partnerships with international educational institutions to continue to update and support informatics education for nurses (O'Connor et al., 2016).

Faculty Informatics Competency

Many countries report a shortage of faculty with education, knowledge and competency in informatics to teach courses at both the undergraduate and graduate levels. Based on this lack of preparation, the content that is delivered can vary greatly from one institution to the next, and the interpretation of what constitutes informatics for nursing education can range from relying on educational technology as the informatics component of nursing education, to computer skills, use of the EHR and other technology. The need for qualified faculty competent to teach informatics to nursing students throughout the world remains a common theme (Forman et al., 2020).

Challenges

Faced with a multitude of challenges that include: faculty unprepared to teach nursing informatics; lack of clarity around the informatics skills and competencies that today's nurses require; a nursing workforce that is lacking informatics competency; and a rapidly changing nursing environment that is increasingly dependent on data, the global nursing community is confronted with a growing need. With multiple groups and organizations working to define and quantify informatics skills and competencies, the ability to produce focused and relevant education is limited. The call for informatics content to be integrated into all BSN and graduate nursing courses, per the newly released educational guidelines (*AACN Essentials*, 2021), has been issued but we are not yet prepared to comply.

Summary

The delivery of informatics education in academic settings across the globe is evolving. While nursing education in general has been forming and improving for over 100 years, training in the field of informatics is still relatively new. Global and even national consensus on the appropriate competencies to include in informatics curricula continues to be an issue despite the availability of several models to choose from. There appears to be no single model with supporting evidence to advocate for: (1) a specific informatics competency list, (2) an effective method of delivery (in-person or online), or (3) where in the nursing academic program to place the content.

Nursing faculty in academic institutions are confronted with a need to address informatics education going forward on a number of levels. First, the integration of core informatics competencies into baccalaureate nursing programs. As mentioned earlier, nurses that are competent in their understanding and use of health information technology experience a fewer healthcare-associated errors, provide safer care, and have higher job satisfaction. This is no surprise given the volume of devices and software our millions of nurses must interact with on a daily basis. Second, the development of graduate-level informatics curriculum that utilizes one of the available competency models. In addition to this, the curriculum must be updated on a routine basis to ensure alignment with advances in technology and evolving industry needs. Third, the development of doctoral-level programs that prepare the nursing informatics leaders of tomorrow. These programs should include not only advanced informatics skills but also leadership concepts to ensure we are creating future change agents and disruptive innovators. Fourth, the development of competent faculty in the field of informatics. This may involve sending faculty members to training courses to help them teach in an area that is not their area of expertise. Each of these four levels represents a call to action that will require partnerships between academic institutions and national/international professional informatics organizations. Ongoing collaboration between these groups can lead to continuous improvement and evolution toward creating a competent and strong informatics workforce.

References

AACN essentials. (2021). American Association of Colleges of Nursing [online]. Available at: https://www.aacnnursing.org/Education-Resources/AACN-Essentials (Accessed 23 September 2021).

About the Australasian Institute of Digital Health. (2021). Australasian Institute of Digital Health [online]. Available at: https://digitalhealth.org.au/about/ (Accessed 2 September 2021).

Aiken, L., Sloane, D., Barnes, H., Cimiotti, J., Jarrín, O., & McHugh, M. (2018). Nurses' and patients' appraisals show patient safety in hospitals remains a concern. *Health Affairs*, 37(11), pp.1744–1751. https://doi.org/10.1377/hlthaff.2018.0711

Al-Rawajfah, O., & Tubaishat, A. (2019). Barriers and facilitators to using electronic healthcare records in Jordanian hospitals from the nurses' perspective: A national survey. *Informatics for Health & Social Care*, 44(1), pp.1–11. https://doi.org/10.1080/17538157.2017.1353998

Aldrich, K. (2017). Trade your open tickets for interoperability. *Nursing Management*, 48(10), pp.25–26. https://doi.org/10.1097/01.NUMA.0000524822.79652.5b

AMIA. (2017). *AMIA 10 domains of competency* [online]. Available at: https://academic.oup.com/jamia/article/25/12/1657/5145365 (Accessed 24 August 2021).

ANA. (2014). *Nursing informatics: Scope and standards of practice*. 2nd ed. Washington, DC: ANA Enterprise.

AONL. (2012). AONE position paper: Nursing informatics executive leader [online]. Available at: https://www.aonl.org/sites/default/files/aone/informatics-executive-leader.pdf. (Accessed 20 August 2021).

Billings, D. M., Kowalski, K., Phillips, J. M., Stalter, A. M., Goldschmidt, K. A., Ruggiero, J. S., Brodhead, J., Bonnett, P. L., Provencio, R. A., McKay, M., Jowell, V., Merriam, D. H., Wiggs, C. M., & Scardaville, D. L. (2019). Using systems thinking to implement the QSEN informatics competency. *Journal of Continuing Education in Nursing*, 50(9), pp.392–397. https://doi.org/10.3928/00220124-20190814-04

Bove, L. A. (2020). Integration of informatics content in baccalaureate and graduate nursing education: An updated status report. *Nurse Educator*, 45(4), pp.206–209. https://doi.org/10.1097/NNE.0000000000000734

Brown, J., Pope, N., Bosco, A. M., Mason, J., & Morgan, A. (2020). Issues affecting nurses' capability to use digital technology at work: An integrative review. *Journal of Clinical Nursing*, 29(15–16), pp.2801–2819. https://doi.org/10.1111/jocn.15321

Colicchio, T. K., Cimino, J. J., & Del Fiol, G. (2019). Unintended consequences of nationwide electronic health record adoption: Challenges and opportunities in the post-meaningful use era. *Journal of Medical Internet Research*, 21(6), p.e13313. https://doi.org/10.2196/13313

Craswell, A., Moxham, L., & Broadbent, M. (2016). Does use of computer technology for perinatal data collection influence data quality? *Health Informatics Journal*, 22(2), pp.293–303. https://doi.org/10.1177/1460458214556372

Crossing the quality chasm: A new health system for the 21st Century. (2001). National Academy Press.

de Fatima Faria Barbosa, S. (2017). Competencies related to informatics and information management for practicing nurses and nurses leaders in Brazil and South America. *Studies in Health Technology & Informatics*, 232, pp.77–85. https://doi.org/10.3233/978-1-61499-738-2-77

De Leeuw, J. A., Woltjer, H., & Kool, R. B. (2020). Identification of factors influencing the adoption of health information technology by nurses who are digitally lagging: In-depth interview study. *Journal of Medical Internet Research*, 22(8), p.e15630. https://doi.org/10.2196/15630

Egbert, N., Thye, J., Hackl, W. O., Müller-Staub, M., Ammenwerth, E., & Hübner, U. (2019). Competencies for nursing in a digital world methodology, results, and use of the DACH-recommendations for nursing informatics core competency areas in Austria, Germany, and Switzerland. *Informatics for Health & Social Care*, 44(4), pp.351–375. https://doi.org/10.1080/17538157.2018.1497635

Farzandipour, M., Mohamadian, H., Akbari, H., Safari, S., & Sharif, R. (2021). Designing a national model for assessment of nursing informatics competency. *BMC Medical Informatics and Decision Making*, 21(1). https://doi.org/10.1186/s12911-021-01405-0

Forman, T. M., Armor, D. A., & Miller, A. S. (2020). A review of clinical informatics competencies in nursing to inform best practices in education and nurse faculty development. *Nursing Education Perspectives*, 41(1), pp.E3–E7. https://doi.org/10.1097/01.nep.0000000000000588

Furst, C. M., Finto, D., Malouf-Todaro, N., Moore, C., Orr, D. A., Santos, J., Sutton, K., & Tipton, P. H. (2013). Changing times: Enhancing clinical practice through evolving technology. *MEDSURG Nursing*, 22(2), pp.131–134.

Furukawa, M. F. (2020). Electronic health record adoption and rates of in-hospital adverse events. *Journal of Patient Safety (Online)*, 16(2), p.137.

Grobe, S. (1989). Nursing informatics competencies. *Methods of Information in Medicine*, 28, pp.267–269.

Health IT curriculum resources for educators. (2020). Office of the National Coordinator for Health Information Technology [online]. Available at: https://www.healthit.gov/topic/health-it-resources/health-it-curriculum-resources-educators (Accessed 23 September 2021).

Hebda, T., & Calderone, T. L. (2010). What nurse educators need to know about the TIGER Initiative. *Nurse Educator*, 35(2), pp.56–60. https://doi.org/10.1097/NNE.0b013e3181ced83d

Honey, M., Collins, E., & Britnell, S. (2020). Education into policy: Embedding health informatics to prepare future nurses: New Zealand case study. *JMIR Nursing*, 3(1), p.e16186. https://doi.org/10.2196/16186

Hübner, U., Shaw, T., Thye, J., Egbert, N., Marin, H., Chang, P., O'Connor, S., Day, K., Honey, M., Blake, R., Hovenga, E., Skiba, D., & Ball, M. (2018). Technology informatics guiding education reform – TIGER. *Methods of Information in Medicine*, 57(S01), pp.e30–e42. https://doi.org/10.3414/me17-01-0155

Hullin, C. (2016). Nursing informatics education: Latino America & Caribe. *Studies in Health Technology & Informatics*, 225, pp.729–731. https://doi.org/10.3233/978-1-61499-658-3-729

Jeon, E., Kim, J., Park, H.-A., Lee, J.-H., Kim, J., Jin, M., Ahn, S., Jun, J., Song, H., On, J., Jung, H., Hong, Y. J., & Yim, S. (2016). Current status of nursing informatics education in Korea. *Healthcare Informatics Research*, 22(2), p.142. https://doi.org/10.4258/hir.2016.22.2.142

Kang, S., Baek, H., Jung, E., Hwang, H., & Yoo, S. (2019). Survey on the demand for adoption of Internet of Things (IoT)-based services in hospitals: Investigation of nurses' perception in a tertiary university hospital. *Applied Nursing Research*, 47, pp.18–23. https://doi.org/10.1016/j.apnr.2019.03.005

Kinnunen, U.-M., Heponiemi, T., Rajalahti, E., Ahonen, O., Korhonen, T., & Hyppönen, H. (2019). Factors related to health informatics competencies for nurses: Results of a national electronic health record survey. *CIN: Computers, Informatics, Nursing*, 37(8), pp.420–429. https://doi.org/10.1097/CIN.0000000000000511

Kinnunen, U.-M., Rajalahti, E., Cummings, E., & Borycki, E. M. (2017). Curricula challenges and informatics competencies for nurse educators. *Studies in Health Technology and Informatics*, 232, pp.41–48.

Koster, Y., & van Houwelingen, C. T. M. (2017). Technology-based healthcare for nursing education within The Netherlands: Past, present and future…NI 2016, Switzerland. *Studies in Health Technology & Informatics*, 232, pp.101–110. https://doi.org/10.3233/978-1-61499-738-2-101

Lambooij, M. S., Drewes, H. W., & Koster, F. (2017). Use of electronic medical records and quality of patient data: Different reaction patterns of doctors and nurses to the hospital organization. *BMC Medical Informatics and Decision Making*, 17(1). https://doi.org/10.1186/s12911-017-0412-x

McBride, S., Tietze, M., Robichaux, C., Stokes, L., & Weber, E. (2018). Identifying and addressing ethical issues with use of electronic health records. *Online Journal of Issues in Nursing*, 23(1). https://doi.org/10.3912/OJIN.Vol23No01Man05

McGowan, B. S., Cantwell, L. P., Conklin, J. L., Raszewski, R., Planchon Wolf, J., Slebodnik, M., McCarthy, S., & Johnson, S. (2020). Evaluating nursing faculty's approach to information literacy instruction: a multi-institutional study. *Journal of the Medical Library Association*, 108(3). https://doi.org/10.5195/jmla.2020.841

Muthee, V., Bochner, A. F., Osterman, A., Liku, N., Akhwale, W., Kwach, J., Prachi, M., Wamicwe, J., Odhiambo, J., Onyango, F., & Puttkammer, N. (2018). The impact of routine data quality assessments on electronic medical record data quality in Kenya. *PLOS ONE*, 13(4), p.e0195362. https://doi.org/10.1371/journal.pone.0195362

Nation, J., & Wangia-Anderson, V. (2019). Applying the data-knowledge-information-wisdom framework to a usability evaluation of electronic health record system for nursing professionals [online]. *Online Journal of Nursing Informatics*, 23(1). Available at: https://www.himss.org/resources/applying-data-knowledge-information-wisdom-framework-usability-evaluation-electronic-health-record (Accessed 27 December 2021).

NLN. (2021). *Competencies* [online]. Available at: https://www.nln.org/professional-development-programs/competencies-for-nursing-education (Accessed 13 August 2021).

Nursing informatics: Scope and standards of practice. (2015). American Nurses Association.

Nursing informatics teaching toolkit. (2014). Canadian Association of Schools of Nursing/Association canadienne des écoles de sciences infirmières (CASN/ACESI) [online]. Available at: https://www.casn.ca/2014/12/nursing-informatics-teaching-toolkit/ (Accessed 10 August 2021).

Nygårdh, A., Sherwood, G., Sandberg, T., Rehn, J., & Knutsson, S. (2017). The visibility of QSEN competencies in clinical assessment tools in Swedish nurse education. *Nurse Education Today*, 59, pp.110–117. https://doi.org/10.1016/j.nedt.2017.09.003

O'Connor, S., Gallagher, J., Wamba, N., Moyo, C., Chirambo, G. B., & O'Donoghue, J. (2016). Establishing long-term nursing informatics capacity in Malawi, Africa. *Studies in Health Technology & Informatics*, 225, pp.1013–1014. https://doi.org/10.3233/978-1-61499-658-3-1013

O'Connor, S., Hubner, U., Shaw, T., Blake, R., & Ball, M. (2017). Time for TIGER to ROAR! Technology informatics guiding education reform. *Nurse Education Today*, 58, pp.78–81. https://doi.org/10.1016/j.nedt.2017.07.014

O'Connor, S., & LaRue, E. (2021). Integrating informatics into undergraduate nursing education: A case study using a spiral learning approach. *Nurse Education in Practice*, 50. https://doi.org/10.1016/j.nepr.2020.102934

Ozbolt, J., & Saba, V. (2008). A brief history of nursing informatics in the United States of America. *Nursing Outlook*, 56(5), p.9.

QSEN Institute. (2021). *QSEN Institute competencies* [online]. Available at: https://qsen.org/competencies/pre-licensure-ksas/ (Accessed 13 August 2021).

Rahman, A. (2015). *Development of a nursing informatics competency assessment tool (NICAT)* (Publication Number 3734182) [D.N.P., Walden University]. Ann Arbor: ProQuest Dissertations & Theses Global.

Sensmeier, J. (2007). The future of IT? Aggressive educational reform: TIGER initiative preps nurses for healthcare's digital era. *Journal of Nursing Administration*, 37(9), pp.2–6.

Sensmeier, J., Anderson, C., & Shaw, T. (2017). International evolution of TIGER informatics competencies. *Studies in Health Technology and Informatics*, 232, pp.69–76.

Shaanika, I., & Iyamu, T. (2019). Health informatics curriculum development for teaching and learning. *Education and Information Technologies*, 24(2), pp.1293–1309.

Smiley, R. A., Lauer, P., Bienemy, C., Berg, J. G., Shireman, E., Reneau, K. A., & Alexander, M. (2018). The 2017 national nursing workforce survey. *Journal of Nursing Regulation*, 9(3), pp.S1–S88. https://doi.org/10.1016/s2155-8256(18)30131-5

Staggers, N., Gassert, C. A., & Curran, C. (2001). Informatics competencies for nurses at four levels of practice. *Journal of Nursing Education*, 40(7), pp.303–316.

Staggers, N., Gassert, C. A., & Curran, C. (2002). A Delphi study to determine informatics competencies for nurses at four levels of practice. *Nursing Research*, 51(6), pp.383–390. https://doi.org/10.1097/00006199-200211000-00006

The TIGER initiative- informatics competencies for every practicing nurse: Recommendations from the TIGER collaborative. (2006). [online]. Available at: http://www.tigersummit.com/uploads/3.Tiger.Report_Competencies_final.pdf (Accessed 27 December 2021).

TIGER virtual learning environment. (2021). HIMSS [online]. Available at: https://www.himss.org/tiger-virtual-learning-environment (Accessed 22 August 2021).

Verma, M. P., & Gupta, S. (2019). Competency in informatics for nursing professional in India: Imbibing the tech-culture among nursing professionals. *International Journal of Nursing Education*, 11(1), pp.67–73. https://doi.org/10.5958/0974-9357.2019.00015.1

Vottero, B. (2017). Teaching informatics to prelicensure, RN-to-BSN, and graduate level students. *Nurse Educator*, 42(5S), pp.S22–S26. https://doi.org/10.1097/NNE.0000000000000414

Weaver, C. A., & Skiba, D. (2006). ANI connection. TIGER initiative: Addressing information technology competencies in curriculum and workforce. *CIN: Computers, Informatics, Nursing*, 24(3), pp.175–176.

Ying, W. U., Yanling, W., & Meihua, J. I. (2017). Competencies related to informatics and information management for practicing nurses in select countries in Asia... NI 2016, Switzerland. *Studies in Health Technology & Informatics*, 232, pp.86–96. https://doi.org/10.3233/978-1-61499-738-2-86

Zhang, X., Tai, D., Pforsich, H., & Lin, V. W. (2018). United States registered nurse workforce report card and shortage forecast: A revisit. *American Journal of Medical Quality*, 33(3), pp.229–236. https://doi.org/10.1177/1062860617738328

Chapter 2

International Health and Healthcare Education Current State

Polun Chang, John Mantas, Chiao-Ling Chelsey Hsu,
I-Ching Evita Hou, Yuan Chen, Qian Xiao, Meihua Ji,
Jiwen Sun, Cuihong Liu

Contents

Introduction 20
An Effective Informatics Competency Development Model for Nurses in
    Mainland China and Taiwan 20
The Nursing Informatics Association in Taiwan 21
The Current Nursing Informatics Education Programs in Taiwan 22
The Development of Nursing Informatics in Mainland China 24
The TIGER Competency Model in Mainland China 28
Two Active and Representative Cases Completely Done by Nurses 32
Quality Assurance of Education in Biomedical and Health Informatics
    via Accreditation as Provided in Europe by EFMI 34
    Accreditation 34
    Certification 35
    Strengths, Weaknesses, Opportunities, and Threats (SWOT) Analysis 36
Implementation of Accreditation 36
Code of Conduct 37
    Preparation and Procedure 37
    Independence and Confidentiality..38

Professional Attitude 38
　　Attitude within the Panel 39
　　　　Template of the self-assessment report 39
Preparatory Work by the Applicant 40
Result of the Evaluation Based on the Criteria 41
Conclusions 41
Bibliography 42

Introduction

This chapter presents different perspectives on international health and healthcare education. First, the Taiwan Training Model will be presented. The Taiwanese model on educating clinical nurses has helped to attract many clinical nurses in both Taiwan and mainland China to learn, very cost effectively and efficiently, the nursing informatics and make good practical designs. It is a model inspired and supported by the Technology Informatics Guiding Education Reform (TIGER) Initiative, as well as the unique experiences developed in Taiwan. This second perspective will introduce the development in Taiwan and the part of progress in mainland China. Then, the European scientific body of Biomedical and Health Informatics will provide the European benefit to the programs, how they support cross-national mobility and required national accreditations processes.

An Effective Informatics Competency Development Model for Nurses in Mainland China and Taiwan

Taiwan nursing informatics (NI) education has 20 years of experience. In addition to job-related computer skills and informatics literacy (Chang et al., 2011), the nurses learn the programming skills to satisfy the information they need on their own and that encourage nursing staff to have the second expertise (Hou et al., 2006). Such nursing informatics education can demonstrate the unique model to the other countries (Chang et al., 2008; Hou et al., 2009).

　　This model is called the Taiwan Training Model (TTM), which was widely started in 2003. It has been used in educating many clinical nurses in both Taiwan and mainland China to learn, very cost effectively and efficiently, the nursing informatics and make good practical designs. It is a model inspired and supported by the Technology Informatics Guiding Education Reform (TIGER) Initiative, as well as the unique experiences developed in Taiwan

(Chang & Kuo, 2010). The core feature is to emphasize the hands-on design capability from the end-user computing (EUC) strategy; and makes the trainees capable of not only knowing but being capable of designing, leading and making an innovative impact in care safety and performance effectiveness. Besides that, in Taiwan, there is an independent Nursing Informatics Association and some academic programs to academically train the nursing informatics nurses from universities.

The Nursing Informatics Association in Taiwan

The Taiwan Nursing Informatics Association (TNIA) was established by the hundreds of nurses trained by the early TTM model in 2006, right after the International Congress in Nursing Informatics (NI2006) in Korea. In order to improve the informatics skills of nursing staff, it regularly organizes training courses for nurses every year (Taiwan Nursing Informatics Association, 2021b) and achieves the improvement in the quality of nursing informatics education through a systematic and organized series of curriculum planning. The main objectives of the training course include:

- To understand the current status and role functions of nursing informatics.
- To improve the principles and strategies for the practical application of nursing informatics.
- To enhance the visibility and professional strength of nursing informatics.
- To enhance the ability of nursing informatics communication and coordination.
- To enhance the quality of care through the integration of information technology and innovative services.

Training courses included topics, such as the current status and future of nursing informatics, the concept and application of programming coding, the database management, the application and introduction of medical and nursing informatics system, the role and function of informatics nurses, the system requirement, the assessment and effectiveness analysis, the electronic medical record management, and the information security management.

In addition to providing training courses, the TNIA is also the first nonprofit organization to provide informatics nurses certification in mainland

China and Taiwan. According to the nursing informatics ability, it is divided into beginner informatics nurses and advanced informatics nurse certification (Feng et al., 2015). The nurses applying for beginner informatics nursing have completed the informatics nurse training course and passed the certification exam, and meet the basic requirements, such as a registered nurse license, a member of the TNIA, more than 2 years of clinical practice, school teaching or health industry experience, and a university degree or above. They can apply to the TNIA for the certification of a beginner informatics nurse. This certificate is permanently valid (Taiwan Nursing Informatics Association, 2021a), but it will be revoked or abolished simultaneously with the validity period of the nurse certificate. Beginner informatics nurses can apply for advanced informatics nurses if he or she has obtained the qualification of beginner informatics nurses for more than 2 years, have been engaged in nursing informatics work for more than 1 year, and have obtained a total of 20 educational credits in the first 2 years of the application period. Every 5 years, he or she can apply for the extension of the certification qualification after obtaining the education credits.

The Current Nursing Informatics Education Programs in Taiwan

The majority of nursing informatics education programs in Taiwan are master-based, and only a few provide a PhD degree. Nursing graduates obtain graduate qualifications through the school's admission application channel. Students who have completed the required credits, met the graduation requirements, submitted a thesis, and passed the examination of the Master's or PhD Degree Examination Committee will be awarded a master's or PhD degree.

The teaching units of schools in Taiwan include the School of Nursing, the School of Medicine, the School of Medical Technology, the School of Management, or the School of Electrical Engineering and Information in various universities. Each school arranges compulsory or elective courses for nursing, informatics, and management based on the program's education goals and core capabilities set by the teaching unit, plus common courses, such as research ethics, research methods, and essay writing.

At present, most clinical nurses will give priority to the nursing informatics-related degree programs conducted by the School of Nursing. The main consideration is to link clinical experience and nursing expertise and meet the practical needs of the nursing workplace. For example, after obtaining a master's degree, they can obtain The Advanced Nurse Practitioner certificate provided by the Taiwanese Nursing Association that could support them to transfer their original clinical nursing work to information nurse specialist, disease case management specialists and other positions. The degree also meets the educational qualifications for job promotion, as a nursing manager, and promotes upward career development. For those who choose a degree program outside of the School of Nursing, the main consideration is to meet personal interests and obtain a second specialty. Therefore, being able to transfer to an information system developer or medical information manager after acquiring more professional information or management skills can also help personal career development.

The educational goal of the Nursing Informatics Program is to cultivate cross-field talents so that they can become a communication bridge between the two majors of healthcare and informatics technology. In addition to referring to the scope of international nursing information certification, the curriculum planning includes administrative management and leadership, system analysis, safety and compliance, interoperability, system design and development, professional development and education, advocacy and policy development, nursing evidence and research (Bickford, 2015; Cummins et al., 2016). At the same time, referring to the Taiwan Nursing Association's position on necessary educational qualification for advanced nurses, they cover six advanced professional capabilities including advanced nursing, teaching, consulting, coordination, leadership, and research and development (Taiwan Nurse Association, 2018). The nursing informatics curriculum is mainly divided into advanced nursing professional courses that include nursing theory and nursing research and health informatics technology courses, such as application programming, system analysis and development, and database management.

More than half of the 26 medical centers in Taiwan have 1–3 full-time informatics nurses serving as hospital information system development coordinators. For others, the nursing supervisor will serve in the nursing informatics committee, as a nursing information system planner, project coordinator, educator, analyst and quality monitor in the institution. In addition, there are nursing staff transferred to hospital information systems related positions, including project managers, programmers, system analysts, data analysts, etc., in healthcare information system companies. There are also nurses who have obtained doctoral degrees and transferred to teaching positions, and at the same time they are responsible for nursing professional

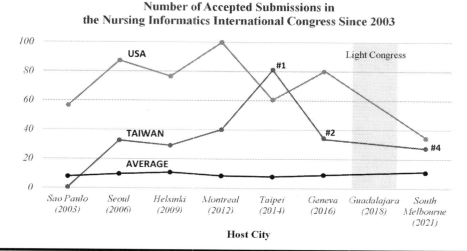

Figure 2.1 The number of accepted submissions from the Nursing Informatics International Congress since 2003 for the United States, almost the benchmark group with the highest acceptance number, average and Taiwan.

education and interdisciplinary teaching. The amount of nursing informatics research is even more significant. According to the statistics from the accepted submission to the Nursing Informatics International Congress since 2003, Taiwan has played a very active role and maintained a leading position (Figure 2.1).

The Development of Nursing Informatics in Mainland China

The computer was first introduced into hospitals in the late 1970s in mainland China for the processing of basic administrative tasks and became more extensive in the 1980s. It was introduced into nursing practice in the late 1980s to the 1990s (Guo, 2000; Li et al., 2009; Zhang, 1992). There were three stages. The first stage was a stand-alone system, mainly in office management. Computers were operated independently and there was no data sharing at all. To meet the needs of nursing practice and management, nurses in some hospitals work with information technicians (ITs) to develop more complicated functions, such as unit management and nursing error analysis (Wang & Zhang, 1993; Wang, 1994) to assist nursing practice.

The second stage started in the late 1990s, along with the rapid development of computer technology, especially broadband and multimedia technology. In 1993, the 'Creation of Chinese Hospital Information System Project' was launched as the 8th five-year National Key Science and Technology Project, which developed the 'China Hospital Information System' named as 'Military Health No 1' in 1997. It was recognized as the first integrated clinical hospital information system developed in mainland China (China E Commerce, 2000; Li et al., 2009) and was widely implemented among large tertiary hospitals thereafter (Qi et al., 2000). It enabled an inpatient nursing workstation system to be built based on that. This second stage was characterized by the utilization of broadband networking and hospital information systems. An integrated nursing record information system (mainly free text) was included in this system (Liu et al., 2002). In 2002, Peking University People's Hospital developed a nursing record system which included four modules: collection of medical and nursing history data, nursing care planning, printing the nursing record, and a nursing knowledge database (Ji, 2012).

Since 2010, the third stage has been characterized by the wide use of a mobile information system along with the development of wireless network technology in nursing practice. Mobile nursing information technologies were first introduced to nursing practice as pilot projects and sporadically emerged at the beginning of this century. The popularity of mobile nursing was accompanied by the improvement of various mobile information technologies. With advancements in the functions of mainland China's Hospital Information System (HIS), increased speed of wireless Wi-Fi, adoption of Radio Frequency Integration Technology (RFIT), mobile nursing carts and mobile devices, the use of mobile electronic nursing records became one of the most important parts in nursing practice. Since 2011, the use of personal digital assistant (PDA) and mobile nursing carts to provide bedside nursing care has become more and more popular in a vast majority of hospitals in mainland China (Ji, 2012). The functions of the mobile nursing information system cover many aspects of nursing practice, such as input and retrieval of patients' demographic and clinical data, patient identification, entry of assessment data and documentation at the point of care, as well as the implementation and management of doctors' orders, nursing quality control and nursing workload tracking (Zeng et al., 2015; Zhang et al., 2014). In particular, closed-loop medication management, dynamic tracking, quality control and quality improvement are used widely in more recent years.

With the rapid development of systems in hospitals, the need for nurses to have informatics competencies increased dramatically. In some hospitals, positions for nurses to translate nursing practice needs between bedside nurses and the information technology department emerged to close the gap between clinical practice and technology (hereafter, this position will be referred to as 'informatics nurse'). Therefore, nursing schools in mainland China began providing computer courses or related content to nursing students, mainly at the baccalaureate level, in addition to courses such as 'Introduction to Computer Science' and 'Literature Searching,' which are mandatory for all bachelor degree students in mainland China. Some nursing schools of universities in mainland China have established master's programs to prepare nurses working in the practice sector as an informatics nurse or in the academic sector as a NI educator and researcher. In order to provide adequate training on knowledge, skills, and ability related to NI for entry-to-practice nursing graduates, a competency model or a set of nursing informatics competencies for graduates who will work as bedside nurses are an urgent need.

Research on nursing informatics competencies emerged in the early 21st century. Early studies mainly focused on information literacy, and various studies viewed this concept differently. Some authors considered information literacy as the awareness, ability, and ethics of using information (Jiang & Shen, 2004), while others considered it as the acquisition, recognition, identification, evaluation, processing, transmission, and the ability to create information (Chen et al., 2015; Huang et al., 2012; Wang & He, 2008). Liu (Liu et al., 2010) and Shi (Shi et al., 2011) considered information literacy as the ability of using information and applying Information and Communication Technologies (ICT) to facilitate problem solving in their workplaces.

Studies have also been conducted on the purpose of identifying the contents and standards for nursing information literacy. In 2008, a core nursing competency model for baccalaureate degree graduates was developed, which included the item 'search and retrieve information through electronic databases' as one of the six core competencies under the domain of 'professionalism' (Yang et al., 2013). In another study, Jiang et al. (Jiang & Shen, 2004) initiated a theoretical model of information literacy for undergraduate nursing students through structural analysis and Delphi method in 2004. They proposed that nursing information literacy consisted of three elements: informatics awareness, informatics capabilities, and informatics ethics.

Through theoretical evaluation and experience analysis, Wang et al. (Wang & He, 2008) constructed a set of nursing information literacy evaluation standards for vocational nursing students. They summarized that the evaluation standard for nursing information literacy should include four domains: information awareness, information knowledge, information capability, and information ethics. Eleven sub-dimensions were identified under these four domains. In 2012, basic skills in searching and retrieving literature, collecting data, as well as effectively acquiring, evaluating and applying nursing informatics skills via modern ICT are included in the 'Essentials of National Undergraduate Nursing Education Standard.'

Xu (2012) conducted a study related to NI competencies among undergraduate nursing students by using a questionnaire survey, factor analysis and three rounds of Delphi in 2012. A framework for NI competencies was developed in which four domains with 13 categories and 33 items were identified. The four domains are information knowledge, information skills, information management ability, and information attitude. Because there was no nationally recognized nursing informatics or nursing information management competency model for nurses in mainland China, a research project was conducted to identify nursing informatics and nursing information management competencies for nurses and informatics nurses to inform nurse professionals from both the educational sector and the practice sector nationwide.

The project was based on NI competencies and NI management competencies described by the American Nurses Association (The American Nurses Association, 2015a, 2015b) and the Nursing Informatics Competencies Model from the TIGER (Technology Informatics Guiding Education Reform) initiative and was carried out in four stages. During the first stage, an initial pool of nursing informatics and information management competency items was developed through extensive literature review. In the second stage, semi-structured in-depth interviews of bedside nurses, 'informatics nurses' (coordinating and communicating with ITs regarding the needs for clinical nursing information system as part of their daily responsibility) and nursing managers were conducted. A questionnaire named Chinese NI and information management competency (NIAIMC) was developed based on the revised competency items using Delphi method during the third stage. Finally, a national survey of more than 1,000 nurses across mainland China was conducted and an exploratory factor analysis was used to generate the NI competency and NI management competency model for nurses in mainland China. The model includes four domains (with a total of 36 items): basic computer knowledge, computer and network operating ability, information literacy, and operating ability of health information systems.

The first formal TTM workshop for nursing informatics specialists (middle level) organized by the national NI interest group was held in Beijing in late 2019 by Dr Polun Chang, as shown in Figure 2.2, when the first one started in 2014 at the School of Nursing, Capital Medical University in Beijing. More than 30 nursing staff attended the training. This training course lasted for 6 days and successfully improved nurses' informatics competencies, including nursing information system needs assessment, program language foundation, process reengineering, form design, application design, data information system application, and interface design.

Figure 2.2 The First Proficient Nursing Informatics Competency Training Program endorsed by the Chinese NI Interest Group in 2019.

The TIGER Competency Model in Mainland China

Though the first nation-initiated TTM training workshop was held in 2019, many NI workshops have been delivered in mainland China since 2014 (Hübner et al., 2016) and got its momentum along with the global movement (Hübner et al., 2018). The TTM training first started as a hospital program in the Shanxi Provincial People's Hospital in Shanxi, fully supported by the Director of Nursing Department, Zhen-Xian Shi, in 2015. In 2016, it was further regarded as a hospital strategy to develop the hospital informatics competencies in a 350-bed Cardiovascular Medical Center in Xiamen, led by the Director of Nursing Department, Yuan Chen.

The workshop lasted for 6–7 days and two 3-hour sessions every day. Hands-on design cases were required for each trainee as homework, so two sessions on days 4 and 6 were reserved for preparation, reporting and discussion. The workshop contents could be found at the fourth edition of nursing informatics (Chen et al., 2020) and the following four ideas were highly pinpointed during the workshop:

- The informatics competency building-up could always start with the tools at hand, such as the most commonly used spreadsheets; and the ideas could be inspired from daily activities such as using smartphone

International Health and Healthcare Education ■ 29

Apps to order foods when we could easily, with confidence, know what to order, where the food is, when it will arrive and finish the payment in seconds.
- The informatics is neither magic nor relic. It is a tool, which is supposed to improve patient care, working environment and professional development. Any nurse could reply on instinct and experience to tell whether the tool is useful or intelligent.
- We need to change the traditional paper-based mindset to a totally new and exciting digital one because the informatics could bring about revolutionary opportunities for intelligently caring for patients, changing working environments and reshaping future nursing professionalism, see Figure 2.3.
- Everyone can do it. The design is just like playing a Lego set to integrate each function to an integrated application with a programming language simpler than daily English, as shown in Figure 2.4, which was clearly introduced in the workshop step by step.

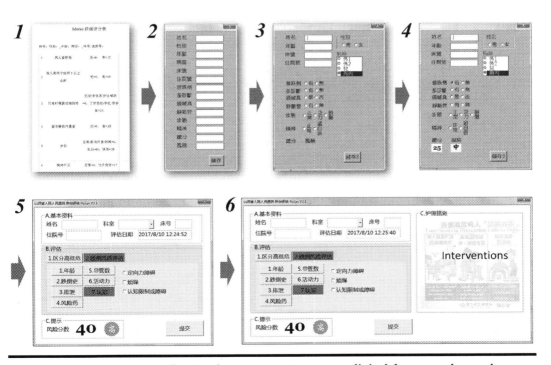

Figure 2.3 Concept transferring from Paper Form 1 to digital forms under various interface designs 2–5 and intelligent form models 5 and 6 with automation and decision supports.

30 ■ *Nursing and Informatics for the 21st Century*

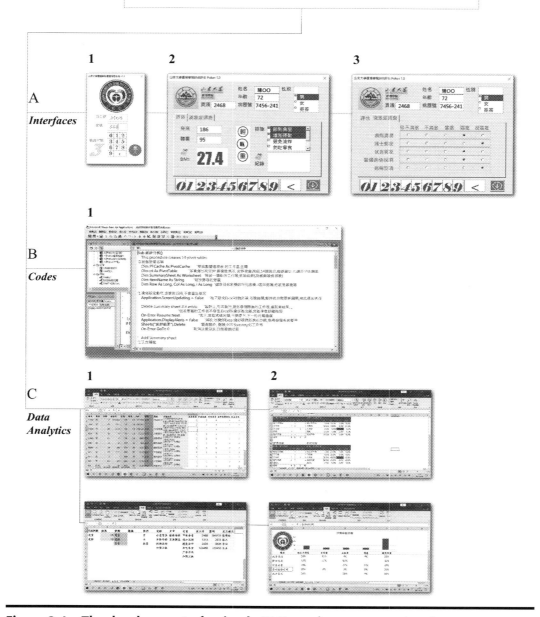

Figure 2.4 The development of a simple BMI nursing assessment and care supports with satisfaction survey system, composed of (A) interfaces, (B) codes and (C) data analytics modules, was experienced by every attendee.

One inspiring story is about what has been done by around 50 clinical nurses, out of 400 nurses, in Xiamen. Nurses from this model, under long-term informatics competency development starting from 2016, they had no idea what nursing informatics was and what they could benefit from the informatics competencies. This group was highly supported by their director and the entire hospital leadership. So far, this group of nurses has led 24 information system projects in hospitals, designed 28 subsystems, and applied for 4 informatics-related patents, and 7 items of intelligent property. They were successfully awarded 3 city research grants, published 3 Chinese journal articles, and submitted 47 domestic conference papers and 33 international ones. Of which, 5 were accepted for oral presentation and 33 were posters. In the 2nd Chinese National Nursing Informatics Conference, this team published 2 oral presentations out of 8, and 8 posters out of 20. In the International Congress in Nursing Informatics (NI2020), there were 63 submissions from China and 11 from this hospital, with 9 accepted.

On April 26, 2020, the Taiwan/China TIGER program was recognized by the Healthcare Information and Management Systems Society (HIMSS) TIGER to be qualified as a program for training the second level of informatics competencies, out of four, which is the Proficient Competency. In June 2020, 38 of 43 nurses applied and were granted the HIMSS TIGER certificates, the first and largest nursing informatics group in a hospital in China, as shown in Figure 2.5. In July 2021, this group was the most active team

Figure 2.5 The first group of nurses granted with the HIMSS TIGER certificates of proficient-level informatics competency.

registered at the Summer Institute in Nursing Informatics (SINI) 2021 and their work was well recognized, winning the Podium and the Best Poster Awards.

Two Active and Representative Cases Completely Done by Nurses

One very basic feature of the TTM workshop is to educate nurses to build up their capability to design their own applications. The following two cases demonstrate what they could make in their real daily practical settings.

Case 1. Pediatric Medication Dosage Calculator (Sun et al., 2021). The pediatric medication dosage calculator is a quick simple reference tool for pediatric nurses to calculate intravenous medication dosages and rates. The system was designed to meet the needs of nurses to effectively avoid calculation errors caused by manual calculation, thus saving nurses a considerable amount of time in calculation and reduce labor costs in double check. This calculator works to ensure each patient receives the right medicine and the right dose at the right time. The system is composed of one standardized database and four modules to deal with the calculation algorithm: intravenous medication database, overdose alert module, unit conversion module, calculation module, nursing considerations module, and the design of system flow and user interface. After calculating, the result will be shown in the result area with the formula used and nursing considerations about the medication to follow. Figure 2.6 presents the logic of system process and flow.

Case 2. The Quality Management Application for Discharge Summaries (Chen et al., 2017). This application involved a simple medical record audit tool to administer clinical audits. It was built by a clinic provider in the Affiliated Eye Hospital of Shandong University of Traditional Chinese Medicine in China. It has already been implemented in the clinical audits of the hospital and was highly praised and appreciated by clinicians and hospital managers. After identifying users' requirements, four function modules were designed to assist with medical record audits: database design, the login module, the result management module, and the operation setting module. This application was built by Excel VBA (Visual Basic for Applications) and all the data were stored in an Excel spreadsheet. Figure 2.7 shows an example of the operation setting interface, every kind of record has its own result item set.

International Health and Healthcare Education ■ 33

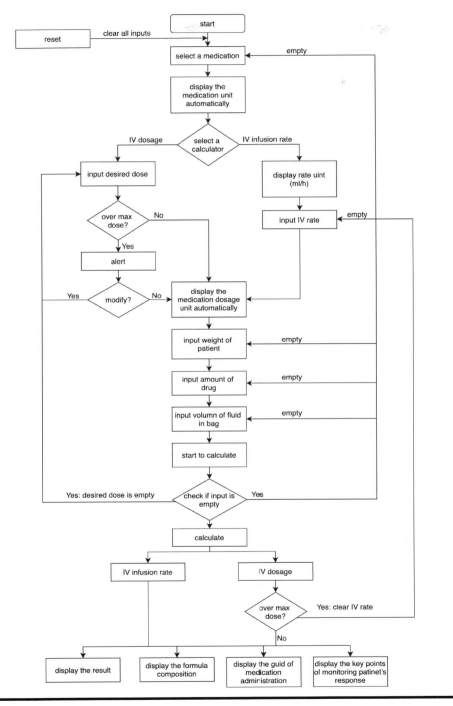

Figure 2.6 The flow chart of pediatric medication dosage calculation.

34 ■ Nursing and Informatics for the 21st Century

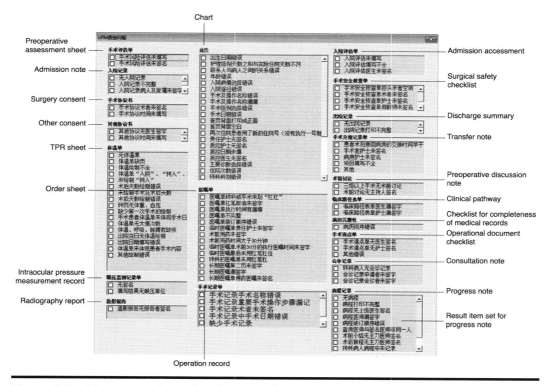

Figure 2.7 The screenshot of main operation setting.

Quality Assurance of Education in Biomedical and Health Informatics via Accreditation as Provided in Europe by EFMI

Accreditation

Accreditation is a diligent evaluation and monitoring peer-review process assuring that educational programs and institutions meet academic standards and operational integrity and quality. There are a great number of European Universities and Institutions implementing and having established programs (undergraduate and postgraduate) in the field of Biomedical and Health Informatics. A mechanism should be applied by EFMI (European Federation for Medical Informatics) to accredit those programs, since EFMI is the European scientific body of Biomedical and Health Informatics, where all national associations have joined in our Federation (EFMI). This accreditation will provide European added value to the programs, be supportive of cross-national mobility and be complementary to the required national accreditations processes.

Certification

Certification is a credentialing process that demonstrates and honors qualifications that an individual can perform a specific professional role or set of tasks. Certification in Health Informatics is a requirement for many professionals in many clinical institutions in a number of countries. Specifically, Clinical Health Informatics is a special concern, as many professionals who are using or implementing health information systems or applications of instrumentation in their professional life. Even those professionals having acquired earlier degrees in Health Informatics or in related fields are required to update and certify their current knowledge and skills. Therefore, eligibility and content requirements combining (1) clinical *practice focus*, (2) *education* and (3) *significant experience* in real-world health informatics accomplishment is urgently needed to ensure qualified expertise and develop 'best practices.' EFMI as the scientific federation in this discipline has the obligation to offer certification processes and certify the professionals of the current skills in the field of Biomedical and Health Informatics.

Actions for accreditation required:

1. Accreditation standard operating procedures defined.
2. Accreditation evaluation rules defined.
3. Site-visit experts catalog should be prepared based on eligibility criteria.
4. Accreditation secretariat should be established as mentioned above.
5. Logistical support required.
6. Clear rules of engagement should be defined ensuring transparency and equality.

Actions for certification required:

1. Certification standard operating procedures should be defined.
2. Certification task forces should be established to develop certification interprofessional programs for Health Informatics, in subdisciplines and in any other required specific applications.
3. The Secretariat should monitor diligently the process, ensuring transparency and equality.
4. Secretariat should be established to support the process throughout all stages.
5. Logistical support should be clearly defined.
6. Clear rules of engagement should be defined.

Strengths, Weaknesses, Opportunities, and Threats (SWOT) Analysis

Strengths. EFMI is a European Federation of National Associations situated in most European countries. The scientific and professional community of Biomedical and Health Informatics is reflected in EFMI as it is yearly depicted in the Medical Informatics Europe (MIE) Conferences.

Opportunities. Very few universities/institutions with programs in the field of Health Informatics have been accredited by an international organization. Similar initiatives had little effect in Europe. In addition, no certification programs have been established yet in Europe in our field.

Weaknesses. EFMI is a volunteer organization without solid professional secretariat support. Also, decisions are delayed due to the internal procedures. Clear mandates should be given to the Accreditation and Certification Committee to ensure the minimization of bureaucracy leading to delays in implementation and decisions taken.

Threats. Other international organizations, some of them, more professional ones than EFMI, have initiated similar actions, and they may apply them in Europe very soon.

Implementation of Accreditation

The EFMI AC2 Accreditation (Mantras, 2020) assessment process is based on well-established assessment processes applied in most European countries. The EFMI Accreditation does not replace any National Accreditation required by the law in each country. It is a complimentary Accreditation judged by a peer-review process in a collegiate way assisting and supporting to achieve high-quality educational programs in the field of Biomedical and Health Informatics.

The assessment consists of five criteria. For each criterion there are several norms required to be met, therefore facilitating the assessment. The criteria are based on the Dublin descriptors, as they have been presented and applied at all academic levels (bachelor's, master's and doctoral degrees). The criteria are the following, and they should be judged by the site-visit panel as either satisfactory or unsatisfactory: (1) needs and relevance; (2) intended learning outcomes; (3) academic/teaching-learning environment; (4) organization and implementation and (5) internal quality assurance and development.

If all five criteria are judged by the site-visit panel as satisfactory, then the result is positive. Therefore, the final decision by the EFMI AC2 Committee is to grant the EFMI Accreditation to the program. The duration of the EFMI Accreditation of the program is 3 years from the time of the endorsement by the EFMI Board. A re-accreditation process is required at the end of this period. On the other hand, if one of the five criteria is judged by the site-visit panel as unsatisfactory, then a partial EFMI Accreditation is granted for a limited time (1 year) until the applicant remedies this criterion and the site-visit panel approves the remedy. Then the AC2 Committee grants the EFMI Accreditation as mentioned above. If more than two criteria are judged by the site-visit panel as unsatisfactory, then no Accreditation is granted, and the applicant may reapply after at least 1 year when there is a proof of implementation of the major changes required.

The main document requested by the EFMI AC2 Committee from the applicant that facilitates the site-visit panel is the self-assessment report. The self-assessment report should be able to present and address the five above-mentioned criteria, starting with the presentation of the institution; the needs in establishing and implementing such a program; and detailing the curriculum development process, the implementation, the faculty background and tasks assigned; internal reviewing; quality assurance; judgment on achieving targets and learning outcomes; students, alumni and stakeholders involvement at all stages of establishing, evaluating and quality assurance of the program. In particular, the self-assessment report should also address the required involvement of international standards and recommendations in the field of education in Biomedical and Health Informatics.

Code of Conduct

Preparation and Procedure

The AC2 Committee appoints a three-member site-visit panel of experienced colleagues, members of the EFMI Council, preferably with professional academic background at a level of professorship. The AC2 Committee appoints one of the three members as chair of the panel, responsible for coordinating the activities at a local level at the site-visit panel based on the assessment framework. The chair is responsible for preparing the report, contacting the AC2 Committee and addressing on behalf of the panel the hierarchy of the program under the accreditation process. The panel members thoroughly prepare for the preliminary meeting and the site visit by studying all the relevant documents and responding to the proposed visit schedule. The panel members base their assessment on the applicable assessment framework and act along the lines of this framework. The chair draws up a draft report in accordance with the applicable assessment framework, factoring in the panel's judgments. The panel members respond to the draft report. All panel members examine and endorse the report. Subsequently, the report is signed by the panel chair.

Independence and Confidentiality

The panel members have no affiliations with the institution/program to be assessed, and they have the right to inspect all the relevant documents and visit specific locations. Wherever confidentiality is called for, all panel members will deal with documents made available and information regarding the institution/program in a confidential manner. In its declaration of independence and confidentiality, the panel commits to confidentiality in dealing with the data it has been provided with. Following the assessment process, the chair will inform the AC2 Committee regarding their findings during the assessment. During the assessment process, the chair and the panel members will not provide any information to the program/institution regarding their findings during the assessment, other than the feedback provided by the chair at the end of the visit or in the assessment report.

Professional Attitude

The panel members respect the identity and the nature of the institution/program. They adopt a businesslike, yet open and approachable attitude. A pleasant and relaxed atmosphere is conducive to the outcomes of the visit. The way the questions are presented and the subjects to be addressed will be geared to the discussion partners. Lengthy introductions will be avoided; the questions will be open-ended and preferably short. Some measure of tenacity through in-depth questions is desirable; however, within reason. The documentation to be requested will be limited to what is essential. Administrative inconvenience for the institution/program will be avoided. The panel members operate with maximum objectivity, impartiality and factuality. They will refrain from voicing their own opinions in their meetings with the institution/program. Each panel member's individual views are subordinate to the panel's common view. They will operate in a conscientious manner, they will distinguish between desirability and reality, and they will consult multiple sources and substantiate deviations. They will refrain from jumping to conclusions. Finally, the panel members have an eye for both the strengths and the points for attention of the institution/program. These are identified in the assessment report. However, a structural provision of recommendations or solutions to the institution/program will be avoided.

Attitude within the Panel

The chair and the panel members are open to feedback. All interactions within the panel will be conducted with respect to each other's contributions.

Template of the self-assessment report

Preface

Introduction

Criterion 1. Needs and relevance. Social context, developments in Biomedical and Health Informatics (BMHI) and the position of the BMHI program; similar programs existing in the region/country; and relative needs in hospitals, in local companies, small and middle-sized enterprises (SMEs) and industries.

Criterion 2. Intended learning outcomes. Description of the intended learning outcomes of the program, links to international standards of the discipline, and requirements of the professional field.

Criterion 3. The academic/teaching learning environment. Vision on teaching and learning, structure of the curriculum, curriculum of the program, embedding of the program in the clinical and research environment of the University, the staff and its qualifications, and e-learning approaches.

Criterion 4. Organization and implementation. Vision on organization and implementation;, feasibility of the program, regulations on enrolment and intake, workload and student mentoring, progress, and support, laboratories teaching and infrastructure, digital libraries, transparency before and after examinations, mentoring and supervision, dissertation preparation, writing and defense.

Criterion 5. Internal quality assurance and development. Vision on quality assurance, student involvement and satisfaction, consistency, validity, and reliability of the assessment; assessment of skills acquired; evaluating achieved learning outcomes; conforming with international educational standards/recommendations in the BMHI field, quality policy and monitoring; careers monitoring; strengths and weaknesses; and improvements.

Preparatory Work by the Applicant

The applicant (Director of the program) receives a letter by the EFMI AC2 Chair stating: I would like to inform you that the EFMI AC2 Committee has accepted to proceed immediately as you have requested with the Accreditation procedure of your new Program at UMIT. Please find attached the documentation, which is useful to prepare the self-assessment report regarding your University and the Program to be evaluated for possible Accreditation.

- You need to prepare the following material, which should be available in a cloud server, and procedures due to the virtual site-visit.
- Prepare the self-assessment report (assessment process and template attached) and send it to my address (john.mantas@outlook.com) and upload a copy of it at a cloud server. Please send us the appropriate link. It should be uploaded at least one week before the site visit date.
- Prepare supporting electronic material, leaflets, etc. related to your University and the Program, and upload them to the cloud server.
- Prepare a video demonstrating the infrastructure available for the Program, such as, auditorium, classes, laboratories, library, digital facilities, study rooms, etc. Please upload it to the cloud server. Organize, for the day of the virtual visit, meetings with your hierarchy, preferably, Dean or Head of Department, Program Director, Labs Directors, Faculty, Alumni (of similar program within the School), Students (of similar program within the School), liaisons with clinics or hospitals or authorities, stakeholders.
- Prepare a draft agenda of the entire meeting (pay attention to the fixed time items, such as meeting with the Dean or Head of Department, etc.). Final agenda will be issued after mutual agreement. Agenda to be uploaded to the cloud server.

- Prepare the virtual teleconferencing platform with technical support to the site visit members (a prior testing with the members of the site-visit panel is recommended). Ease of use and minimum technical expertise for the platform is recommended.

In the next few days, we will send you the names of the three members of the site-visit panel. In case, you choose that one or more of the panelists are not acceptable to your Institution due to any reason including conflict of interest, we will replace the member or the members in strict confidence.

We have noted your suggested dates and we will select one, accordingly.

We are recommending that you communicate this message to the UMIT's hierarchy indicating the initiation of the EFMI Accreditation process.

Please do not hesitate to send me any question you may have regarding the procedure.

Result of the Evaluation Based on the Criteria

Following the initial letter, a response will look like to the letter-request for Accreditation of the Master's program in Medical Informatics sent in June 2020, EFMI started the procedures established by AC2, the Accreditation Committee of EFMI.

The AC2 site-visit panel for the Accreditation of UMIT's Master's in Medical Informatics: Prof. univ. dr. ing. Lăcrămioara Stoicu-Tivadar, Emeritus Prof. Arie Hasman, and Assoc Prof. Inge Madsen met the UMIT faculty, staff and collaborators during the one-day virtual visit on 20.07.2020.

We are glad to inform you that the site-visit panel Report was accepted by the AC2 Committee and the EFMI Board endorsed this decision on 31.08.2020. The decision states:

The European Federation of Medical Informatics is granting the EFMI accreditation to the UMIT's program 'Master's degree in Medical Informatics' for a duration of 3 years.

Conclusions

Taiwan has demonstrated how the integration of international support and local commitments with the right strategies can help build up mass informatics competency for healthcare professionals in years. Today this group further plays a leading role in building up the smart-hospital projects. The Chinese nurses, as totaled as 4.5 million in mainland China in 2019, are in the early stage of building up their informatics competency. Could we expect what exciting achievements will happen in 10 years in China when we saw the success story in Taiwan and the mainland China has proven to the world that they could and have made many amazing accomplishments? We expect further closer cooperation among the international NI community and those in mainland China and Taiwan to develop more excellent informatics-led healthcare services models.

The EFMI AC2 has already initiated the procedure, and the first applicant was UMIT in Austria. The accreditation to UMIT was awarded during the opening session of MIE conference 2021 in Athens. EFMI has received new applications based on the existing BMHI program in Europe (Kolokathi et al., 2018, 2019), which will be processed in the forthcoming months and will be reported on the EFMI website.

It would be useful in future research to have this process evaluated against the benefits in quality improvement of the educational program as well as on the impact on revising the educational recommendations (Mantras et al., 2010) in BMHI.

Bibliography

Bickford, C. J. (2015). The specialty of nursing informatics: New scope and standards guide practice. *Computers, Informatics, Nursing*, 33(4), pp.129–131. https://doi.org/10.1097/cin.0000000000000150

Chang, J., Poynton, M. R., Gassert, C. A., & Staggers, N. (2011). Nursing informatics competencies required of nurses in Taiwan. *International Journal of Medical Informatics*, 80(5), pp.332–340. https://doi.org/10.1016/j.ijmedinf.2011.01.011

Chang, P., Hsu, C. L., Hou, I. C., Tu, M. H., & Liu, C. W. (2008). The end user computing strategy of using Excel VBA in promoting nursing informatics in Taiwan. *Perspectives in Nursing Science*, 5(1), pp.45–58. Available at: https://www.koreascience.or.kr/article/JAKO200813036233965

Chang, P., & Kuo, M. C. (2010). Taiwan model: Nursing informatics training. In M. J. Ball, J. V. Douglas, P. H. Walker, D. DuLong, B. Gugerty, K. J. Hannah, J. Kiel, S. K. Newbold, J. E. Sensmeier, D. J. Skiba, & M. R. Troseth, eds., *Nursing informatics: Where caring and technologies meet*. 4th ed. New York: Springer, pp. 411–428.

Chen, D. I., Su, J., Hong, Y. J., Gong, D. C., Zhu, Y. Y., et al. (2017). Problem oriented medical record quality monitoring. *Chinese Medical Records*, 12(18), pp.36–38.

Chen, Y., Yan, L., Zheng, W., Lin, B., Wu, L., Wu, Z., & Chang, P. (2020). Establishment of nursing informatics competency evaluation index system of clinical nurses. *Chinese Nursing Management*, 20(6), pp.921–924.

Chen, Y., Xu, X., & Yang, H. (2015). Analysis of nurses' information ability and influencing factors in age of big data. *Chinese Journal of Modern Nursing*, 21(20), pp.2390–2394.

China E Commerce. (2000). Current status of the hospital information systems development in China. *China Ecommerce Report*, 14, pp.18–19.

Cummins, M. R., Gundlapalli, A. V., Gundlapalli, A. V., Murray, P., Park, H. A., & Lehmann, C. U. (2016). Nursing informatics certification worldwide: History, pathway, roles, and motivation. *Yearbook of Medical Informatics*, 25(01), pp.264–271. https://doi.org/10.15265/IY-2016-039

Feng, R. C., Lee, Y. L., & Lee, T. Y. (2015). The role development of informatics nurse specialists in Taiwan. *The Journal of Nursing*, 62(3), pp.23. https://doi.org/10.6224/JN.62.3.23

Guo, C. (2000). Experience of using no. 1 military medical project in nursing work station (in Chinese). *Medical Information*, 13(8), pp.445–446.

Hou, I. C., Chang, P., & Wang, T. Y. (2006). Qualitative analysis of end user computing strategy and experiences in promoting nursing informatics in Taiwan. *Studies in Health Technology Informatics*, 122, pp.613–615.

Hou, I. C., Liu, C. W., Hsu, C. L., & Chang, P. (2009). The evaluation of using roadmap guided excel VBA training to promote nursing informatics in Taiwan. *Studies in health Technology and Informatics*, 146, pp.253–257.

Huang, H., Yu-lan, D., Chun-mei, R., Li-li, S. & Su-wei, C. (2012). A survey on the information literacy of head nurses in the wards of "high quality nursing service demonstration project". *Journal of Nursing Administration*, 12(2), pp.99–100.

Hübner, U., Ball, M. J., Marin, H. D. F., Chang, P., Wilson, M., & Anderson, C. (2016). Towards implementing a global competency-based nursing and clinical informatics curriculum: Applying the TIGER initiative. In *Nursing Informatics 2016—eHealth for All: Every Level Collaboration—From Project to Realization*. Studies in Health Technology and Informatics, Vol. 225. IOS Press, pp. 762–764. https://doi.org/10.3233/978-1-61499-658-3-762

Hübner, U., Shaw, T., Thye, J., Egbert, N., Marin, H. F., Chang, P., O'Connor, S., Day, K., Honey, M., Blake, R., Hovenga, E., Skiba, D., & Ball, M. J. (2018). Technology informatics guiding education reform - TIGER. *Methods of Information in Medicine*, 57(S01), pp.e30–e42. doi:10.3414/ME17-01-0155

Ji, H. (2012). Wireless mobile nursing cart actualizing the extention of information system to patient's bedside (Chinese). *China Information Field: eMedicine*, 3, pp.48–49.

Jiang, A., & Shen, J. (2004). Study on the concept and compositions of information literacy of nursing undergraduates. *Chinese Journal of Nursing*, 39(2), pp.84–86.

Kolokathi, A., Hasman, A., Chronaki, C., Madsen, I., Moen, A., Randell, R., & Mantas, J. (2019). Education in biomedical and health informatics: A European perspective. *Studies in Health Technology and Informatics*, 264, pp.1951–1952. https://doi.org/10.3233/SHTI190729

Kolokathi, A., & Mantas, J. (2018). Education in biomedical and health informatics: A mapping approach. *Studies in Health Technology and Informatics*, 251, pp.313–316.

Li, B. L., Ma, L., & Xu, Y. (2009). The application of nursing informatics and communication technology (in Chinese). *Chinese Nursing Management*, 9(3), pp.76–78.

Liu, J., et al. (2002). Developing an electronic nursing record system. *Chinese Journal of Nursing*, 37(8), pp.595–598.

Liu, L., et al. (2010). The ability of nursing undergraduates in acquiring nursing information (in Chinese). *Journal of Nursing Administration*, 17(3A), pp.24–26.

Mantas, J. (2020). The accreditation procedure ensures quality of education in biomedical and health informatics. *Studies in Health Technology and Informatics*, 272, pp.484–486. https://doi.org/10.3233/SHTI200601

Mantas, J., Ammenwerth, E., Demiris, G., Hasman, A., Haux, R., Hersh, W., Hovenga, E., Lun, K. C., Marin, H., Martin-Sanchez, F., Wright, G.; IMIA Recommendations on Education Task Force. (2010). Recommendations of the International Medical Informatics Association (IMIA) on education in biomedical and health informatics. First revision. *Methods of Information in Medicine*, 49(2), pp.105–120. https://doi.org/10.3414/ME5119

National Chung Cheng University. (2021). Department of Information Management. Available at: https://www.mis.ccu.edu.tw

National Taipei University of Nursing and Health Sciences. (2021a). Department of Information Management. Available at: http://im.ntunhs.edu.tw

National Taipei University of Nursing and Health Sciences. (2021b). School of Nursing. Available at: https://ntunhsson.ntunhs.edu.tw/files/90-1031-16.php?Lang=zh-tw

National Taiwan University. (2021). Graduate Institute of Biomedical Electronics and Bioinformatics. Available at: http://www.bebi.ntu.edu.tw/web/about/about.jsp?lang=en

National Yang Ming Chiao Tung University. (2021a). Institute of Biomedical Informatics. Available at: http://bmi.ym.edu.tw/wp/

National Yang Ming Chiao Tung University. (2021b). School of Nursing. Available at: https://son.nycu.edu.tw

Qi, L. F., et al. (2000). The use of 'Military Health No 1' in nursing case management in a holistic approach through informatization. *Medical Information*, 13(9), pp.499–500.

Shi, F., et al. (2011). Current status of information competency of nursing undergraduate students (in Chinese). *General Nursing*, 9(9), pp.2525–2526.

Sun, J. W., Qian, Y., Luo, W. Y., Xue, P. P., & Lu, H. (2021). Development and usability of a pediatric intravenous maintenance drug calculation small program based on user-built concept. *Chinese Journal of Modern Nursing*, 27(9), pp.1171–1175. https://doi.org/10.3760/cma.j.cn115682-20200710-04326

Taipei Medical University. (2021). Graduate Institute of Biomedical Informatics. Available at: http://gibi.tmu.edu.tw

Taiwan Nurse Association. (2018). Advanced Practice Nurse. Available at: https://www.twna.org.tw/Laws/Law_Detail.aspx?oD9oKv122m7ZbtPHHYLPs39EOyYLopP5

Taiwan Nursing Informatics Association. (2021a). Informatics Nurse Certification Policy (Basic Level). Available at: https://www.ni.org.tw/v2/doc2_cload.aspx

Taiwan Nursing Informatics Association. (2021b). Informatics Nurse Training Program (Basic Level). Available at: https://www.ni.org.tw/v2/newsm_cload3.aspx?pidm=158

Technology Informatics Guiding Education Reform. (2009). Informatics competencies for every registered nurse: Recommendations from the TIGER collaborative. Available at: http://www.tigersummit.com/uploads/3.Tiger.Report_Competencies_final.pdf

The American Nurses Association. (2015a). The scope of nursing informatics practice. In *Nursing informatics: Scope and standards of practice*. 2nd ed. Silver Spring: American Nurses Association, Inc., pp. 1–2.

The American Nursing Association. (2015b). The scope of nursing informatics practice: Informatics competencies requisite for all registered nurses. In *Nursing informatics: Scope and standards of practice*. 2nd ed. Silver Spring: American Nurses Association, Inc., pp. 37–38.

Tzu Chi University. (2021). Department of Medical Informatics. Available at: http://tcumi.tcu.edu.tw/?page_id=178

Wang, G., & Zhang, J. (1993). Application of computer software in analyzing nursing errors. *Chinese Journal of Nursing*, 28(5), pp.262–264.

Wang, G. J. (1994). Experiences of involving the development of computer software. *Chinese Journal of Nursing*, 29(9), pp.544–546.

Wang, T., & He, S. (2008). On the evaluation criteria of information literacy of higher vocational student nurses (in Chinese). *China Medical Education Technology*, 22(5), pp.419–421.

Xu, R. (2012). *Study on framework of nursing information competencies for undergraduate students (in Chinese)*. Hangzhou: Department of Nursing, Hongzou Normal University, p.127.

Yang, F., et al. (2013). A core competency model for Chinese baccalaureate nursing graduates: A descriptive correlational study in Beijing. *Nurse Education Today*, 33, pp.1465–1470.

Zeng, F., et al. (2015). Development and application of mobile nursing information system. *China Medical Equipment*, 12(4), pp.18–22.

Zhang, B., et al. (2014). Application of mobile nursing information system in clinical settings. *Chinese Nursing Management*, z1, pp.88–89.

Zhang, Q. (1992). Use of computer systems in nursing management system (in Chinese). *Journal of Chinese Nursing*, 27(2), pp.84–86.

Chapter 3

Health and Healthcare Education Current State

Jane Marie Kirschling and Mary Etta Mills

Contents

Introduction 47
Re-envisioning the Nursing Education Roadmap 48
Leading Dimensions of Professional Nursing Education 49
Technology and Practice Innovation...52
Healthcare Education 55
Attention to the Intangibles 57
Conclusion 59
References...59

Introduction

Nursing education in the United States continues to transform in response to the evolving needs of our nation's complex healthcare system. This transformation has been shaped by the Institute of Medicine's report *The Future of Nursing: Leading Change, Advancing Health* (2011). This report puts forward recommendations to be accomplished by 2020—including the need for nurses to join with other health professionals in leading the redesign of care, that residency training for nurses be deployed, that 80% of the nursing workforce be baccalaureate prepared, that the number of doctorally prepared nurses double, and that full scope of practice barriers be removed.

DOI: 10.4324/9781003281009-3

While there is still work to be done, good progress has been made on a number of the recommendations.

Re-envisioning the Nursing Education Roadmap

How nursing education will evolve over the next decade is being shaped by a variety of factors. *The Future of Nursing 2020–2030* articulates the role that nurses must play in addressing health inequity and requires that the profession engage 'in the complex work of aligning public health, healthcare, social services and public polices to eliminate health disparities and achieve health equity' (National Academies of Sciences, Engineering, and Medicine, 2021, p. 1). This call to action has broad implications for the nursing workforce but also requires that nursing education for entry-into-practice, as well as advanced nursing practice, and the preparation of nursing scientists focus on health disparities.

Community-based care, caring for vulnerable populations and population health will need greater emphasis within various curricula, and it will be essential that nursing students, as well as practicing nurses, are further challenged to go beyond the episodic care that is delivered in hospitals to consider the whole person, their support systems and other available resources. Academic–practice partnerships are emerging across the United States that bridge care coordination across settings and levels of care. For example, the University of Maryland Medical Center in Baltimore has partnered with the University of Maryland School of Nursing (UMSON) to promote care coordination and patient-centered care across Maryland hospitals and expand Registered Nurse to Bachelor of Science in Nursing (RN-to-BSN) care coordination and health information technology in the School as well as community college nursing programs (Nahm et al., 2021).

Nursing education programs also need to continue to work closely with their clinical partners on transition-into-practice residency programs for both entry-into-practice and advanced practice registered nurses. The Maryland Nurse Residency Collaborative received a $1.8 million grant from Maryland's Who Will Care fund in 2018. The Collaborative includes 44 hospitals and is a partnership between the Maryland Organization of Nurse Leaders, Vizient, and the American Association of Colleges of Nursing (AACN). The 12-month program is for entry-into-practice graduates and includes online training materials, onsite education, leadership development, career planning and guidance from nurse experts.

UMSON nursing faculty have implemented a collaborative education and practice partnership with University of Maryland Upper Chesapeake Medical Center nurses (Akintade et al., 2020). The partnership includes increased clinical practice opportunities for nurse practitioner students, the development of a post-advanced practice fellowship program and a faculty practice position at the Medical Center's Comprehensive Care Center.

These academic–practice partnerships are critical as we look toward the future of nursing education and practice and leverage our collective expertise. And new partnerships will need to emerge as we collectively work to reduce health disparities in the United States.

Leading Dimensions of Professional Nursing Education

In 2004, the Sullivan Commission on Diversity in the Healthcare Workforce (Sullivan, 2004) highlighted the lack of diversity of America's healthcare providers. And now, nearly two decades later, we are finally seeing progress in diversifying the nursing workforce in terms of race and ethnicity. The 2020 National Nursing Workforce Survey reported that of the 4,198,031 active licenses in the United States, nearly 81% of RNs reported being White/Caucasian, RNs who reported being Asian accounted for 7.2% of the workforce, representing the largest non-Caucasian racial group in the RN workforce. Black/African-American RNs increased from 6.0% in 2013 to 6.7% in 2020 and the proportion of RNs reporting being Hispanic/Latinx also increased from 2017 (Smiley et al., 2021, p. S6).

The key to diversifying the nursing profession is the pipeline of new graduates. The AACN (Fang et al., 2021) reported that in Fall 2020, 62.1% of nursing students enrolled in undergraduate programs were white, 13.7% were Hispanic or Latino, 12.4% were Black or African American, 7.7% were Asian and 3.2% reported being from two or more races. Less than 1% of enrolled students were American Indian or Alaskan Native (0.6%) or Native Hawaiian or Pacific Islander (0.4%). The 'changing face' of the nursing workforce is critical given The Sullivan Commission's (2004) stance that 'The lack of minority health professionals is compounding the nation's persistent racial and ethnic health disparities' (p. i).

Nursing programs throughout the United States are, and will continue to be, engaged in curriculum revision given a number of forces. These include the National Council of State Boards of Nursing (NCSBN) 'Next Generation National Council Licensure Examination for Registered Nurses (NCLEX)

Project' (NCSBN, no date), AACN's (2021) *The Essentials: Core Competencies for Professional Nursing Education* (*The Essentials*), the growth of associate to baccalaureate partnerships and associate to master's degree programs, and the evolution of doctoral education in nursing, including the Doctor of Nursing Practice and PhD. The Next Generation NCLEX Project is redesigning the registered nurse licensing exam to move beyond testing nursing knowledge to assessing decision-making and clinical judgment in nursing practice through 'real-world' case studies. It is projected that the earliest the new testing format will go into effect is 2023.

The Essentials reflects a new 'framework for preparing individuals as members of the discipline of nursing, reflecting expectations across the trajectory of nursing education and applied experience' (AACN, 2021, p. 2). This framework provides '10 domains that represent the essence of professional nursing practice and the expected competencies for each domain' (p. 2). *The Essentials* defines entry and advanced levels of education. Baccalaureate and graduate nursing programs will have to do major curriculum work to redesign and realign the various curricula.

For many individuals interested in a nursing career, the associate degree continues to be their point of entry. 'Approximately 42% of nurses in 2020 reported the baccalaureate nursing degree as their first U.S. nursing license,' which reflected growth of 5.8% from 2013 (Smiley et al., 2021, p. S5). During this same time period, persons who initially earned a diploma or associate degree in nursing dropped by 7.5%. One of the recommendations in the 2011 report *The future of nursing* was to increase the number of nurses who attained a baccalaureate degree to 80% by 2020. In order to address this recommendation, baccalaureate and graduate nursing programs expanded their partnerships with associate degree programs to reduce barriers to enrolling in RN-to-BSN and RN-to-master's programs. The concerted focus on articulation between associate degree and baccalaureate programs in the United States resulted in a 93% increase in enrollments between 2011 and 2018, from 65,074 to 125,279; in 2020, enrollments in RN-to-BSN declined to 119,769 (Fang, 2021, p. 24).

UMSON now has agreements with all 15 of Maryland's associate degree programs. Additionally, associate degree students can enroll as 'special students' in the RN-to-BSN program while still completing their associate degree requirements, which allows them to reduce the time to completion of the BSN. The Registered Nurse to Master of Science in Nursing (RN-to-MSN) program combines elements of the BSN and MSN programs by substituting the master's core courses for BSN electives, which reduces the overall cost of the program and allows students to specialize in community/public health nursing, health services leadership and management, or nursing informatics. For associate degree nurses who graduated without yet having earned the BSN or MSN degree, a Nurse Support Program II initiative supports academic–practice partnerships with Maryland hospitals to engage, recruit and graduate hospital-based staff as MSN graduates prepared for leadership and educator roles. With this preparation, these hospital-based graduates can concurrently serve as clinical instructors to assist schools of nursing in the preparation of new nurses (Mills et al., 2020).

The expansion of graduate education, and especially doctoral education, in nursing in the United States is also noteworthy and will continue to require schools of nursing to assure that the curricula for the various avenues for preparing nurses for advanced nursing practice and for careers as nurse scientists are responsive to the needs of the ever-evolving healthcare system. A recommendation in the 2011 report *The future of nursing* was to double the number of doctorally prepared nurses by 2020, this recommendation has been far exceeded. While enrollment in 146 research-focused doctoral programs decreased by 5.9% between 2016 (4,883 students) and 2020 (4,597 students), enrollment in 378 Doctorate of Nursing Practice (DNP) programs increased by 56.3% (2016 25,258 students, 2020 39,485 students) (Smiley et al., 2021, pp. 53, 66). The growth in DNP programs has placed considerable pressure on faculty resources as programs have worked to assure that they were meeting *The Essentials of Doctoral Education for Advanced Nursing Practice* and especially the requirement of a final DNP project (AACN, 2006). In addition, the advanced practice registered nurse programs have to meet the requirements of the various specialties. All of the DNP curricula, including BSN-to-DNP and post-master's DNP, will have to be re-envisioned given the 2021 *Essentials*.

In 2018, the AACN hosted an invitational discussion with the National Institute of Nursing Research—National Institutes of Health focused on the PhD pathway in nursing. The outcomes included three recommendations—promoting recruitment, providing mentoring and professional development, and funding new researchers (AACN, 2018). Expanding the pipeline of the next generation of nurse scientists is important, and the pipeline needs to continue to advance strategies that attract nurses earlier in their careers, including streamlined BSN-to-PhD options. PhD curricula also have to be continually refined to address the evolving areas of science and new research methods. A final area of development for doctoral education in nursing is combining the DNP and PhD to support DNP-prepared nurses who decide to pursue research careers.

Technology and Practice Innovation

Rapid advances in technology have enabled nursing education to prepare students for practice in diverse settings and under a multitude of clinical conditions. Information systems have grown to encompass processes such as data analytics, encrypted information, cybersecurity, digitized clinical records and automated physiologic data capture. These systems depend on defining and capturing data that once combined can provide information and support knowledge generation. Nursing informatics as a field of practice has experienced rapid growth since the initiation of formalized nursing informatics education, with the first master's program established at UMSON in 1989 and the first PhD program in nursing informatics, also at UMSON, in 1991. Expanding beyond the first DNP program in nursing informatics at the University of Minnesota launched in 2007, DNP programs with a nursing informatics focus continue to expand. A formal certification in nursing informatics first became available through the American Nurses Credentialing Center in 1992. Since that time, the importance of information and communication technology has become one of the underpinnings of support for care and provider communication across all levels of care delivery. In 2021, AACN included Informatics and Healthcare Technology as the eighth domain of *The Essentials*. Faculty will need to further integrate core information and communication technologies' competencies into nursing curricula. There is an emphasis on 'the use of technology to support healthcare processes and clinical thinking; and the ability of informatics and technology to positively impact patient outcomes' (AACN, 2021, p. 8).

While the use of electronic health records (EHR) has become the norm, the capacity of information technology to support a person's care continues to grow exponentially. Mobile healthcare (mHealth) applications, for example, involve the use of mobile and wireless devices to support wearables for self-health monitoring of physiologic parameters such as cardiac rate and rhythm status, to provide information to individuals and their providers and can be used 'to improve health outcomes, healthcare services, and health research' (Department of Health and Human Services, 2013, p. 3). These applications support wearables for self-health monitoring and have allowed growth of telemedicine and telehealth that enable healthcare providers to remotely evaluate data in real time (Chang et al., 2017). Patient portals allow information stored in the EHR to be accessed and viewed by patients. In this way, individuals can review their recorded health information and choose how—and what—additional data to share with their healthcare provider.

Although the interconnectivity of multiple sources of data can increasingly support continuity and coordination of care across levels and settings, it also creates new challenges and opportunities for healthcare providers to consider, such as health information privacy, legal and regulatory requirements, patient and provider health information technology literacy, and health literacy. With the increasing focus on preventive and primary care, patient participation in managing their care becomes ever more essential. The ability of persons to participate fully as a partner in their care is an important social determinant of health, since it is influenced by multiple factors such as culture, income, education and access to basic resources—including access and understanding of supportive technology. Preparation of nurse educators, as well as of students, in advances in technology is essential when considering the multiple facets of health information technology and the interrelationship of data collection, access, and use by both consumers and healthcare professionals.

With advances in computational design, artificial intelligence (AI) as a field is increasingly able to assist in providing information support for care and treatment (Mansour et al., 2021). This field of science supports unique rapid data analysis to propose the results of diagnostic assessments and monitor and control physiologic support systems. Collection of data from multiple sources, including the EHR, further allows the analysis of large data sets for clinical decisions and quality improvement. The use of big data for case tracking of COVID, such as that used by the Minnesota Department of Health, is one example of real-world application (MDH, 2022). Preparation of nurses to understand the scientific principles underlying AI can support the adoption and use of future technology. Educational tools supported by AI, such as virtual reality by which novel situations can be generated for simulated patient care experiences and robotics (British Broadcasting Company, 2020, paragraph 26), will further support the nursing process. Nursing education needs not only to prepare the next generation of nurses to utilize technologic support but also to participate in its development (Pruinelli and Michalowski, 2021).

Clinical practice preparation of students is increasingly supported by clinical simulation and virtual clinical simulation experience. High-fidelity, or manikin-based, simulation dates back to the 1960s as a way of giving students clinical experiences before interacting with patients in an actual care setting. While manikin-based simulation provides a psychomotor-based clinical education, the growing interest in distance education—only made more critical by the COVID-19 pandemic—has fostered development of new simulation tools including virtual clinical simulation. This tool provides flexibility with an emphasis on cognitive tasks such as diagnostic reasoning to help build clinical judgment. This is also an emphasis in the 2021 *Essentials*. For example, virtual clinical simulation can be used to offer virtual patient encounters to assist with communication and medical record interpretation. Work in this field has grown to include physiologic audio such as breath and heart sounds, virtual intravenous starts, medical images, interactive communication, client assessment, and outcome evaluation. Experience with medical records is provided through systems such as EHR Go (2021), a learning platform with customizable patient cases. It enables students to document patient care and administer medication in a barcoded electronic medication administration record (eMAR). These systems have allowed schools of nursing to increase competencies and reduce clinical placement time in actual healthcare settings while still developing student clinical abilities. The use of simulation in the curriculum as a replacement for direct patient clinical hours or experiences is 'determined by requirements of national specialty education, certification entities, and regulatory entities' (AACN, 2021, p. 25). As virtual reality applications grow, there will be greater degrees of immersion and interactivity in virtual environments.

The use of standardized patients has been demonstrated to be an excellent opportunity for interprofessional education to prepare students to 'transition to cohesive, collaborative, patient-centered practice' (Luctkar-Flude et al., 2016, p. 25). Standardized patients are actors who simulate patients with specific conditions. Students interact with them just as they would with actual patients by taking a history, conducting a physical examination, documenting findings, and constructing a plan of treatment. This preparation increases both skills and knowledge attainment prior to actual patient encounters. When used as part of interprofessional education, standardized patients can increase participation in clinical decision-making across disciplines.

Supported by a diverse set of technologies, growth in mobile computing and improved Internet capability, distance education has also taken on new precedence with the onset of COVID-19 as a worldwide pandemic. The fully online learning environment has enabled students to engage in both structured mastery of content through video presentations, interactive exercises, assignments, readings, and asynchronous discussions with instructors and classmates. Web-enhanced course delivery involves courses being offered face-to-face supplemented by web-based materials. Hybrid instruction combines online learning with either synchronous class sessions or in-person instruction on a defined schedule. As a method of instruction, distance education has provided increased flexibility and convenience for the learner. It has also been instrumental in negating geographic boundaries, allowing students to complete studies in programs far from their places of residence and work.

Learning management systems, also referred to as course management systems, such as Blackboard, Brightspace, Canvas and Schoology, are used to support course content, communication, access, and use of course materials, testing, grading and record-keeping. Learning management systems can further support course development through a database of instructional resources such as videos or other course content that can be accessed or modified.

Challenges of distance education include assisting instructors with support to refocus their role to connecting with students as a coach and assisting with active learning. Likewise, students need assistance in structuring time to meet course requirements. Time commitment also changes, since students can access materials anytime and anywhere and are able to reach out to instructors through posted questions and conversations at any point in the day or night, seven days a week. This requires an adjustment by students and instructors regarding expectations for timely responses and flexibility for document submissions.

Technologic advances will continue to grow as virtual and augmented reality experiences are incorporated into online learning platforms. This approach can lead to adaptive learning where the content and assessment are responsive to the demonstrated level of comprehension by individual learners and progresses in level as the learner advances. As the development of virtual environments advances, students will increasingly have an opportunity to experience settings that mimic the real world, including avatars simulating patients or healthcare team members with whom they can interact to practice and apply educational content.

Healthcare Education

Just as nursing education continues to evolve, similar work is being done across other programs in health professions education. For example, the American Association of Medical Colleges highlights that both the content and structure of medical student education is changing. Changes in content 'reflect scientific advancements, medical breakthroughs, delivery-system changes, and social issues' (no date, p. 2). Examples of the changes in structure include 'earlier clinical experiences, curriculum structures integrating the basic and clinical sciences, emphasis on interprofessional educational opportunities, and case-based learning' (p. 2).

The majority of programs in health professions education in the United States have moved to professional doctorates, consistent with medicine. The movement to professional doctorates has allowed for expanding the curricula in terms of content and practice experiences.

Health professions education in the United States has also embraced a greater emphasis on interprofessional education. While there have been focused opportunities for decades in areas such as geriatrics and end-of-life care, a broader adoption of interprofessional education was sparked by the development of the Interprofessional Education Collaborative (IPEC) Core Competencies in 2011, which were updated in 2016 to 'broaden the interprofessional competencies to better achieve the Triple Aim (improve the patient experience of care, improve the health of populations, and reduce the per capita cost of healthcare), with particular reference to population health' (IPEC, 2016, p. 1). The four core competency domains include values and ethics, roles and responsibilities for collaborative practice, interprofessional communication, and teamwork and team-based care. These core competencies underpin the 'vision of interprofessional collaborative practice as key to the safe, high quality, accessible, patient-centered care desired by all' (IPEC Expert Panel, 2011, p. i).

Six health professions organizations formed IPEC which provided the foundation for the renewed focus on interprofessional education. The founding organizations included AACN, the American Association of Colleges of Osteopathic Medicine, the American Association of Colleges of Pharmacy, the American Dental Education Association, the Association of American Medical Colleges and the Association of Schools and Programs of Public Health. In 2021, there are 21 IPEC members. Similarly, the National Center for Interprofessional Practice and Education was founded in 2012 with support from the Josiah Macy Jr. Foundation, the Robert Wood Johnson Foundation, the Gordon and Betty Moore Foundation, the United States Health and Human Services Health Resources and Services Administration, and the University of Minnesota. This first public–private partnership in the United States provides the leadership, evidence and resources needed to guide the nation on interprofessional education and collaborative practice driven by data (Interprofessional Practice and Education, 2021).

At the University of Maryland, Baltimore, the Center for Interprofessional Education was formed in 2013. The Center offers 15 hours of interprofessional care content to students in the Schools of Dentistry, Medicine, Nursing, and Pharmacy as well as the Graduate School and holds an annual workshop where students come together with faculty to do a case-based scenario that includes standardized patients. In addition, the Center provides faculty development and seed funding for interprofessional education initiatives that involve students from two or more disciplines on campus (including the Schools of Law and Social Work) with a primary focus on practice and field application.

In general, affordability of higher education continues to be a concern in America and this holds true for health professions education. The most expensive health professions program is dental school, the class of 2018 had an average debt of $285,184, which is two times a dentist's average annual income (Proctor, 2020). Fortunately, entry-level nursing student debt is much lower but still of concern at an average debt in 2019 between $19,928 (Associate Degree in Nursing), $23,711 (Bachelor of Science in Nursing) and $47,321 (Master of Science in Nursing), according to the US Department of Education's College Scorecard (Lane, 2021).

Health professions workforce shortages have been, and will continue to be, an issue that impacts the delivery and availability of healthcare in America. Of the 20 occupations projected to have the highest growth between 2019 and 2029, six are in healthcare—nurse practitioners (52% growth), occupational therapist assistants (35%), home health and personal care aides (34%), physical therapist assistants (33%), physician assistants (31%), and speech and language pathologists (25%) (U.S. Bureau of Labor Statistics, 2021a). It is projected that the demand for registered nurses will grow by 7% (faster than average), and there will be an additional 221,900 positions by 2029 (U.S. Bureau of Labor Statistics, 2021b).

Attention to the Intangibles

The development of professionals in whom the care of individuals is entrusted has important underpinnings, some of which include ethical decision-making and philosophical value systems supporting leadership. They are also key elements related to accomplishment of the 2021 *Essentials*, which importantly include professionalism (domain 9) and personal, professional and leadership development (domain 10).

The American Nurses Association Code of Ethics for Nurses (ANA, 2015) is a guide for carrying out nursing responsibilities in a manner consistent with quality in nursing care and the ethical obligations of the profession. The formation of a personal ethical framework is built on an abstract system of thinking that can be fostered by including studies and reflections on moral phenomena, for example, considering what an individual professes to do versus what they actually do. A utilitarian code of ethics acts to distinguish between areas that may be deceptively similar by removing ambiguity through rules and procedures. Going beyond utility, nursing education can assist students in developing justification premises for valid arguments and processes to decide if something is 'right.' This process can extend to questioning 'facts' that are based on unseen data. For example, clinical decision support systems may be based on historical data that is biased 'against minority groups, persons with disabilities, or those with mental health conditions' (Johnson, 2019, p. 434). Likewise, AI and systems of care dependent on access to technologies and high-speed Internet are examples of areas where there are risks for bias and exclusion. Ethical principles would 'ensure that all populations are included in the data so that they all benefit from predictions by the AI algorithms that could impact healthcare delivery' (Johnson, 2019, p. 436). Examination at this level requires progressively moving from rule to principle to ethical decision-making. These considerations go beyond the basic principles of ethics in healthcare that refer to respect for patient autonomy (the right to make their own decisions), beneficence (treatment must contain the intention of benefiting the patient), nonmaleficence (treatment offered does not afford harm to the patient), and justice (distribution of scarce resource, fairness and equity in access to services).

Philosophical underpinnings of ethics include the Socratic method leading to the examination of internal consistency within a point of view and criticism, reflection, and examination of the justification for a particular point of view. Aristotle distinguished between the broad (what is right) and narrow senses (what is fair and equal distribution). This creates competing theories of justice that can drive important differences in personal beliefs between individuals. Nurse educators are charged with including scenarios within the curriculum to allow students to discuss distributive justice: how services and opportunities should be distributed (not just scarce resources).

Leadership in nursing builds on these ethical and philosophical principles. Leaders are charged with assessment of what resources are being distributed, the population that needs to be served, and the personnel and resources that are available. The film *Code gray: Ethical dilemmas in nursing* portrays nurses in dilemmas of autonomy, authority and power conflicts (Achtenberg and Sawyer, 1984). This 1984 American short documentary film is still a resource designed to stimulate conversation. The Hastings Center Reports are another resource for exploring the ethical, legal and social issues in healthcare.

Conclusion

Nursing education in the United States continues to evolve in response to the needs of the healthcare system and social needs. Academic–practice partnerships allow us to accelerate the necessary changes since they leverage our collective expertise. The pipeline of new graduates reflects a more diverse nursing workforce, which will help to address longstanding racial and ethnic health disparities.

A number of factors are influencing health professions education, including but not limited to technology in practice and education, a heightened focus on interprofessional education, and ongoing concerns about the cost of education and workforce needs. As the future unfolds, nursing leadership must continue to build on ethical and philosophical principles to guide how resources are being distributed to meet the needs of the population being served.

References

Achtenbert, B., & Sawyer, J. (1984). *Code gray ethical dilemmas in nursing* [online], film, Fanlight Productions. Available at: http://fanlight.com/catalog/films/004_cg.php (Accessed 25 May 2021).

Akintade, B. F., Idzik, S., Fornili, K., Montgomery, K. L., Gourley, B., Novak, K., & Indenbaum-Bates, K. (2020). *Development and implementation of a collaborative nurse practitioner clinical training program* [online]. Poster presented at the 2020 Maryland Action Coalition Annual Summit. Available at: https://www.nursing.umaryland.edu/media/son/academics/professional-education/mdac-2020/presentations/Akintade-PPT---Development-and-Implementation-of-a-Collaborative-Nurse-Practitioner-Clinical-Training-Program.pdf (Accessed 24 May 2021).

American Association of Colleges of Nursing. (2006). *The essentials of doctoral education for advanced nursing practice* [online]. Washington, DC: American Association of Colleges of Nursing. Available at: https://www.aacnnursing.org/DNP/DNP-Essentials.pdf (Accessed 24 May 2021).

American Association of Colleges of Nursing. (2018). *The PhD pathway in nursing* [online]. Report on an invitational conversation done in collaboration with the National Institute of Nursing Research, National Institutes of Health. Washington, DC: American Association of Colleges of Nursing. Available at: https://www.aacnnursing.org/Portals/42/news/surveys-data/PhD-Pathway.pdf (Accessed 24 May 2021).

American Association of Colleges of Nursing. (2021, April 6). *The essentials: Core competencies for professional nursing education* [online]. Washington, DC: American Association of Colleges of Nursing. Available at: https://www.aacnnursing.org/Portals/42/AcademicNursing/pdf/ Essentials-2021.pdf (Accessed 24 May 2021).

American Association of Medical Colleges. (n.d.). *Policy priorities to improve our nation's health: How medical education is changing* [online]. Washington, DC: American Association of Colleges of Nursing. Available at: https://www.aamc.org/media/19151/download (Accessed 24 May 2021).

American Nurses Association. (2015). *Code of ethics for nurses with interpretive statements* [online]. Available at: https://www.nursingworld.org/practice-policy/nursing-excellence/ethics/code-of-ethics-for-nurses/coe-view-only/ (Accessed 24 May 2021).

British Broadcasting Company. (2020). *What the world can learn from Japan's robots* [online]. Available at: https://www.bbc.com/worklife/article/20200205-what-the-world-can-learn-from-japans-robots (Accessed 24 May 2021).

Chang, D. P., Lee, T. T., Mills, M. E., & Lee, H. L. (2017). Experience of home telehealth technology in older patients with diabetes. *Computers, Informatics, Nursing*, 36(2), pp.59–66.

Department of Health and Human Services. (2013). *Definition of mHealth* [online]. Available at: https://grants.nih.gov/grants/guide/pa-files/PAR-14-028.html (Accessed 25 May 2021).

EHR Go. (2021). [online]. Available at: https://ehrgo.com/ (Accessed 24 May 2021).

Fang, D., Keyt, J. C., McFadden, T., & Trautman, DE. (2021). *2020–2021 enrollment and graduations in baccalaureate and graduate programs in nursing*. Washington, DC: American Association of Colleges of Nursing.

Institute of Medicine Committee on the Robert Wood Johnson Foundation Initiative on the Future of Nursing. (2011). *The future of nursing: Leading change, advancing health*. Washington, DC: National Academies Press.

Interprofessional Education Collaborative. (2016). *Core competencies for interprofessional collaborative practice: 2016 update* [online]. Washington, DC: Interprofessional Education Collaborative. Available at: https://ipec.memberclicks.net/assets/2016-Update.pdf (Accessed 24 May 2021).

Interprofessional Education Collaborative Expert Panel. (2011). *Core competencies for interprofessional collaborative practice: Report of an expert panel* [online]. Washington, DC: Interprofessional Education Collaborative. Available at: https://ipec.memberclicks.net/ assets/2011-Original.pdf (Accessed 24 May 2021).

Interprofessional Practice and Education. (2021). *Bringing together practice and education in a new Nexus for better care, added value and healthier communities* [online]. National Center for Interprofessional Practice and Education. Available at: https://nexusipe.org/ (Accessed 24 August 2021).

Johnson, S. L. (2019). A.I., machine learning and ethics in healthcare', *Journal of Legal Medicine*, 39(4), pp.427–441.

Lane, R. (2021, May 6). Average nursing student debt: How much debt do nurses have? *Nerdwallet* [online]. Available at: https://www.nerdwallet.com/article/loans/student-loans/average-nursing-student-debt (Accessed 24 May 2021).

Luctkar-Flude, M., Hopkins-Rosseel, D., Jones-Hiscock, C., Pulling, C., Gauthier, J., Knapp, A., Pinchin, S., & Brown, C. A. (2016). 'Interprofessional infection control education using standardized patients for nursing, medical and physiotherapy students', *Journal of Interprofessional Education & Practice*, 2(March), pp.25–31.

Mansour, R. F., Amraqui, A. E., Nouaouri, I., Diaz, V. G., Gupta, D., & Kumar, S. (2021). 'Artificial intelligence and Internet of things enabled disease diagnosis model for smart healthcare systems'. *IEEE Access* (Open Journal), 9(2021), pp.45137–45146.

MDH. (2022). *COVID-19 dashboard / COVID-19 Updates and Information - State of Minnesota* [online]. Available at: https://mn.gov/covid19/data/covid-dashboard/index.jsp (Accessed 24 January 2022).

Mills, M. E., Hickman, L. J., Lucci, S., & Pratt, J. (2020). *Impact of academic-practice partnerships on nursing entry level clinical rotations and graduations* [online]. Poster presented at the 2020 Maryland Action Coalition Summit. Available at: https://nursesupport.org/assets/ files/1/files/nspii/mills_poster__impact_of_a cademicpractice_partnerships-1-.pdf (Accessed 24 May 2021).

Nahm, E. S., Raymond, G., Mills, M. E., Tyler, R., Doyle, K., Rowen, L., & Kirschling, J. (2021). *The future of nursing 2020–2030: UMNursing as an example for academic-practice partnership efforts* [online]. Poster presented at the 2021 Maryland Action Coalition Virtual Leadership Summit. Available at: https://www.nursing.umaryland.edu/media/son/academics/ professional-education/mdac-20 21/posters/49_Nahm_Eun-Shim-MDAC-Web-Only.pdf (Accessed 25 may 2021).

National Academies of Sciences, Engineering, and Medicine. (2021). *The future of nursing 2020–2030: Charting a path to achieve health equity* [online]. Washington, DC: The National Academies Press. Available at: https://doi.org/10.17226/25982 (Accessed 24 May 2021).

National Council of State Boards of Nursing. (n.d.). *Next generation NCLEX project* [online]. Available at: https://www.ncsbn.org/next-generation-nclex.htm (Accessed 24 May 2021).

Proctor, G. (2020, February 18). 15 most affordable dental schools in the U.S', *Student Loan Planner* [online]. Available at: https://www.studentloanplanner.com/best-affordable-dental-schools/ (Accessed 24 May 2021).

Pruinelli, L., & Michalowski, M. (2021). Toward an augmented nursing: Artificial intelligence future. *Computers, Informatics, Nursing*, 39(6), pp.296–297.

Smiley, R. A., Ruttinger, C., Oliveira, C. M., Hudson, L. R., Allgeyer, R., Reneau, K. A., Silvestre, J. H., & Alexander, M. (2021). The 2020 national nursing workforce survey. *Journal of Nursing Regulation*, 12(1), pp.S4–S96.

Sullivan, L. W. (2004). *Missing persons: Minorities in the health professions: A report of the Sullivan commission on diversity in the healthcare workforce* [online]. Available at: https://drum.lib.umd.edu/bitstream/handle/1903/22267/Sullivan_Final_Report_000.pdf?sequence=1&isAllowed=y (Accessed 24 May 2021).

U.S. Bureau of Labor Statistics. (2021a, April 9). *Occupational outlook handbook: Fastest growing occupations* [online]. Available at: https://www.bls.gov/ooh/fastest-growing.htm (Accessed 24 May 2021).

U.S. Bureau of Labor Statistics. (2021b, April 9). *Occupational outlook handbook: Registered nurses* [online]. Available at: https://www.bls.gov/ooh/healthcare/registered-nurses.htm (Accessed 24 May 2021).

Chapter 4

Using Digital as a Tool, Not Being the Tool of the Technology Giants

Peter Klein, Bob Barker, Kevin Bryant and Alexander M.K. Mackenzie

Contents

Introduction	64
Digital Devices Get Upgrades—When Is Yours Scheduled?	64
Digital Wellness and You as a Professional	65
Digital Psychology	66
Personal Processes	67
People Skills and Digital	69
Digital and Wellness	70
Digital Wellness and Your Family, Friends and Coworkers	71
Phubbing	72
Family Media Agreements	72
Social Media and Relationships	72
Your Personal Digital Brand	73
Your Profile Photo—Identification and First Impression	73
The 'About You' Part	74
The Trust Factor	74
Caring for the Digital You and Security	74
The Five Key Cyber–Health Outcomes	75

DOI: 10.4324/9781003281009-4

Best Practices: What You Can Do to Protect Your Patients, Your Colleagues and Yourself 75
Summary: The Secret of Success—Your Community 77
References 78

Introduction

Digital Devices Get Upgrades—When Is Yours Scheduled?

Transport yourself back to Silicon Valley, the year is 2007, the iPhone is new, and Google and Apple are hiring the best and brightest data scientists, psychologists, scientists and business people for one reason: to keep people looking at their devices or software.

In Silicon Valley, the result is generations of people obsessed with their phones and software. A 2013 stage adaptation of George Orwell's book *1984* suggested that addiction to the device would happen: 'The people will not revolt. They will not look up from their screens long enough to notice what's happening' (Icke & Macmillan, 2013). Today, the line resonates louder than ever.

Since their founding, companies such as Google, Facebook, Apple, Twitter (and many others) have been receiving investments to fund the development of technology to keep people looking at their devices so shareholders could get higher returns. According to Eyal, these tech companies are building their digital technology to get you to behave in a certain way—to buy the goods and services their advertisers want you to consume. These companies want you to get addicted to them because it will increase their revenue (Eyal, 2021). These big tech companies collect and sell your data, and then use your data to power artificial intelligence (AI) to get you to think about what they want you to purchase. This is why most of the software you download is 'free.' Is it free? It comes at a cost: your data and attention.

Data is collected in multiple ways. When you use Gmail, you give Google permission to read your emails and they use this data to customize the ads they send you and what shows up in your news feed. When you visit a website and click 'OK' to share information and acknowledge the use of browser 'cookies,' you are granting the company broad privileges. These privileges allow the company to use your data to customize your experience and what you receive in the form of advertising (each company can do this differently and collect different types and levels of your data). Because cookies can collect sensitive personal data, tracking cookies is sometimes considered to be a potential privacy concern.

In 2021, Americans was expected to spend an average of 6 hours and 43 minutes online per day (Kemp, 2020)—that is about 100 days of your year. Every second, 15.5 new people join social networks (Kemp, 2021). And yet, 64% of Americans say social media has a mostly negative effect on the way things are going in the United States today (Auxier, 2020). Ask yourself: what is technology doing to you, your patients, healthcare, your family and your life?

Most people get a new smartphone approximately every 3 years (Ng, 2019). The software on your phone is updated on average ten times a year (Lustosa, 2018). When was the last time you upgraded your brain with the knowledge you need to live your life to the fullest, where you are in control of your life, and not your phone controlling you? Your phone has had 30 software updates since you purchased it. Have *you* had an upgrade? Do you know how to use your phone wisely? Do you understand security and how to set your phone preferences to your advantage? Or do you just keep scrolling?

This is the time to upgrade your knowledge about controlling your devices and software, not the other way around. It is time to control your knowledge and intellect. In this chapter, we provide you with ideas that have worked across different industries to empower your control of your devices and not let the device and the companies behind them control what you are thinking and doing. We will explore ways of ensuring digital wellness, establishing your digital brand and maintaining digital security.

Digital Wellness and You as a Professional

Beyond the core tasks of caring for patients, digital technology enables most work and indeed how we get most communication and tasks done in our personal lives. Because we use our devices for many hours each day, as mentioned in the introduction, we should be prioritizing continually improving how we use the available devices, applications and systems to increase effectiveness, efficiency and responsibility, allowing us more time for nursing care and interacting with our friends, families and loved ones.

We all face a digital dilemma. On the one hand, we know improving our digital skills and learning new technologies are important: yet on the other, we find excuses not to do anything about it—we say: 'I don't have time'; 'I'm a bit of a dinosaur'; 'It doesn't interest me'; or 'I get someone else to do it.'

The starting point for resolving this dilemma is understanding the basics of digital psychology.

Digital Psychology

As Tony Robbins says about success in life, it's 80% about what is going on in your head and only 20% mechanics (Robbins, 2017). We can apply Robbins's 80/20 rule to our digital psychology too. Consider the following areas as part of the 80% that is going on in your head when it comes to success with digital technology:

- *Frustration.* Recognize that your past relationship with technology stretches over many years, building up frustrations and experiences that affect your motivation and interest in improving. If you get frustrated, know where to ask for help: the IT help desk, a colleague or a query into Google or YouTube.
- *Limiting beliefs.* If you keep telling yourself 'I can't do this,' or 'I can't work this out,' and 'I'm a technophobe,' it will become a self-fulfilling prophecy. Instead, try to develop an attitude of curiosity when it comes to technology, by asking others how they do things. Consider making it an exchange where you show them something or share an application (app) that you use.
- *Unhealthy habits.* You may have developed bad habits, such as spending too much time on email or social media and constantly scrolling for no particular reason. This can make you become more self-centered, less socially tuned in and waste time that you could use on more positive activities. At worst, you form a mobile phone addiction. The answer here is to recognize these habits and their triggers. Take back control by limiting the time you spend on your smartphone, and look for a substitute approach or behavior change, as we discuss below.
- *Less informed technology set-up.* This is the '20% mechanics' piece. If you have an old, slow phone or laptop, or lose your passwords, or have an untidy digital environment and can't find things you know you have stored, then these are areas to improve. It will add significantly to your overall positive feelings about, and therefore optimum use of, technology.

The key to improving your digital professionalism and competence is 'getting out of your head' and being curious and asking others how they operate or get things done digitally/online. No one can be an expert in all the plethora of digital technology in both their professional and personal lives, so we have to develop the habit of learning from others.

Personal Processes

We all have a set of personal processes we follow to get our jobs done, and many are now technology-based. There is seldom one single, 'right way'; we all learn strategies along the way; consequently, it is important sometimes to stop and find out what others do. Here are a few practices to review.

- *Time management.* What controls everything about how you use your time is your role, and within that, your objectives. So when you are planning your time, you need to have these in mind and not be distracted from your main tasks. That means having a clear direction/contribution to life/work and related goals and writing them down, so they are visible every day. You create time to achieve them: 'if it's in the diary it gets done.' Three useful time management techniques are *blocking out time*—if you are using an electronic calendar, block out time to actually work within the boundaries of your role, and prevent loss of your time in other non-priority directions. This blocking time strategy includes things like your breaks, learning time, meditation/prayer—whatever is important to you in order to maintain your well-being in the context of your duties. Also, key is *meeting discipline*—which means not necessarily having an hour-long meeting (the default on most computer systems) when 15, 30 or 45 minutes will do, and maintaining productive practices at meetings (such as agenda, chair, inclusion, breaks and minutes). In the context of your work day, have *agreed working times*—when you are engaged in a variety of activities such as a shift at the hospital, working at a clinic, doing home visits, and especially when you have to work from home, establish your working time parameters with the other members of your household or work environment so that they are mindful of your workload. Also adopt a transition time or action between work mode and home mode to help you to set clear boundaries, e.g., changing your clothes or shoes, shutting the laptop/office door, putting the phone down.
- *Focus and distraction.* Self-interruption is 50% of distraction (Jin & Dabbish, 2009), so it's important to understand the common triggers that distract us and how to control them.

Common distractions include *notifications on your phone or desktop*—turn them off, and ideally, put your phone out of sight; *lots of tabs open*—close unwanted tabs when focusing on a task, especially your email tab; multiple tabs encourage multitasking, which is the opposite of focus; *allowing people to disturb you*—tell your work colleagues when you are focusing, perhaps with a sign on your screen or note on your door; and *emotional states of boredom, fear and uncertainty*—make sure your objectives are clear, to motivate you and give you traction. If you are being distracted, note the sensation you had when you looked for escape and 'surf the urge' for 10 minutes to see if it subsides (Eyal, 2019).

Good practices to avoid getting distracted are *a well-planned schedule*— set realistic blocks of time focused on your key objectives and include time for thinking, exercise and reading; *a tidy desk* so you can focus on the task at hand; *creating friction* ('putting the cookie jar on the top shelf') by turning off notifications, closing unwanted tabs including browser and email, hiding your phone, and if you need it, using a focusing app like *Freedom*, *Forest* or *Focus Keeper* to help stop interruptions on the computer, or *Flipd* which turns your phone into a dumb phone for a designated time. Also *take regular breaks* to refresh the mind.

- *Processing.* Office workers spend 28% of their time processing email (Chui et al., 2012)—which is a third of their workday, yet not many people are taught how to manage their email efficiently and effectively. *Harvard Business Review* highlights time-wasting habits that waste time every day: over-checking email (21 minutes), re-reading email (27 minutes), foldering (10 minutes), processing unwanted email (8 minutes) (Plummer, 2019).

You experience how the time soon adds up. The solutions to these challenges are to *process email at set times*—if your job is dependent on closely monitoring email this tactic is not possible, but with so many other forms of chat-based, real-time communications available, it is possible to establish a rule of processing email at set times and avoid those re-reading, time-wasting traps; *have a process*—such as the '4 D's' of email management (if it can be done in less than 2 minutes, *DO* it; *DELEGATE* the action to your team; if it's an action to be done later, *DEFER* by moving it to a pending folder or sending a to-do to your Task Manager; or *DELETE* or archive it immediately); and simply *send less*— the more you send, the more you will get, since every message sent generates four more (Gallo, 2012). Use asynchronous communications instead like chat in Teams, Google, Slack and WhatsApp.

There are many tasks and list management apps and approaches, and your choice depends on how you operate and the systems you have in place. If you do use software, the key function you need is to be able to send tasks to your Task Manager directly from your email.

- *Weekly reviews*. It's important to set time aside for a weekly review. This is a chance to ensure processing of your email, review your objectives, projects and calendar for the following week, and challenge yourself to do better. As Brendon Burchard says: 'The more productive you are, the more successful you feel' (Burchard, 2017). You will probably need a couple of hours to do this properly. It's as important as any meeting, so ideally do it in work time.

People Skills and Digital

While you may be great with people and caring for people, how do those skills translate when you go online? The challenge with technology is that though it offers many choices as to how to communicate, by its very natural we are not meeting face-to-face but through a digital filter, which can affect our cognitive load and make us feel tired. An example is the new 'Zoom fatigue' (Lee, 2020) that has emerged since the COVID-19 pandemic.

Here are three practices that will help you become a better communicator online:

- *Draw up a communications charter* within your team which clarifies how you will function online. Here are some headings to consider: core values, working hours and commitments, meeting disciplines, platform choices, response times, 'in office' days.
- *Establish best practices for video conferences*. More remote working and remote patient care mean more video meetings. But because you do not get all the normal signals of face-to-face communication, they can create fatigue or lack of concentration. You need to put methods in place to combat these effects, including *having an efficient technology set-up*—if you cannot be seen or heard well online, people are going to find it hard to focus on what you are saying. Think about lighting, screen and eye position, framing your picture (is your room okay or do you need a custom background?) and getting your sound checked by

someone. *During the call*, avoid multitasking (hide your smartphone), change your view from gallery view to reduce online stimulation, suggest breaks, smile more and take part.
- *Consider the communications value chain*—communication from start to finish is especially important in the health professions where communications could be a matter of life and death. For example, this means ensuring your communications are clear, so they are not misinterpreted as they progress through the communication line; and verifying through another channel that urgent messages have been received. Saying, 'but I sent them an email' might not be good enough. In the Deepwater Horizon oil disaster in the Gulf of Mexico (BBC, 2010), an email was sent about the impending blowout, but no one checked that it had been received.

Here are some tips for sending clear emails: write clear titles, put the ask at the top, make it clear who should respond, give a deadline and send five emails not one. If very task orientated, be upbeat: remember, when you send an email with positivity gets downgraded a few notches (Glei, 2016), radiate warmth and use emojis ☺. If there's no response, *resend the email*: try again with a slightly different message; ask about their spam filters, or *try a different channel*, such as call their assistant; use messaging; telephone them; or send a message on LinkedIn. Whatever you do, don't leave communications to chance.

Digital and Wellness

As telemedicine, applications and information available to us keep advancing, so too does the technology to track our own personal wellness. Wellness underpins everything we do professionally. If we do not look after ourselves, this will impact our ability to do a good job. One of the main wellness issues at work is stress, which has risen dramatically during the COVID-19 crisis with now 70% of all workers reporting feeling more stressed than at any other point in their career (Ginger, 2020).

We all have a personal stress threshold, and if we pass over it, stress will start manifesting itself in our bodies and minds through depression and other symptoms. We can build up resilience to stress by making *wellness deposits* each day which keep stress at bay. Digital technology can help us keep ourselves on track. Below are five areas to consider to create a stress resilience plan of wellness deposits:

- *Steps.* The easiest physical activity to track is steps, and a wearable device is the simplest way to do it and can be reinforced by adding friends on social media. Studies have shown (10,000 STEPS, 2021) how beneficial the goal of doing 10,000 steps a day can be.
- *Screen time.* Technology companies (such as Google and Apple) have recently acknowledged the issues of phone addiction and the effects of too much screen time, and have included functionality in their software to allow you to track your screen use. Screen dependency is driven by the dopamine hits of new content and app design (Haynes, 2018). From a stress perspective, aim to reduce your screen time through a number of approaches to find the right balance between totally turning off your phones at one end of the scale (a *digital detox*) and being addicted to them at the other end of the scale.
- *Self-care.* Address your physical health when using digital devices. Avoid back pain, forward head posture (damaging the spine), headaches and carpal tunnel syndrome in the hands.
- *State of mind.* There are many approaches to incorporating some form of *mindfulness as* part of your stress reduction routine. A huge number of digital applications, online tutorials and resources are available to help people develop skills such as mindfulness to improve their mental health.
- *Sleep.* Sleep is the key to restoring the body, having energy in the day and being less stressed. Digital devices such as wearables allow you to track your sleep and act as a reminder to get a healthy amount and quantity of sleep. But digital devices can also adversely affect sleep, especially the blue light emitted from any screen. So, from a digital perspective, to get a night of good sleep: *use the 321 routine*—3 hours before bed, no food; 2 hours before bed, no work; 1 hour before, no technology/screens; *don't have technology in your bedroom*—use a real alarm clock, not your phone; and *track your sleep*—use the app data to teach you more about your optimal approach to sleep.

Digital Wellness and Your Family, Friends and Coworkers

Because most of us are 'always on' some kind of digital device—smartphone, computer, laptop, TV or gaming station—we need to become more aware of how this affects our relationships and mental health and how to take steps to prevent issues and optimize well-being.

Phubbing

Phubbing is snubbing someone you are with in favor of your phone. Choosing to have a digital conversation, or worse, scrolling through social media, rather than talking to the person you are with, makes them feel undervalued, unappreciated and research shows it has detrimental effects on our real-life relationships. One study (Chotpitayasunondh & Douglas, 2016) found that more than *17% of people phub others at least four times a day* and *almost 32% of people report being phubbed two to three times a day.*

We all need to be more aware of how we are using our devices and who we may be ignoring/affecting. It's also important to know that patients may be phubbing you without knowing it and may struggle to stop. Awareness and thinking about your actions to avoid becoming a phubber are the first steps to well-being.

Family Media Agreements

Having escaped the computers and systems at work, coming home where children are all attached to their devices is not good for healthy family relationships. Common Sense Media is an organization that provides education and advocacy to families to promote safe technology and media for children. Their Family Media Agreement (Common Sense Media, n.d.) and device contract set realistic rules so you and your children can make the most of media and technology.

Social Media and Relationships

Do technology and social media strengthen or weaken relationships? Broadly speaking, access to the Internet and active communications with others on social media where people are supporting each other either individually or in groups are both good engagements (Digital Wellness Collective, 2021). Many people become too dependent or suffer from excessive use because they lack a healthy social support infrastructure. Pointers when considering your relationships on social media include:

- It is always better to communicate face to face.
- Recognize how the platform impacts the message. Think about the impact of a short text versus a voice message; a one-line email versus a chatty email with emojis; a Facebook post shared with many versus a direct message to an individual; a voice call versus a Zoom call.

- Recognize that active use—posting, commenting, sharing, reacting—is good; just scrolling, watching, hovering are not.
- Write your thoughts and feelings down before engaging in a difficult conversation.
- Avoid negative comparisons. Social comparison—comparing yourself to others who all seem to be 'crushing life'—can have a negative effect on you. To counter this, look and follow inspiring content and discover what on social media brings you joy.
- Limit your time on social media to 1–2 hours a day. It's okay to look at Instagram, but not to get obsessed by it.
- Limit the number of platforms—the more platforms you use, the more time you will spend on them, and potentially the more addicted you will become.

Your Personal Digital Brand

A confluence of events has made 'personal branding' and 'digital branding' more important than ever for health professionals. The COVID-19 pandemic has only accelerated the trend toward telehealth and remote work. Patients can now learn a tremendous amount about nursing, medicine or medical teams responsible for their care from online bios and social media. From a trust and confidence perspective, this can cut both ways.

Human beings are visual people; we make assessments based on snapshots all the time: rightly and wrongly. This is particularly true in hiring. If you are active on social media, there is every chance that you will be noticed by a prospective employer at some point in the hiring process. There is another less recognized factor that makes online branding a key consideration for healthcare professionals. Once a patient has chosen a nurse practitioner, doctor or specialist they may then be introduced to other members of the health team, including the nursing staff. Good treatment and recovery, especially for serious illnesses or injuries, depend on the patient's emotional and psychological state. Imagine the dismay, for example, of a patient in the process of recovery who sees that one of their doctors or nurses is sharing contradictory treatment protocols online.

Your Profile Photo—Identification and First Impression

Your profile picture is the first place a person's eyes go when they arrive on your profile page. Make it count. Another purpose of your profile photo is to *create the right feeling and tone*—professional and also engaging. Other recommendations to note when adding your photo are: use a headshot, color is best, your image should take up no more than 60% of the total photo, a plain background is normally best and look straight at the camera.

The 'About You' Part

What LinkedIn calls your 'Headline Summary' appears just below your name. Every platform is different—currently, you can use 240 characters on LinkedIn to include key details, while on Twitter you have a maximum of 160 characters. This is where the LinkedIn and Google spiders visit first and rely on in the indexing process. You are trying to increase the likelihood that people will come to your profile, so the headline summary is the most important field in your profile, especially if you are new to your role. So spend time writing your summary to clarify your brand. Make it easy to read, avoid complex sentences and be sure that the first sentence or two are especially engaging.

The Trust Factor

Keep in mind that employers are looking for congruence—that your desire to be a nursing professional is consistent with your other life choices and interests. Borrowing from Edelman, one of the largest public relations agencies: 'People don't buy the "what," they buy the "why."' Trust begins when people understand and believe your motivation.

Caring for the Digital You and Security

Healthcare organizations are a prime target for cybercriminals and rival nation-state actors due to the resale value of stolen medical, research or financial data and the disruption that cyberattacks can cause. Healthcare records can bring up to ten times more than payment information on the dark web and can cost three times more than average to remediate (IBM, 2020). The fact that since the pandemic began, cyberattacks on healthcare organizations have surged by 45% (Check Point, 2021) makes good cybersecurity vital to the safe, effective and efficient operation of any healthcare organization and the safety of patients and employees.

The Five Key Cyber–Health Outcomes

These are *safety* of patients, which can be endangered if records are altered or equipment compromised; *security* of patients' records, which need to be protected against theft, corruption and loss—note the laws that have been passed to promote this (HHS, 2020; General Data Protection Regulation, 2018; California Consumer Privacy Act, 2021); *availability* of healthcare services, whose disruption can have significant implications for patients; *protected intellectual property* (IP) such as experimental drug formulae, clinical trial data and results; and *trust* by the patient, which would be eroded by cyberattacks and security breaches.

These five outcomes underline the importance of information security to the organization and the health outcomes of patients. This is not simply an IT problem. Healthcare practitioners have an important role to play, and the next section details what you can do.

Best Practices: What You Can Do to Protect Your Patients, Your Colleagues and Yourself

Don't be an easy target. 81% of hacking-related breaches occur because of compromised (guessed or stolen) *passwords* (Verizon, 2020). Password best practice has changed over the years as we learn more about the technical and behavioral pros and cons. The National Institute of Standards and Technology (NIST) recommends Password Guidelines (NIST Special Publication 800-63B). First, *length is more effective than complexity.* Longer passwords take far longer to decrypt (in some cases thousands of years longer), so if a database of passwords has been stolen, the shorter ones will be decrypted first and the longest ones might not even be worth the effort of the attacker. NIST guidelines call for a strict eight-character minimum length.

Many sites and services require you to create passwords with one lower case letter, one upper case letter, one special character, one number, etc. This is why users tend to reuse passwords, with predictable minor changes (e.g., an '!' at the end, or a '3' instead of an 'E'). It helps if the system *does not require frequent password changes* since it is even more difficult to remember passwords that have to be frequently changed, leading to weaker, shorter and more memorable passwords. If an attacker knows one such password, it can be simple to guess others. Also, *check your password against 'blacklists'* of compromised passwords (e.g., dictionary words, stolen passwords and variations on the organization's name) can be checked to ensure that you are not using one. Your IT or security department may provide this, but you can also check at haveibeenpwned.com.

Use multi-factor authentication (MFA). This requires two or more types of authentications, usually combining 'something you know' (e.g., a password) with 'something you have' (e.g., a phone or physical token) and/or 'something you are' (e.g., a fingerprint or retinal scan). This prevents an attacker from gaining access to a system if just one form of authentication has been compromised. Microsoft (Maynes, 2019) reported that 99.9% of automated cyberattacks on their platforms were blocked by MFA. That's why NIST recommends that MFA is used to secure Personal Identifying Information (PII) (including Personal Health Information (PHI)) accessible online.

Be protective—look after tokens. Even MFA is vulnerable. Write a password down, leave a phone unlocked or a key fob token lying around, and the strengths melt away. It's important to be mindful of the security of the 'something you have' at all times. Providing MFA through a smartphone app not only provides the computing power necessary but uses something the owner cares about and keeps on their person. Physical tokens, or key fobs, have tougher security in themselves but tend to be more expensive and less user-friendly. Some organizations still use SMS messages to provide one-time passcodes as a second form of authentication, but NIST does not recommend this as SMS messages can be intercepted.

Be mindful—ransomware and phishing. Ransomware attacks typically infect a system with malware (e.g., a virus) that encrypts the hard drive making the data on it inaccessible. The attackers then demand payment to return access to the data. Administrators might disinfect the affected system/s and restore the data from an uninfected backup, but this takes time during which the system is unusable, which is why so many victims pay the demanded payment. However, paying a ransom does not prevent it from happening again, nor does it ensure the data has not been stolen or manipulated by the attacker.

Many ransomware attacks begin with *phishing* emails. This technique uses social engineering techniques to persuade people to perform a particular action (e.g., provide access credentials or download malware through an infected link or document). Phishing attempts range in sophistication, from emails that are clearly suspicious (spelling mistakes, poor English/sentence construction, links that have no connection to the reported source, etc.) to sophisticated targeted attacks (e.g., referring to activity such as a conference attended) to make the email convincing. It's best to be suspicious of all emails ('Think Before You Click'), particularly those from an unknown source or that appear out of the ordinary. The Federal Trade Commission (Federal Trade Commission, 2021) provides up-to-date advice and examples of phishing scams.

Be in touch—build a security community. Everyone can take part in some way to ensure greater communication, collaboration and security for their patients. Some will have a keen interest in learning about threats or in keeping up with best practices, while others just want to avoid being locked out of their workstation. All have a part to play. Some can become security advocates, helping colleagues and leading communications with security teams. Others can share their awareness of the importance of security with their colleagues through their work behaviors. Management can take the risks seriously and champion security initiatives. Bringing these interested parties together builds a community and encourages communication. It can be as much a social activity as serious security and a lot of fun!

Summary: The Secret of Success—Your Community

Stop scrolling and start listening to the people that matter most. We assume that the people who work for the companies that created these addictive technologies are all good people. They did not set out to have you be addicted to your device(s). They were creating a platform they thought would make access to information more accessible, allow you to connect to friends and family, and stay up to date on the news. The phone and most apps are all good inventions. They only distract us because we let them. Distraction and attention are a choice, and we have been living the distraction and inattention long before the smartphone. According to Harvard professors (Kemp, 2019), our mind is wired to wander, and being aware of this is the first step to controlling our phones, health and relationships.

For over 10 years, Educated Change has been working with organizations worldwide, helping them use social media to influence, change minds and create value. In that work and with the ten thousand plus people we have touched, we have found that the best way to tackle all aspects of digital wellness is through the *community*. This community understands the importance of relationships, and members want the people in their lives to be healthy. If you care about the people in your life and want to improve in your work, you will begin to notice your smartphone usage and begin to focus on what matters most to you. As your awareness grows, you will begin to use your phone as a tool and also focus on what matters to others.

You will stop scrolling, checking your news feeds, and replace them with relationships and shared interests across your community.

> In all our research, we have not found a single person who has said they wished they had spent more time on their phone.

References

10,000 STEPS (2021). *Counting your steps*. 10,000 STEPS [Online]. Available at: https://www.10000steps.org.au/articles/counting-steps/ (Accessed 4 March 2021).

Auxier, B. (2020). *64% of Americans say social media have a mostly negative effect on the way things are going in the U.S. today*. Pew Research Center Factank [Online]. Available at: https://www.pewresearch.org/fact-tank/2020/10/15/64-of-americans-say-social-media-have-a-mostly-negative-effect-on-the-way-things-are-going-in-the-u-s-today/ (Accessed: 2 March 2021).

BBC (2010). Congress tells Hayward BP ignored oil well dangers. *BBC News* [Online]. Available at: https://www.bbc.co.uk/news/10337146 (Accessed 4 March 2021).

Burchard, B. (2017). *High performance habits: Excerpts*. Brendon Burchard [Online]. Available at: https://brendon.com/blog/high-performancehabits/ (Accessed 4 March 2021).

California Consumer Privacy Act of 2018 [1798.100 - 1798.199.100]. *Civil Code Title 1.81.5. California* [online]. Available at: https://leginfo.legislature.ca.gov/faces/codes_displayText.xhtml?division=3.&part=4.&lawCode=CIV&title=1.81.5 (Accessed: 20 March 2021).

Check Point (2021). Attacks targeting healthcare organizations spike globally as COVID-19 cases rise again. *Check Point Blog* [Online]. Available at: https://blog.checkpoint.com/2021/01/05/attacks-targeting-healthcare-organizations-spike-globally-as-covid-19-cases-rise-again/. (Accessed 21 March 2021).

Chotpitayasunondh, V., & Douglas, K.M. (2016). How "phubbing" becomes the norm: The antecedents and consequences of snubbing via smartphone. *Computers in Human Behaviour*, 63 [Online]. Available at: https://www.sciencedirect.com/science/article/pii/S0747563216303454 (Accessed 4 March 2021).

Chui, M., Manyika, J., Bughin, J., Dobbs, R., Roxburgh, C., Sarrazin, H., Sands, G., & Westergren, M. (2012). *The social economy: Unlocking value and productivity through social technologies*. McKinsey Global Institute [Online]. Available at: https://www.mckinsey.com/industries/technology-media-and-telecommunications/our-insights/the-social-economy (Accessed 30 June 2021).

Common Sense Media (n.d.). Family media agreement. *Common Sense Media* [Online]. Available at: https://www.commonsensemedia.org/family-media-agreement (Accessed 4 March 2021).

Digital Wellness Collective (2021). [Online]. Available at: https://digitalwellnesscollective.com/ (Accessed 4 March 2021).

Eyal, N. (2019). How to disarm internal triggers and improve focus. *[Blog] Nir and Far* [Online]. Available at: https://www.nirandfar.com/internal-triggers/ (Accessed 2 March 2021).

Eyal, N. (2021). Tech companies are addicting people! But should they stop? *[Blog] Nir and Far* [Online]. Available at: https://www.nirandfar.com/tech-companies-addicting-people-stop/ (Accessed 2 March 2021).

Federal Trade Commission (2021). *Scams: Phishing* [Online]. Available at: https://www.ftc.gov/scams/phishing. (Accessed 20 March 2021).

Gallo, A. (2012). Stop email overload. *Harvard Business Review*, 21 February 2012 [Online]. Available at: https://hbr.org/2012/02/stop-email-overload-1 (Accessed 4 March 2021).

General Data Protection Regulation (GDPR) (2018). [online]. Available at: https://gdpr-info.eu/ (Accessed 20 March 2021).

Ginger (2020). *2020 workforce attitudes towards mental health report* [Online]. Available at: https://go.ginger.io/annual-behavioral-health-report-2020 (Accessed 5 March 2021).

Glei, J.K. (2016). *Unsubscribe: How to kill email anxiety, avoid distractions, and get real work done.* New York: Public Affairs.

Haynes, T. (2018). *Dopamine, smartphones & you: A battle for your time.* [Blog] Harvard University [Online]. Available at: https://sitn.hms.harvard.edu/flash/2018/dopamine-smartphones-battle-time/ (Accessed 30 June 2021).

HHS (2020). *The HIPAA privacy rule.* HHS.gov. Health Information Privacy [Online]. Available at: https://www.hhs.gov/hipaa/for-professionals/privacy/index.html. (Accessed 20 March 2021).

IBM (2020). *Cost of a data breach report 2020.* IBM [Online]. Available at: https://www.ibm.com/security/data-breach. (Accessed 21 March 2021).

Icke, R., & Macmillan, D. (2013). *1984. Oberon modern plays.* London: Oberon Books.

Jin, J., and Dabbish, L.A. (2009). Self-interruption on the computer: A typology of discretionary task interleaving. In Proceedings of the 27th International Conference on Human Factors in Computing Systems, April 2009 [Online]. Available at: https://www.researchgate.net/publication/221517140_Self-Interruption_on_the_Computer_A_Typology_of_Discretionary_Task_Interleaving (Accessed 4 March 2021).

Kemp, N. (2019). *Harvard psychologists reveal the real reason we're all so distracted.* Inc. [Online]. Available at: https://www.inc.com/nate-klemp/harvard-psychologists-reveal-real-reason-were-all-so-distracted.html (Accessed 4 March 2021).

Kemp, S. (2020). Digital 2020: 3.8 billion people use social media. *wearesocial*, 30 January 2020 [Online]. Available at https://wearesocial.com/ca/2020/01/30/digital-2020-what-you-really-need-to-know/# (Accessed 2 March 2021).

Kemp, S. (2021). 15.5 users join social every 5 seconds (and other key stats to know). *Hootsuite*, 27 January 2021 [Online]. Available at: https://blog.hootsuite.com/simon-kemp-social-media/ (Accessed 2 March 2021).

Lee, J. (2020). A neuropsychological exploration of zoom fatigue. *Psychiatric Times*, 17 November 2020 [Online]. Available at: https://www.psychiatrictimes.com/view/psychological-exploration-zoom-fatigue (Accessed 4 March 2021).

Lustosa, B. (2018). Apple's iOS update frequency has increased 51% under Cook's management. *VentureBeat*, 28 February 2018 [Online]. Available at: https://venturebeat.com/2018/02/28/apples-ios-update-frequency-has-increased-51-under-cooks-management/ (Accessed 2 March 2021).

Maynes, M. (2019). *One simple action you can take to prevent 99.9 percent of attacks on your accounts.* Microsoft [Online]. Available at: https://www.microsoft.com/security/blog/2019/08/20/one-simple-action-you-can-take-to-prevent-99-9-percent-of-account-attacks/. (Accessed 24 March 2021).

Ng, A. (2019). Smartphone users are waiting longer before upgrading: Here's why. *CNBC*, 17 May 2019 [Online]. Available at: https://www.cnbc.com/2019/05/17/smartphone-users-are-waiting-longer-before-upgrading-heres-why.html (Accessed 2 March 2021).

NIST Special Publication 800–63B, U.S. Department of Commerce (2017). *Digital identity guidelines* [Online]. Available at: https://pages.nist.gov/800-63-3/sp800-63b.html (Accessed 1 July 2021).

Plummer, M. (2019). How to spend way less time on email every day. *Harvard Business Review*, 22 January 2019 [Online]. Available at: https://hbr.org/2019/01/how-to-spend-way-less-time-on-email-every-day (Accessed 4 March 2021).

Robbins, T. (2016). *Tony Robbins explains why 80% of success is psychological!* [Online]. Available at: https://www.youtube.com/watch?v=UDjrpZD-uPk (Accessed 2 March 2021).

Verizon (2020). *Data breach investigations report 2020.* Verizon [Online]. Available at: https://enterprise.verizon.com/content/verizonenterprise/us/en/index/resources/reports/2020-data-breach-investigations-report.pdf. (Accessed 24 March 2021).

Chapter 5

Learning from Clients/ Patients to Advance Education and Scholarship

Jennie C. De Gagne, Katrina Green and Margaret H. Sturdivant

Contents

Introduction 81
Nursing Education and Nursing Professional Development 82
The Evolvement of eHealth Literacy (Digital Health Literacy) 83
Assessing Digital Learning Needs of Patients/Families/Communities 85
Advancing Nursing Education and Scholarship 89
Summary 90
References 91

Introduction

Nursing professional development (NPD) is a 'specialized nursing practice that facilitates the professional role development and growth of nurses and other healthcare personnel along the continuum from novice to expert' (Harper & Maloney, 2016, p. 6). NPD educators have consistently been at the forefront of healthcare change, leading the charge by employing adult learning principles to assess readiness and identify the needs of learners (Harper et al., 2017; Johnson & Smith, 2019). Educators specialized in NPD use instructional strategies to 'bridge the knowledge, skills and/or practice gaps identified through a needs assessment' (Harper et

DOI: 10.4324/9781003281009-5

al., 2017, p. 16). In the service of lifelong learning, NPD educators collaborate with a variety of team members to advance new knowledge and best practices and disseminate them through scholarship of teaching and learning (SoTL). This chapter provides an overview of the roles and responsibilities of NPD educators and their contributions to nursing education through various organizations. The chapter first examines the literature on eHealth literacy and digital learning needs of clients, patients and communities, then discusses ways to advance scholarship of teaching for systematic engagement with the community.

Nursing Education and Nursing Professional Development

Information technology is an increasingly important tool for accessing and disseminating nursing information (both patient-specific and general scientific knowledge); therefore, nurse educators in all settings should be aware of their clientele's ability to use information technology effectively. Information technology is affecting every aspect of communication and education; thus, the roles and responsibilities of NPD educators continuously evolve to include new ways of meeting the various learning needs of their clientele.

NPD educators often serve as preceptors for nursing students' clinical experiences, and they collaborate with healthcare team members to facilitate transitions and changes (e.g., orientation of new hires, staff members' continuing education, and introduction of technologies for patient care and patient education). Their learners include diverse groups of adults from various cultural backgrounds with different learning styles or preferences who bring a wide range of experiences, proficiencies, competencies and skills to the learning and care environment. Thus, it is necessary for NPD educators to employ adult learning principles and varied techniques to best meet learners' needs. Ensuring learner engagement and motivation for ongoing professional development and lifelong learning is an important NPD educator responsibility. NPD educators use active teaching strategies to influence behavior change and facilitate an optimum learning environment (Harper et al., 2017; Johnson & Smith, 2019). In addition to their primary roles as facilitators of professional learning, NPD educators may assume responsibilities such as demonstrating expertise in healthcare data management and analysis or promoting the strategic plan of a healthcare system by championing scientific inquiry (Chappell, 2020). As change agents and strong advocates for organizational goals, missions and values, NPD educators lead role-model best practices to ensure that changes evolve and are sustained in our technologically revolutionized healthcare environment.

The Evolvement of eHealth Literacy (Digital Health Literacy)

When it was introduced in the 1970s, health literacy referred to a person's ability to read and complete common math calculations. Over time, the concept evolved into a more complex multidimensional understanding, leading to the definition: 'The degree to which an individual has the capacity to obtain, communicate, process, and understand basic health information and services to make appropriate health decisions' (Institute of Medicine, 2004). This definition was used in the Patient Protection and Affordable Care Act of 2010, Title V, as well as in Healthy People 2010 and 2020. Health literacy includes components of oral language literacy, print literacy and numeracy, and a critical component is an individual's ability to obtain and use information at any given time. For example, regardless of their level of education, an individual or their loved ones may have difficulty in hearing, processing or using information while receiving a serious medical diagnosis or negative test results during a doctor's visit. In such a case, follow-up conversations or a written summary of the material discussed would be critical to ensure appropriate self-care management.

Healthcare providers and health professions educators have a responsibility to promote patient and community health literacy skills. A study by Mackert et al. (2016) found that patients or community members who exhibited poor health literacy were less likely to use available health technology tools. Individuals who are highly eHealth literate are more likely to scrutinize information and gain positive outcomes from information searches about self-management of healthcare needs (Azzopardi-Muscat & Sorensen, 2019). It is important to incorporate technology into community healthcare education so that the needs of individuals are addressed effectively. To ensure that appropriate resources are being used, healthcare providers and educators should assess the resources or references that their clients consult. When in-person meetings with patients occur, members of the healthcare team can demonstrate for patients how to (a) access the websites or applications they recommend, (b) download important applications or resources to a smartphone and (c) set up access. With the help of their healthcare team, the patient and their family members can retrieve important links and access reliable sources of information.

Refinements to the health literacy definition are ongoing as numerous studies have found that individuals with low health literacy have more emergency room visits, hospitalizations, complications from chronic health conditions due to poor self-management and higher mortality (Centers for Disease Control and Prevention [CDC], 2020). Attaining health literacy for all is one of the overarching goals of Healthy People 2030, which outlines personal health literacy as well as organizational health literacy. Three objectives of the US Department of Health and Human Services (HHS) Healthy People 2030 publication, a 10-year plan to improve the health of all Americans (HHS, 2020), include obtaining the patient's perception of whether the healthcare team (1) checked whether they understood instructions given, (2) explained materials in a way that was easy to understand, and (3) involved them in decisions about their healthcare to the extent they desired. Thus, health literacy is a responsibility shared by the healthcare team and the consumer.

Digital health literacy refers to the ability to use emerging information and communication technologies to enable or improve health and healthcare (Levin-Zamir and Bertschi, 2018). Norman and Skinner (2006) introduced the concept of eHealth literacy, describing it as 'the ability to seek, find, understand, and appraise health information from electronic sources and apply the knowledge gained to addressing or solving a health problem' (p. 2). The definition has been defined as 'the ability of people to use emerging information and communication technologies to improve or enable health and healthcare' (Paige et al., 2018, as cited in Neter & Brainin, 2012, p. 1). Digital health literacy, or eHealth literacy, evolved from media health literacy and is relevant for both the non-digital (television, print, radio, etc.) and the digital media (Internet, social media, and mobile tools) (Levin-Zamir and Bertschi, 2018). Brach and Harris (2021) recently highlighted new definitions and an expectation for organizations to make information and services easy to find, understand and use.

O'Connor et al. (2016) named key factors that determine how patients and the public engage with and enroll in digital health interventions, including level of education attained, limited computer skills, literacy skills, age and ability to pay for the technology. Consumers are increasingly utilizing computers and mobile devices for common activities, such as using a patient portal to access their medical records, having a virtual health visit with a provider, searching for health information on the Internet, or using applications to monitor or track a behavior. The Lily Model by Norman and Skinner (2006) claimed that eHealth literacy combines six domains: (1) traditional literacy, (2) information literacy, (3) scientific literacy, (4) media literacy, (5) computer literacy, and (6) health literacy. Being successful or literate in seeking, finding, understanding and evaluating health information from electronic sources and applying the knowledge gained to address or solve a health problem requires that a person be skilled in each of these six domains, with information and computer literacy being the most essential skills.

Assessing Digital Learning Needs of Patients/Families/Communities

Healthcare consumers use Internet health information to make important decisions about their healthcare (Gilmour et al., 2014). Most data to determine community needs is gathered through surveys, questionnaires, focus groups, public meetings, direct observations and interviews. What is considered essential by one community may not be as important for another; thus, it is important that healthcare providers and educators understand the communities they serve in order to develop the most appropriate technology resources for their members. Patient advocacy organizations, such as the National Heart Association or American Cancer Society, provide education, advocacy and support for patients and communities. These organizations have strong community ties, and often many members of the community are also members of the organization (Rose, 2014). Advocacy groups use technological resources to provide education (e.g., through the use of media such as podcasts and videos, and material that can be printed directly from their websites).

Telehealth is a tool that can provide tele-research, tele-consultation and tele-education (Chen et al., 2021). A teleconferencing tool can support patient education and address public health needs, including rehabilitation and mental healthcare. It is a versatile tool, and many healthcare providers are exploring its use for patient and community health education and support. Telehealth can be used to support individuals in rural areas who may not have access to care. In isolated communities where providing even basic healthcare can be challenging, it can be used to arrange follow-up visits with specialists or provide mental wellness appointments. The benefit of utilizing resources such as FaceTime, Zoom or Webex-like platforms is that healthcare providers can assess both verbal and nonverbal communication during a conversation, supporting a more comprehensive assessment when a face-to-face visit with a patient is not possible; this can be immensely helpful during a public health crisis when it is unsafe for individuals to attend in-person appointments, and can significantly enhance communication between the healthcare provider and patient, and family members (White et al., 2021).

During the COVID-19 pandemic, in-person visitations were halted, making patient and caregiver communication a challenge. Healthcare team members partnered with technology experts to find innovative ways to use communication tools; for example, technologies employing tablets or portable computers have enabled family members to participate in patient rounds with the medical team or in teaching sessions. In areas such as pediatric ICUs, virtual discharge teaching with tablets allows parents or loved ones who may not be able to be at the bedside due to visitor restrictions to participate in the learning experience.

Although in-person appointments differ from virtual experiences, in some ways technology can offer enhanced experiences. Whether the experience involves a virtual visit or a class, it can be enriched by following the clear communication tips for telehealth outlined by Coleman (2020): (1) prepare for encounters (ask patient to gather data in advance of call, have a back-up phone number for the patient); (2) ensure privacy (both parties should be in a quiet and private space, turn up the volume on devices); (3) ensure hearing adequacy (confirm patient is able to hear); (4) use clear or plain language (use interpreters if necessary, set an agenda, use one to three key messages, use teach-back techniques); and (5) use memory aids (discharge summary, patient education materials, etc.). The Hospital at Home model is an innovative method that allows patients who meet specific health criteria to receive hospital-level care at home; digital resources monitor their pulse, heart rhythm and vital signs remotely. Members of the health team are alerted to changes in the patient's health and provide in-person care daily.

During the COVID-19 pandemic, technology has facilitated equity in health service and delivery. For example, when COVID vaccines became available for the various communities, clinics were set up to be able to provide vaccine education, information and administration. In many locations across the nation, it was recognized that we were missing the opportunities to vaccinate those members of our more vulnerable populations. Multiple challenges had been identified that were impacting the ability of the members of these communities from being able to get vaccinated. Transportation resources was identified as a factor for consideration as many did not have personal vehicles and relied on public transportation. Public transportation may or may not have been available to clinic sites. Trusting the vaccine and those administering them was also a concern of some. With the newness of the COVID vaccines and so much unreliable information, many did not know what to believe. These challenges were overcome by listening to the members of the community. 'Pop-up' clinics were created and placed through these communities that provided a closer to home location which allowed easier access. Often, key members from the neighborhood, such as from a local church or school, served as volunteers in the clinics to help with the communication struggles and build trust with the process. Other strategies also included some neighborhoods doing door-to-door vaccines, mobile vaccine clinics that would run through the neighborhoods, and even programs with various ride-share businesses to provide free rides to where they needed to go. By listening to the member of the community, vaccine clinics staff were able to address the needs and deliver vaccines to those who needed.

Similarly, electronic health records are a flexible resource for patients and families. Access to the content in electronic records can contribute to better preparation for healthcare visits by providing patients and their families with access to lab values, test results and provider notes so that they can formulate thoughtful questions for the healthcare team prior to a visit. Healthcare providers can use electronic charts to disseminate patient education and provide answers to important health questions, and they can complete telehealth visits through various applications. By connecting patients with their healthcare team, electronic health records encourage accountability for an active participation in healthcare. For example, individuals with comorbidities and very complex care may be followed by a variety of specialists. An electronic healthcare record can connect all members of the healthcare team, including the patient, electronically, allowing them to receive and review the same patient information. Thus, technology can improve communication, facilitate collaboration, provide preventative care, and support ongoing education for the patient, family or community (Vest et al., 2010).

Given the plethora of websites available today that the community can search for information, it is essential that the healthcare team remain aware of current reliable resources and can show patients how to locate them (Gilmour et al., 2014). The National Institute on Aging (NIH, 2018) provides guidelines for locating reliable resources or determining the reliability of a website, such as maintaining awareness of (a) its sponsors, (b) its authors, (c) when was it written, and (d) whether it is privacy protected.

Patients and community members should understand that their best source of factual information is their healthcare team. Healthcare providers and nurse educators can utilize reliable websites such as MedlinePlus (www.medlineplus.gov), Centers for Medicare & Medicaid Services (www.cms.gov), MyHealthfinder (www.healthfinder.gov), and US Food and Drug Administration (www.fda.gov) to facilitate patient education and develop teaching materials.

There are numerous resources available to help patients and families learn about health conditions, but not all are based on scientific evidence. Patients may encounter medical misinformation from a variety of online sources that can lead to serious health consequences (Southwell et al., 2020). Fortunately, most patients trust healthcare team members to provide accurate and reliable information. Nursing continues to be the most trusted profession; nurses earned a high score of 89% for honesty and ethics in the 2020 Gallup Poll Honesty and Ethics Survey, four points higher than their strong score in 2019 (Saad, 2020). Nurses can build on trusting relationships to invite conversations with patients about potential misinformation; however, there are limited programs available to train healthcare team members to acknowledge misinformation, listen with empathy and share appropriate information sources (Leask et al., 2012). Southwell et al. (2020) strongly asserted that addressing incorrect information or misinformation properly requires more than simply stating that it is false. Discussions about the reliability and accuracy of information present opportunities to learn about the patient's values, preferences, comprehension and health literacy. Clinicians can foster an open dialogue with a patient who holds inaccurate beliefs by using an open and caring approach. Asking patients what they have learned about the topic, what worries them or what beliefs are important to them will provide valuable insights. Southwell et al. (2020) emphasized the importance of listening, acknowledging and empathizing while determining whether the person has a desire to learn more.

Lyles and Sarkar (2015) identified three main challenges to using technology to provide education to consumers. Basic access is one of the main concerns. Many vulnerable populations may not have the ability to use, or be able to afford, Internet services (Chen et al., 2021). Technology training is also a concern given the variety of users and technologies. Not all community members have access to smartphones, tablets or computers, and those who do have access may not understand how to use them to find needed information. Customized client-focused support can be provided through written directions or focus groups for members who experience difficulty accessing required information and using it effectively. The final challenge identified was the usability of the website or platform the consumer is trying to access. This concern can be addressed by using more user-friendly access points such as learner portals (Lyles & Sakar, 2015).

Many health systems and advocacy groups have adapted the use of portals to give the patient and community a reliable access point to needed information. Patient portals often contain libraries of patient education materials that include written materials designed according to best practices of health literacy (e.g., complex terms are defined, icons or images are used to promote the content, and statements are action-oriented and patient-centered). Organizations can ensure that materials are based on current evidence to help control misinformation of medical topics. Short videos focusing on one or two key messages are especially effective for patients with low literacy. Many patient education libraries include images, symptom checkers and other patient-friendly resources. These materials are often available on a smartphone app for the patient portal. This is one approach for health systems to provide organizational health literacy for patients, although building awareness of these resources continues to be a challenge.

Advancing Nursing Education and Scholarship

The critical roles and responsibilities of NPD educators involve protecting the public by supporting a workforce of members who provide health services. NPD educators do more than precepting students or facilitating learning; they engage in scholarship of teaching and learning (SoTL), thus contributing to the development of nursing education as a science and art. Dissemination of SoTL is not a causal or ad hoc activity in that it involves a target audience and appropriate setting to communicate findings to accelerate both practice and decision-making processes. In short, the goal of the dissemination is to give findings of a project to a target audience who can make maximal use of them without delays. To be most effective, dissemination strategies must be incorporated into the earlier planning stages of a project. However, it is important to note the differences between *educational scholarship* and *engaging in scholarship*. The former is defined as 'any material, product or resource originally developed to fulfill a specific educational purpose that has been successfully peer-reviewed and is subsequently made public through appropriate dissemination for use by others' (Association of American Medical Colleges, 2021, para 2). On the other hand, the latter is the responsibility of all nurse educators including NPD educators. As a champion for engaging in scholarship, the NPD educator 'promotes the generation and dissemination of new knowledge and the use of evidence to advance NPD practice, guide clinical practice, and improve patient care' (Harper & Maloney, 2016, p. 17). Using many venues to disseminate the products of scholarship, NPD educators make the outcomes of their efforts public and accessible for critique and use by others.

Summary

Information technology plays a critical role in all aspects of education from communication to facilitation of teaching and learning. NPD educators often use computers and digital technologies to promote consumers' eHealth literacy. Digital technologies offer many options for deeper patient engagement in self-management such as frequent monitoring of specific actions (e.g., daily weights, heart rate). Often, technologies allow communications between regular fitness devices to be shared with healthcare team members. Prompts or nudges can be pushed to patients via a text message reminder or call if patients need to provide information. Text messages are also used to remind patients of upcoming appointments or actions (e.g., reminders not to eat prior to a procedure). Short videos of correct techniques for exercises a patient has been instructed to complete may be pushed to the patient. Apps may also offer content such as recipes and wellness tips.

Quick links and clearly written instructions aimed at meeting the needs of patients with low health literacy can be good tools to guide these users if health literacy best practices for providing healthcare education are followed. NPD educators can design and develop printed materials about various advocacy groups including online resources, phone numbers and other points of access information. Several national organizations are campaigning to promote health equity by increasing health literacy, specifically eHealth literacy. For example, the National Institute of Children's Health Quality advocates that producers of medical literature use plain language that avoids vague wording to address specific actions that should be taken. Policymakers can take advantage of opportunities to positively influence health literacy. Enhancing health literacy will require effort from personal, organizational, commercial and public policy perspectives.

The COVID-19 pandemic has forced healthcare teams to adopt new ways of communicating. Telehealth, once considered a means of connecting with individuals in remote areas, has emerged as an effective way for providers and patients to share information. Virtual visits can occur in the comfort of an individual's home, a more convenient and less costly option than visiting a clinic. Group classes are conducted virtually for complex chronic health conditions, and virtual group sessions can be easily arranged prior to large, complex surgical procedures. Converting in-person sessions into virtual classes using a variety of technologies has increased options for engaging patients and communities in their care. When used judiciously and according to best practices, technology enables a healthcare team to have greater connection to the community during times of high acuity in emergency departments and hospitals while improving the patient experience. Time will tell whether these trends continue. NPD educators will have an integral role in promoting research, evidence-based practice and quality improvement while partaking in a broad dissemination of lessons learned from these projects to advance education and scholarship in nursing.

References

Association of American Medical Colleges. (2021). *Educational scholarship for residents* [online]. Available at: https://students-residents.aamc.org/training-opportunities-residents-and-fellows/educational-scholarship-residents (Accessed 07 June 2021).

Azzopardi-Muscat, N., & Sorensen, K. (2019). Towards an equitable digital public health era: Promoting equity through a health literacy perspective. *European Journal of Public Health*, 29(3), pp.13–17. https://doi.org/10.1093/eurpub/ckz166

Brach, C., & Harris, L. M. (2021). Healthy people 2030 health literacy definition tells organizations: Make information and services easy to find, understand, and use. *Journal of General Internal Medicine*, 36(4), pp.1084–1085. https://doi.org/10.1007/s11606-020-06384-y

Chappell, K. (2020). Leaders for learning and change. *Journal for Nurses in Professional Development*, 36(1), pp.52–53. https://doi.org/10.1097/NND.0000000000000603

Centers for Disease Control and Prevention. (2020, September 25). *Patients with low health literacy* [online]. Available at: https://www.cdc.gov/cpr/infographics/healthliteracy.htm (Accessed 23 May 2021).

Chen, Y., Kathirithamby, D. R., Li, J., Candelario-Velazquez, C., Bloomfield, A., & Felicia, A. (2021). Telemedicine in the Coronavirus disease 2019 pandemic: A pediatric rehabilitation perspective. *American Journal of Physical Medicine & Rehabilitation*, 100(4), pp.321–326. https://doi.org/10.1097/PHM.0000000000001698

Coleman, C. (2020). Health literacy and clear communication best practices for telemedicine. *Health Literacy Research & Practice*, 4(4), pp.e224–229. https://doi.org/10.3928/24748307-20200924-01

Gilmour, J., Hanna, S., Chan, H., Strong, A., & Huntington, A. (2014). Engaging with patient online health information use: A survey of primary health care nurses. *Sage Open*, p1–10. http://doi.org/10.1177/2158244014550617

Harper, M. G., & Maloney, P. (eds.) (2016). *Nursing professional development: Scope and standards of practice*. 3rd ed. Association for Nursing Professional Development.

Harper, M. G., Maloney, P., & Shinners, J. (2017). Looking back and looking forward through the lens of the nursing professional development: Scope and standards of practice (3rd ed.). *Journal for Nurses in Professional Development*, 33(6), pp.329–332. https://doi.org/10.1097/NND.0000000000000402

Institute of Medicine. (2004). *Health literacy: A prescription to end confusion* [online]. Available at: https://www.nap.edu/catalog/10883/health-literacy-a-prescription-to-end-confusion (Accessed 13 May 2021).

Johnson, C., & Smith, C. (2019). The evolution from staff development to nursing professional development and continuing professional development. *Journal for Nurses in Professional Development*, 35(2), pp.104–106. https://doi.10.1097/NND.0000000000000506

Leask, J., Kinnersley, P., Jackson, C., Cheater, F., Bedford, H., & Rowles, G. (2012). Communicating with parents about vaccination: A framework for health professionals. *BMC Pediatrics*, 12(1), p.154. https://doi.org/10.1186/1471-2431-12-154

Levin-Zamir, D., & Bertschi, I. (2018). Media health literacy, Ehealth literacy, and the role of the social environment in context. *International Journal of Environmental Research and Public Health*, 15(8), p.1643. doi: 10.3390/ijerph15081643.

Lyles, C. R., & Sarkar, U. (2015). Health literacy, vulnerable patients, and health information technology use: Where do we go from here? *Journal of Internal Medicine*, 30(3), pp.271–272. https://doi.org/10.1007/s11606-014-3166-5

Mackert, M., Mabry-Flynn, A., Champlin, S., Donovan, E. E., & Pounders, K. (2016). Health literacy and health information technology adoption: The potential for a new digital divide. *Journal of Medical Internet Research*, 18(10), p.264. https://doi.org/10.2196/jmir.6349

National Institutes of Health. (2018, October 31). *Online health information: Is it reliable?* [online]. Available at: https://www.nia.nih.gov/health/online-health-information-it-reliable (Accessed 08 June 2021).

Norman, C. D. (2006). eHealth literacy: Essential skills for consumer health in a networked world. *Journal of Medical Internet Research*, 8(2). https://doi.org/10.2196/jmir.8.2.e9

O'Connor, S., Hanlon, P., O'Donnell, C. A., Garcia, S., Glanville, J., & Mair, F. S. (2016). Understanding factors affecting patient and public engagement and recruitment to digital health interventions: A systematic review of qualitative studies. *BMC Medical Inform Decision Making*, 16(120). https://doi.org/10.1186/s12911-016-0359-3

Paige, S. R., Stellefson, M., Krieger, J. L., Anderson-Lewis, C., Cheong, J., & Stopka, C. (2018). Proposing a transactional model of eHealth literacy: Concept analysis. *Journal of Medical Internet Research*, 20(10), p.e10175. https://doi.org/10.2196/10175

Rose, S. L. (2014). Patient advocacy organizations: Institutional conflicts of interest, trust and trustworthiness. *Journal of Law, Medicine & Ethics*, 41(3), pp.680–687. https://doi.org/10.1111.jlme.12078

Saad, L. (2020, December 22). *U.S. ethics ratings rise for medical workers and teachers* [online]. Available at: https://news.gallup.com/poll/328136/ethics-ratings-rise-medical-workers-teachers.aspx (Accessed 08 June 2021).

Southwell, B. G., Wood, J. L., & Navar, A. M. (2020). Roles for health care professionals in addressing patient-held misinformation beyond fact correction. *American Journal of Public Health*, 110, pp.288–289 [online]. Available at: https://ajph.aphapublications.org/doi/abs/10.2105/AJPH.2020.305729 (Accessed 22 May 2021).

U.S. Department of Health and Human Services. (2020). *Healthy people 2030 health literacy definitions* [online]. Available at: https://health.gov/healthypeople/about/workgroups/health-communication-and-health-information-technology-workgroup (Accessed 02 June 2021).

Vest, J. R., Bolin, J. N., Miller, T. R., Gamm, L. D., Siegrist, T. E., & Martinez., L. E. (2010). Medical homes: "Where you stand on definitions depends on where you sit." *Medical Care Research & Review*, 67(4), pp.393–411. https://doi.org/10.1177/1077558710367794

White, H., Tuck, A., Pyrke, B., Murphy, E., Figg, K., Cartwright, G., & Abdalla, B. (2021). 141 FaceTime for the first time: Patients, families, and junior doctors. *Age & Ageing*, 50(1), pp.12–42. https://doi.org/10/1093/ageing/afab030.102

Chapter 6

Cultivating a Workforce of Nurse Disruptors: An Academic–Practice Innovation Hub

Linda McCauley, Sharon Pappas and Rose Hayes

Contents

Introduction	96
It Starts with a Shared Vision	97
Big Debts, Bad Data and Bureaucratic Messes	99
Reversing Biases against Women and Nurses in Innovation	99
The Need Is Great; the Jobs Are Waiting	101
When the Going Gets Tough, Nurses Innovate	102
Where Innovation Starts: The Emory Nursing Learning Center	103
Curious Nurses Welcome	104
The Center for Data Science	106
Project NeLL	106
National Continuing Education	107
What We Have Learned: Implications for Academia and Practice	108
Conclusion and Recommendations for the Future	108
References	109

DOI: 10.4324/9781003281009-6

Introduction

> Were there none who were discontented, the world would never reach anything better.
>
> **Florence Nightingale**

When a health system is faced with a problem, regardless of whether it is an emerging threat or a long-standing challenge, it is often a nurse who comes up with the solution. The nurse—exposed to the issue every day—probably has already maneuvered a work-around solution that could be patented, scaled up and disseminated to advance healthcare standards. As the profession with the most constant patient interaction, in every setting, nurses have seen what works and what does not work in clinical care. Nurses are therefore uniquely poised to develop innovative mechanisms to improve care delivery.

However, many nurse-led ideas for practice innovation never move beyond conception. There are countless steps between ideation, implementation and widespread adoption of an idea that can change the world. And the challenges facing innovators in any industry are compounded for nurses. In acute care, for instance, nurses are often doing everything they can just to keep people alive right now: working 12+ hour shifts, staying late and picking up shifts when their unit needs them. This does not leave much time for business plans or stakeholder meetings. In clinics, hospice and home health settings, the long hours, unexpected challenges and care coordination spill over into time that might otherwise be spent on innovation work as well. For many nurses, going home means a 'second shift' of housework and caregiving when the day is done. With limited time, resources and infrastructure, for every forward-thinking student or frontline leader, there has probably been at least one good idea that has been dismissed or lost somewhere in the voids of convoluted systems.

What's more, in many instances nurses fill support roles, which too often lead to handing their creative ideas over to someone else to implement. In hospitals that lack the nursing governance required for Magnet® certification, professional governance—wherein clinical nurses have ownership in how practice changes are implemented—is often missing. With only 10% of the US hospitals and few ambulatory settings holding Magnet® designations (Laseter et al., 2020), the presence of professional governance over nursing practice is not yet a standard.

It doesn't have to be this way. It's time to reward nurse innovators and dreamers. We can create the mechanisms necessary for nurses to lead patients and colleagues into the 21st century. This chapter explores the strategies that have enabled one academic–practice partnership (APP) to propel nurse-led innovation, including through the careful cultivation of a digitally enabled, nursing workforce. The tactics we discuss may be replicated, and the resources we have developed are meant to be shared. Leaders create the context for how we interact, how decisions are made and how space is created for nurses to advance patient care. We hope nurse leaders across the United States and globally will join us in applauding nurse disruptors and advancing imperfect nursing ideas that carry the spark of potential.

It Starts with a Shared Vision

Many academic–practice partnerships (APPs) never move past a transactional state; but Emory Nursing leadership realized early on the benefits of solving common problems together. We could think better as partners and saw clearly that relationships would be at the core of our approach to addressing health system challenges. Stimulated by the American Association of Colleges of Nursing's (AACN) *New Era Report*, our teams did not want to allow outdated leadership practices to limit the innovation that would be necessary for successful joint endeavors (AACN, 2016). We understood that traditional, individual-based leadership behaviors would not support the transformation necessary for Emory nurses to thrive (Weberg, 2014). In order to prepare future nurse leaders, we recognized that those who contributed to their clinical learning had to reimagine how they led (Pappas et al., 2019).

To move together effectively, we developed a shared mission and vision. The mission of the Emory Nursing APP is to build a workforce of highly competent and compassionate nurse leaders with the ability to influence change. This partnership, referred to collectively as 'Emory Nursing,' is composed of Emory Healthcare (EHC) and Emory Nell Hodgson Woodruff School of Nursing (NHSWN).

EHC is the most comprehensive health system in Georgia, with 13 hospitals (four are Magnet® designated), a large-scale outpatient clinic and 250 provider locations (Emory Healthcare, 2021). EHC brings a legacy of innovative clinicians, including nurses who developed systems to predict Medical Emergency Team activation (Still, 2018), as well as a nurse-led team that studied nurses' perceptions of telehealth adoption in the Intensive Care Unit (ICU) (Kaplow

& Zellinger, 2021). The Nell Hodgson Woodruff School of Nursing (NHWSN) is the home of the fourth-ranked undergraduate nursing program and the second-ranked graduate nursing program in the United States (US News and World Report, 2021). Emory nursing faculty are extensively engaged in scholarship that transforms healthcare delivery across the lifespan (Clasen et al., 2020; Emory University, 2021; Epps et al., 2019), including large-scale studies in new care models for people with dementia (Kovaleva et al., 2020) and adaptation of sensors and smart-connected devices to empower vulnerable populations (Hertzberg et al., 2021; Chandler et al., 2020; Bussenius et al., 2018).

Emory Nursing is led by a governing body called the Joint Leadership Council (JLC), composed of executives, frontline leaders and stakeholders from both the medical center (EHC) and the school of nursing (NHWSN). The JLC meets quarterly to evaluate and refine its alignment, allowing a continuous exchange of support. This partnership enables academia to leverage real-time insights from practice to ensure that graduating students are ready to address pressing healthcare needs. Students are better prepared to enter the workforce trained in emerging competencies, with skill sets tailored to clinical vacancies. One example is the InEmory Program, which matches students to understaffed medical-surgical units across EHC (Emory Nursing, 2021a). Practice, in turn, can provide the questions (and divulge the clinical problems) necessary to fuel effective academic research and development. It also provides student rotations for the academic process, gives access to diverse settings for academic research and fosters relationships with patient and provider communities (Pappas et al., 2019).

The JLC draws upon a handful of core tactics to execute these functions. Tactics include (1) real-time, mutual data sharing, (2) alignment of Doctor of Nursing Practice (DNP) projects with health system needs and (3) the creation of innovation resources that are not only accessible to nurses in both organizations but built into each organization's infrastructure. These resources, such as Project NeLL (a suite of applications for teaching and practicing nursing data science—developed by the School and powered by EHC big data), are democratizing the means of change so that nurses of every level can contribute to advancing our APP's mission.

Given our profession's decades-long attempts to catch up with innovation curricular standards, our partnership's focus on nursing innovation is significant. The *2021 AACN Essentials* and *2021 Future of Nursing Report* are only the most recent in repeated calls to educate current and future generations in innovation skills (AACN, 2021; NAM, 2021). And yet, deeply rooted barriers—such as time, cost, accessibility of data and outdated assumptions about what it means to be innovative—persist (Blumenstyk, 2019; Conners and Herbert, 2016; Larson, 2017). For instance, nursing curricula have historically focused on inputting data into the electronic health record (EHR), with little to no time spent on strategies for using the data in meaningful ways to influence care (McCauley & Delaney, 2017). Too often, nursing curricula require coursework on statistics, but do not discuss how to use data in meaningful ways. Furthermore, many widely available databases do not include key nursing-sensitive data, such as nurses' notes and National Database of Nursing Quality Indicator (NDNQI) relevant fields. To address this limitation, we are creating accessible, nurse-centered mechanisms to drive innovation, including databases with nursing-sensitive data.

Big Debts, Bad Data and Bureaucratic Messes

Leaders in academia and practice continue to face deeply rooted barriers to cultivating a workforce of nurse disruptors. One major barrier is the professional glass ceiling(s) that women—particularly women of color—face across industries, and because nursing continues to be a predominantly female workforce. Across professions, women have historically faced disproportionate challenges in bringing new ideas to market. These challenges include hiring practices, workplace expectations and the biases of supervisors, among other factors. To illustrate this point, only 0.28% of global patent applications come from women-only teams, whereas 96% name one or more male inventor (Collins, 2018; UK Intellectual Property Office Informatics Team, 2016). Collins (2018) adds, 'If the proportion of female inventors increases at the same rate as the last 40 years, it will take until the year 2198 to achieve an equal proportion of female and male inventors.' These roadblocks are amplified by the lack of required innovation assignments in nursing curricula. Instead, decades of nursing education have focused on applying standards of care, albeit with an important focus on quality and safety. Few nursing students have opportunities to participate in design-thinking assignments or to join extracurricular hackathons on clinical problems.

Reversing Biases against Women and Nurses in Innovation

Emory Nursing's approach has been to lead frank conversations about intersectional barriers to inclusion and to develop strategies for their elimination.

Based on internal and external conversations with stakeholders, we have identified four core needs or opportunities for improvement across academia and practice. We are using these improvement areas to devise pathways for more inclusive, nurse-centered problem-solving.

People power: This category includes the widespread need for (1) representation and advancement of diverse nurse innovators, (2) inclusive professional development in innovation skills, (3) buy-in from stakeholders for transformation processes across the innovation lifecycle and (4) leadership's readiness to reward disruptive thinking. Change begins at the top. Leaders of all levels, including faculty and clinical mentors, must encourage the spirit of innovation. However, as Ellis (2019) describes, clinical mentors and faculty can, themselves, function as roadblocks to innovation: '[Some] professors have a reputation … when it comes to change [as being] skeptical, recalcitrant, resentful, even obstructionist, the "Party of No."' This phenomenon can be due, at least in part, to professors/mentors being incentivized to uphold clinical protocols, rather than challenging students to find 'a better way.' In fact, students who do not deliver care in alignment with strict protocols are often graded unfavorably. Consistency and repetitiveness can be crucial to quality assurance, but unwavering adherence to procedure can stifle creativity. Consistency and disruption are not mutually exclusive: Nursing can cultivate cultures of change, while also ensuring dependable care.

Time: This category includes the time necessary for faculty and frontline leaders' development and curricular change. Any discussions about nurses pursuing new skills or assuming transformation projects beyond role expectations must account for burnout, work–life balance and fair/equitable compensation. As Gephart et al. (2018) put it, 'amid calls for more nursing engagement with big data, there is a shortage of those with the knowledge and skills to do so.' A vicious cycle exists in which nursing faculty and clinical nurse leaders across the United States lack the time to learn innovation skills themselves, and/or to build innovation principles into curricula and continuing education. Consequently, faculty and clinical leaders often cannot adequately train the next generation, and the shortage of innovation faculty/mentors intensifies year after year. How do we break this cycle? Our answer is to develop innovation resources 'by nurses for nurses'—and insist that the solutions be fast, accessible and fit seamlessly into nurses' work.

Resources: tools for research, learning and teaching. NHWSN's strategic initiative on innovation, described in Figure 6.1, recognizes the widespread need for straightforward innovation resources across nursing domains. We are developing dynamic resources, such as Project NeLL and Emory Nursing

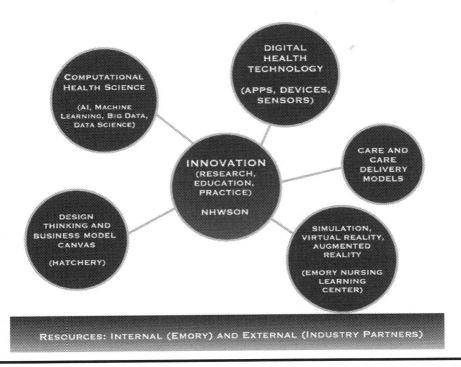

Figure 6.1 Emory Nursing Innovation Model, developed by Dr. Beth Ann Swan, Associate Dean and Vice President of Academic-Practice Partnerships, 2021.

Experience, to facilitate nursing innovation. Beyond resource development, the figure illustrates the breath of innovation that can be cultivated in nursing education, research and practice.

Confusing 'data based' and 'evidence based': an area of concern is the disconnect between 'evidence-based' and 'data-driven' practice. Nurses are driving practice forward—with a massive data blind spot. Nurse disruptors rarely are prompted to use health records data to justify a study or intervention. That means nurse-led solutions may not account for the reality of what is happening across healthcare today. We must close the disconnect between evidence-based practice (EBP) and data-driven leadership, increase nurses' access to big data and ensure nurses know how to use it.

The Need Is Great; the Jobs Are Waiting

There is no question that nurses require training in innovation competencies. In one 2018 report by GlobalData, 50% of surveyed healthcare organizations were in the midst of implementing a formal digital transformation strategy, and another 26% were developing a strategy. These organizations need workers with knowledge spanning leadership, clinical best practices and informatics. In a 2020 HIMSS Nursing Informatics Workforce Survey, 41% of respondents reported their organization had created a Chief Nursing Informatics Officer (CNIO) role, and these positions are expected to be in even greater demand over time (HIMSS, 2020). Furthermore, HIMSS workforce surveys (conducted annually since 2004) have consistently indicated that nurses with informatics and analytics skills are more marketable to employers, higher paid and receive more job offers than nurses without these skills.

Nursing employers in particular are recognizing that digital preparedness and a disruptive mindset are not just attractive from a hiring perspective—they may be critical to professional survival. One topic that has been in the nursing literature for over three decades is clinician burnout. Recently, the National Academies of Science, Engineering and Medicine (NASEM) committed multiple resources to examine the problem of burnout and improve care by addressing clinician well-being (NASEM, 2019). In the NASEM report, the conceptual framework specifies that burnout is not addressed solely by improving the resilience of the individual, but also by addressing the systems in which clinicians practice. Systems managers, ever concerned with process and liability, ought to regularly assess the processes that are seen as exhausting and unnecessary in the eyes of frontline clinicians. Once those issues are exposed, it would be powerful to have frontline clinicians develop new approaches—instead of introducing top-down solutions that may be resented or rejected. Those who provide patient care are best positioned to describe the processes/tools that should be eliminated and offer alternatives.

The philosophy of our APP is that innovation is not just one more thing to teach students and one more thing for nurses to do. We believe nurses will be empowered and energized IF they work in environments that encourage and reward innovation. Believing in one's expertise and having the opportunity to improve systems can go a long way in building joy for work, reducing burnout and connecting to purpose.

When the Going Gets Tough, Nurses Innovate

Throughout its history, our academic and practice partnership (APP) has risen to meet profound challenges thanks to (1) our alignment across academia and practice and (2), our willingness to listen to nurses who come forward with suggestions for solving big problems. In 2020, we were recognized for this approach through the American Association of Colleges of Nursing's Academic Practice Partnership Award, which cited our successful joint ventures. These included the Integrated Memory Care Clinic (IMCC), the first, nurse-led clinic in the United States specializing in primary care for people with dementia, InEmory, Emory Nursing Experience and others.

The next 5 years will build upon this foundation, leveraging innovative tools, technologies and resources to accelerate partnership activities. Our APP alignment over the next 5 years will enable us to (1) prepare a national workforce of highly competent, compassionate and *digitally enabled* nurse leaders who are prepared to disrupt health systems that no longer work and (2) advance nurse-led solutions that reflect design-thinking, best practices in informatics and an entrepreneurial spirit. The following programs will be critical to realizing this vision. The values of accessibility and inclusion run throughout our Innovation Initiatives, meaning our colleagues across the United States and around the globe may leverage these resources as well (Figure 6.2).

Where Innovation Starts: The Emory Nursing Learning Center

The Emory Nursing Learning Center (ENLC) will launch in phases, beginning in August 2021. The ENLC provides a hub for nurses and collaborators

Figure 6.2 The Emory Nursing Learning Center in Downtown Decatur, Ga.

to share in learning, discovery, and innovation (Sams, 2020). The physical spaces that make up the ENLC are located in Downtown Decatur, Georgia, close to both the emerging 'Atlanta Silicone Valley' (i.e., corporate-tech organizations headquartered in Atlanta) and high foot-traffic, community locations (i.e., City Hall, religious venues, an event pavilion and parks). This proximity to thriving centers for stakeholder engagement is central to the ENLC's aim to catalyze interdisciplinary, community-led solutions.

Housed in the ENLC are an Innovation Hub, augmented reality (AR)/virtual reality (VR) rooms, an interactive 'apartment' to practice home and hospice care, and interdisciplinary collision spaces. A *'collision space'* is a shared location for casual conversations, fun and tinkering (e.g., Legos), and flow-state activities (e.g., knitting, coloring). Why would a very serious center for nursing advancement come with crayons? Because exceptional ideas can't be forced: when people can step away from a perplexing problem, color and think about nothing for a while, science shows the answers are bound to come (Agnoli et al., 2018; Lebuda et al., 2015).

The simulation labs and classrooms within the ENLC are *smart connected*. A smart-connected space is one that you can interact with via touch, voice, motion sensors and other features designed to facilitate learning. Here is just one illustration: a smart-connected sim lab might have the capability to prompt a simulated, veteran panic-attack whenever a student inadvertently makes a loud noise that could mimic fireworks or gunshots. The students would then have to stop their current task to intervene, just as they would in real life. However, in this setting, secondary inputs like voice strain and provider heart rate could be used to understand and refine factors like group stress, interpersonal dynamics and students' learning needs.

Curious Nurses Welcome

ENLC spaces are made to welcome nurses from academia and practice, patients, communities and collaborators across sectors. People can access our smart-connected spaces from anywhere. In the scenario above, we might be joined by Distance Accelerated Bachelor of Science in Nursing students and a guest lecturer from the Department of Veterans Affairs. Real-time translation and closed captioning mean people can weigh in on discussions regardless of language, location and learning needs. The ability to opt in to either real-time or asynchronous sessions mean time zone is not a concern either. These approaches have been rigorously tested over more than half a decade through the Emory-Ethiopia PhD in Nursing Program. This program is the first PhD in Nursing Program in Ethiopia and is the first PhD program of its kind (hybrid, remote/in person, international and smart connected) in Africa (Gary et al., 2020).

Within the Emory innovation ecosystem, which includes several centers, the ENLC's Innovation Hub stands out—and complements the work of peer centers—by bringing the engineering, business and practice perspectives together. We are creating a place for people to build and do—to execute the entire lifecycle of patient and community-centered innovation, including prototyping and testing. Because Emory University does not have an engineering school, it was especially important for us to welcome partners such as Georgia Tech, and to provide material assets for hands-on creation. If inspiration strikes over coffee and Legos at midnight, you can't break the creative process due to a lack of silicone and piping! And how powerful to have a practicing nurse, a business student and an engineer creating together, knowing what will and won't work within their respective industries—all of which are necessary to implement effective solutions.

Physical spaces are complemented by virtual playgrounds and practice suites like Project NeLL, Emory Nursing Experience and immersive AR/VR landscapes. Our intention for the AR/VR library (currently in planning/development) is to afford nurses the ability to test their mental, emotional and logistical readiness for any new or unexpected scenario they may encounter. Whether you are deploying to a Mercy Ship, an outpost of our Emory-Ethiopia network, or the fallout of a terrorist attack—you should be able to step into a simulation, before plunging into reality. Imagine how impactful it would have been for reserve nurses and students across the United States to have had this capability in the early days of the COVID-19 pandemic.

The following sections describe some of the projects within the ENLC in more detail. Each of these items is informed by—and supports—APP alignment and is contributing to our mission to prepare a workforce of nurse disruptors. In order to cultivate such a workforce, practice leaders must pivot to meet new standards in academic preparation and foster a culture that doesn't just support but expects continuous process improvement from employees. Furthermore, innovation is not truly 'innovative' until it is implemented and measured. With these simple truths in mind, we have methodically incorporated the following mechanisms for advancing innovation into programs across our organizations.

The Center for Data Science

The Center for Data Science (CDS) is housed within the School, but supports transformation work across academia and practice. The CDS was established in 2015 with the recruitment of Dr. Vicki Stover Hertzberg, a world-renowned biostatistician, to the School's faculty. Dr. Hertzberg is known for many accomplishments including the use of big data to map the spread of viral pathogens on airplanes (Hertzberg, 2018). Drs. Hertzberg and McCauley founded the Center to bring the power of data-driven thinking to bear on the greatest challenges in healthcare and scientific discovery today. Each of the nurse leaders whose professional growth is accelerated by CDS goes on to solve problems, discover knowledge and change lives. Some of the research and practice services offered through the Center include (1) immediate access to organized, downloadable, healthcare big data through Project NeLL; (2) access and scientific mentorship on how to analyze and apply 'omics' data; (3) the means to create, patent, and learn from real-time biological and environmental sensors; and (4) the professional support and industry connections necessary to develop and protect nurse-designed products.

CDS faculty and staff support mechanisms for process improvement, from grant writing and execution on the academic side, to implementation, evaluation and sustainability on the practice side. Since its founding, CDS has helped to secure more than US$ 56.1 million in external research grants, with more than US$ 26.5 million in active grants today.

Project NeLL

Project NeLL is a suite of applications (Apps) for teaching, learning and practicing nursing data science. NeLL is transforming the way nurses think about research and empowering nurses of all levels to solve the problems they encounter at the frontlines of care (Hayes, 2021). NeLL includes a searchable big database containing 37+ trillion data points from 2.7+ billion EHR records (15+ billion patient encounters), representing 1.2+ million patient journeys across the care continuum. Designed by nurses for nurses, it doesn't matter how much an end user already knows about analytics: NeLL is made to be intuitive so that nurses may download the data they need on first use. Its learning and teaching apps include a comprehensive data dictionary and a self-paced, e-learning course being developed through Emory Nursing Experience, our continuing education enterprise. NeLL is already being utilized to transform healthcare, for example, with students investigating the care of patients with Hepatitis C, the cost value of nurse anesthetists, age and race disparities in opioid administration, and more (Nakayama et al., 2021).

Project NeLL is a strong illustration of academic–practice synergy. The EHR data in NeLL's repository come from Emory Healthcare; these data are de-identified by the health system's Clinical Data Warehouse before being sent to NHWSN. Once the data arrive at the School, a team of CDS scientists clean, index and organize it for use within NeLL's interface. Emory nurses from the undergraduate to advanced practice level may query the data whenever systems-level questions arise.

In order for NeLL to be sustainable, we recognize that champions will be needed to teach analytics to nurses in practice (i.e., it is not enough to teach students entering practice; we also need to train the existing workforce). Thus, we are developing a NeLL Fellowship program, to launch in 2022, which will provide a mini-sabbatical for clinical leaders to immerse themselves in using NeLL. These nursing leaders can then teach their colleagues and mentor DNP students completing dissertation projects.

National Continuing Education

Emory Nursing Experience (ENE) is our nationally accessible catalog of immersive continuing education courses, accredited by the American Nurses Credentialing Centers Commission on Accreditation. ENE courses, developed by the School and Emory Healthcare Nursing Education, are informed by data and insights regarding workforce knowledge gaps. Courses are taught by faculty experts and complemented by virtual, in-person and hybrid opportunities to apply new knowledge. Nurses in practice, hoping to maintain their licensing or advance their career, are our primary audience. They may receive contact hours and certifications from anywhere in the world through ENE. However, a broad range of other nursing users, including faculty, students and staff, tap into the ENE catalog to supplement their work and teaching. The ENE team addresses real nursing needs by moving quickly to fill knowledge gaps when they arise. One example is a series of COVID-related learning experiences, released at the start of the pandemic (Emory Nursing, 2021b).

What We Have Learned: Implications for Academia and Practice

During the pandemic, when routine professional governance meetings were almost eliminated, EHC continued to work with individuals that were part of system councils to make decisions. The re-processing of isolation gowns and placement of IV pumps outside the patient room required clinician input, and dormant council members were called into service to provide guidance. We learned the value of the habit of clinician governance—the individuals were prepared in decision-making, risk taking and boundary spanning (the ability to make connections in otherwise unconnected groups) (Weberg & Davidson, 2021). We needed those clinician skills every day as we responded to the unknown. Relationships are key to making risk-taking and boundary spanning possible; and because academia and practice routinely worked together, we were able to recognize deficits in knowledge and acquire information from internal and external sources so others could adapt to changing conditions. These same capabilities are important in non-crisis times as well. Leading innovation requires us to resist a command-and-control approach to leadership, and instead build relationships and lead together through daily complexities. Bottom line, we created the context for disruption, where a network of people came together to set a direction for the healthcare system to evolve.

Conclusion and Recommendations for the Future

In Spring 2021, the AACN passed a new *Essentials* document focused on preparing nursing to meet the needs of the 21st century, differentiating between 'change' and 'transformation.' The authors state that 'change' fixes the past, while 'transformation' creates the future—modifying values, core beliefs and desires. Innovation may not, right now, be an expectation for all nursing graduates, but we believe it is a bridge to the future of nursing and will soon be recognized as central to effective nursing practice. Nursing students who are disruptors, who desire to find new ways of thinking and doing, who are ready-to-use new technologies to improve care, have to be nurtured. Academic–practice partnerships are key to building a future in which such nurse leaders can thrive.

References

Agnoli, S., Vanucci, M., Pelagatti, C., & Corazza, G. E. (2018). Exploring the link between mind wandering, mindfulness, and creativity: A multidimensional approach. *Creativity Research Journal*, 30, pp.1–53.

American Association of Colleges of Nursing. (2016). *Advancing healthcare transformation: A new era for academic nursing* [online]. Available at: https://www.aacnnursing.org/portals/42/publications/aacn-new-era-report.pdf (Accessed 6 September 2021).

American Association of Colleges of Nursing. (2021). *The essentials: Core competencies for professional nursing* [online]. Available at: https://www.aacnnursing.org/Store/product-info/productcd/PUB_NEWESSENTIALS (Accessed 6 September 2021).

Blumenstyk, G. (2019). Beyond the buzz. In G. Blumenstyk & L. Gardner, eds., *The innovation imperative: The buzz, the barriers, and what real change looks like*. The Chronicle of Higher Education [online]. Available at: https://store.chronicle.com/collections/reports-guides/products/the-innovation-imperative (Accessed 6 September 2021).

Bussenius, H., Zeck, A., Williams, B., & Haynes, A. (2018). Surveillance of pediatric hypertension using smartphone technology. *Journal of Pediatric Health Care*, 32(5), pp.e98–e104. https://doi.org/10.1016/j.pedhc.2018.04.003

Chandler, R., Hernandez, N., Guillaume, D., Grandoit, S., Branch-Ellis, D., & Lightfoot, M. (2020). A community-engaged approach to creating a mobile HIV prevention application for Black women: Focus group study to determine preferences via prototype demos. *Journal of Internet Research (JMIR) mHealth and uHealth*, 8(7), p.e18437. https://doi.org/10.2196/18437

Clasen, T., et al. (2020). Design and rationale of the HAPIN study: A multicountry randomized controlled trial to assess the effect of liquified petroleum gas stove and continuous fuel distribution. *Environmental Health Perspectives*. https://doi.org/10.1289/EHP6407

Collins, E. (2018). *How likely is little miss inventor to be awarded a patent?* Kilburn & Strode [online]. Available at: https://bit.ly/3vZ3BCt (Accessed 4 September 2021).

Connors, H., & Herbert, V. (2016). Integrating an academic electronic health record: Challenges and success strategies. *Computers, Informatics, Nursing*, 34(8), pp.345–354. 10.1097/CIN.0000000000000264.

Ellis, L. (2019). How one bold reinvention plan went bellyup. In G. Blumenstyk & L. Gardner, eds., *The innovation imperative: The buzz, the barriers, and what real change looks like*. The Chronical of Higher Education [online]. Available at: https://store.chronicle.com/collections/reports-guides/products/the-innovation-imperative (Accessed 6 September 2021).

Emory Healthcare. (2021). *About us*. [online]. Available at: https://www.usnews.com/best-graduate-schools/top-nursing-schools (Accessed 3 August 2021).

Emory Nursing. (2021a). *In Emory: Program details* [online]. Available at https://bit.ly/3mJH4aC (Accessed 4 September 2021).

Emory Nursing. (2021b). *Emory nursing experience* [online]. Available at https://bit.ly/3p5vFkG (Accessed 4 September 2021).

Emory University. (2021). *I am an Emory researcher* [online]. Available at https://news.emory.edu/features/2021/08/emory-researcher-dunn-amore/index.html (Accessed 3 September 2021).

Epps, F., Brewster, G., Alexander, K., Choe, J., Heidbreder, V., & Hepburn, K. (2019). Dementia-friendly faith village worship services to support African American families: Research protocol. *Research in Nursing and Health*, 42, pp.189–197. https://doi.org/10.1002/nur.21940

Gary, B., Rogers, M., Demisse, L., Hayes, R., & McCauley, L. (2020). The Emory-Addis Ababa PhD in nursing program: A sustainable model for strengthening nursing research capacity in Ethiopia. *Journal of Professional Nursing*, 36(6), pp.531–537. https://doi.org/10.1016/j.profnurs.2020.08.004

Gephart, S., Davis, M., & Shea, K. (2018). Perspectives on policy and the value of nursing science. *Nursing Science Quarterly*, 31(1), pp.78–81. https://doi.org/10.1177/0894318417741122

GlobalData. (2018). Digital transformations and emerging technology in healthcare industry. *GlobalData Reports GDHCHT014* [online]. Available at: https://store.globaldata.com/report/gdhcht014--digital-transformations-and-emerging-technologies-in-the-healthcare-industry-h2-2018/ (Accessed 6 September 2021).

Hayes, R. (2021). Transforming the future of nursing research. *Emory Nursing Magazine* [online]. Available at https://bit.ly/3wGpLZO (Accessed 4 September 2021).

Hertzberg, V. S., Mac, V. T., Mitchell, R. M., Tansey, M. G., Chicas, R., Tovar-Aguilar, J. A., & McCauley, L. (2021). Heat exposure, heat-related illness, dehydration, inflammation, muscle breakdown, and renal dysfunction: A machine learning model of biomarkers. *Biological Research for Nursing*. https://doi.org/10.1177/10998004211016070

Hertzberg, V. S., Weiss, H., Elon, L., Si, W., Norris, S., & the Fly Healthy Research Team. (2018). Behaviors, movements, and transmission of droplet-mediated respiratory diseases during transcontinental airline flights. *PNAS*, 115(14), pp.3623–3627. https://doi.org/10.1073/pnas.1711611115

HIMSS. (2020). *HIMSS 2020 nursing informatics workforce survey: Executive summary* [online]. Available at: https://bit.ly/38nmK6w (Accessed 4 September 2021).

Kaplow, R., & Zellinger, M. (2021). Nurses' perception of telemedicine adoption in the intensive care unit. *American Journal of Critical Care*, 30(2), pp.122–127. https://doi.org/10.4037/ajcc2021205

Kovaleva, M., Higgins, M., Jennings, B., Song, M., Clevenger, C., Griffiths, P., & Hepburn, K. (2020). Patient and caregiver outcomes at the integrated memory care clinic. *Geriatric Nurse*, 41(6), pp.761–768. https://doi.org/10.1016/j.gerinurse.2020.05.006

Larson, L. R. (2017). *Perceptions and experiences of baccalaureate nursing program leaders related to nursing informatics*. University of Kansas [doctoral dissertation, online]. Available at: https://bit.ly/34mTUAt (Accessed 4 September 2021).

Laseter, K., Richards, M., Dandapani, N., Burns, L., & McHugh, M. (2020). Magnet hospital recognition in hospital systems over time. *Healthcare Manage Review*, 44(1), pp.19–29. https://doi.org/10.1097/HMR.0000000000000167

Lebuda, I., Zabelina, D. L., & Karwowski, M. (2015). Mind-full of ideas: A meta-analysis of the mindfulness–creativity link. *Personality and Individual Differences*, pp.1–5. https://doi.org/10.1016/j.paid.2015.09.040

McCauley, L. A., & Delaney, C. W. (2017). What big data and data science mean for schools of nursing and academia. In C. W. Delaney, C. A. Weaver, J. J. Warren, R. R. Clancy, & R. Simpson, eds., *Big data-enabled nursing: Education, research and practice*. Springer: Switzerland, pp.374–384.

Nakayama, J. Y., Ho, J., Cartwright, E., Simpson, R., & Hertzberg, V. S. (2021). Predictors of progression through the cascade of care to a cure for hepatitis C patients using decision trees and random forests. *Computers in Biology and Medicine*, 134, p.104461. https://doi.org/10.1016/j.compbiomed.2021.104461

National Academies of Medicine. (2021). *The future of nursing: 2020–2030: Charting a path to achieve health equity*. Washington, DC: The National Academies Press [online]. Available at: https://nam.edu/publications/the-future-of-nursing-2020-2030/ (Accessed 6 September 2021).

National Academies of Sciences, Engineering, and Medicine. (2019). *Taking action against clinician burnout: A systems approach to professional well-being*. Washington, DC: The National Academies Press, p.334. https://doi.org/10.17226/25521

Pappas, S., Hayes, R., & McCauley, L. (2019). Implementation of new era strategic initiatives across an academic health center. *Nurse Leader*, 18(3), pp.237–242. https://doi.org/10.1016/j.mnl.2019.10.004

Sams, D. (2020). Emory's fast-growing nursing school will soon be towering over downtown Decatur. *Atlanta Business Chronicle* [online]. Available at: https://bit.ly/2S2q5U2. (Accessed 4 September 2021).

Still, M., Vanderlaan, J., Brown, C., Gordon, M., Holder, C., McMurtry, J. P., Meyer, E., Morelock, V., & Shapiro, S. (2018). Predictors of second medical emergency team activation within 24 hours of index event. *Journal of Nursing Care Quality*, 33(2), pp.157–165. https://doi.org/10.1098/NCQ.0000000000000272

UK Intellectual Property Office Informatics Team. (2016). *Gender profiles in UK patenting: An analysis of female inventorship* [online]. Available at: https://bit.ly/34HwZkt (Accessed 4 September 2021).

US News and World Report. (2021). 2022 best *nursing schools* [online]. Available at: https://www.usnews.com/best-graduate-schools/top-nursing-schools (Accessed 4 September 2021).

Weberg, D., & Davidson, S., eds. (2021). *Leadership for evidence-based innovation in nursing and health professions*. Burlington, MA: Jones & Bartlett Learning, p.480.

Weberg, D. & Weberg, K. (2014). Seven behaviors to advance teamwork findings form a study of innovation leadership in a simulation center. *Nursing Administration Quarterly*, 38(3), pp.230–237. https://doi.org/10.1097/NAQ.0000000000000041

Chapter 7

Nursing Education and Digital Health Strategies

Marisa L. Wilson

Contents

Introduction	113
Informatics, Technology and Digital Health	115
Nurses Engage with Data and Technology	117
Nursing: A Long History of Change Using Informatics Processes and Technology	118
The AACN Re-envisioned Essentials—Domain 8: Informatics and Healthcare Technology	121
Preparing Faculty	123
Faculty Teaching All Nurses	123
Resources to Assist Development	124
Digital Health Framework	125
Summary	126
Key Take-Away Points	126
References	127

Introduction

Health systems have long relied on established, evidence-based disease strategies and approaches to manage the care of individual patients who live in communities and are part of a population served by a provider. Despite using evidence-supported strategies for individual patients by the entire healthcare team, the prevalence of chronic disease and illness continues to grow. In 2019, the Centers for Disease Control and Prevention (CDC) notes that 60% of adults in the United States have one chronic illness and 40% have two or more accounting for US$ 3.3 trillion in healthcare costs annually (Centers for Disease Control and Prevention [CDC], 2019). Chronic illness is now responsible for 75% of the total healthcare burden in North America, and recent evidence suggests that the current models of care delivery are neither sufficient nor well constructed to effectively manage the demands that this level of chronic illness places on the system (Milani et al., 2017). The CDC (2021) estimates that heart disease and stroke cost the US$ 214 billion in care and lost productivity per year, cancer care US$ 174 billion, diabetes US$ 327 billion, obesity US$ 147 billion, and arthritis US$ 304 billion. Current funding models and cost pressures will make life-changing therapies unaffordable and inaccessible for many unless the health system can transform care delivery and new models of care can be developed and implemented and this includes digital and virtual models. Health systems struggle to manage growing demand for service while trying to remain fiscally sound, meet consumers and populations expectations on the providers and systems for personalization of care that encompasses health and wellness (Statista, 2019).

Healthcare consumers now demand personalized care that encompasses their unique circumstances, values, needs and risks. Consumers expect patient-centered care but often receive formulaic care pathways and models that rely on prescriptive approaches delivered using in-person modalities and models not designed for them. Consumers receive care often not where or when they need it. Consumers can connect virtually via the Internet to global experts and organizations, and they have access to information and services through Internet-based technologies already. Calixte et al. (2020), in a secondary analysis of Health Information National Trends Survey, determined that 43% of consumers used the Internet to find a doctor and 80% looked online for their health information. Patients, consumers and caregivers are there in the digital space and they expect their care providers to meet them where they are. There is a gap between what is currently delivered and how it is delivered, and what the consumer wants and what they access. The key to closing this gap and to advance and strengthen the healthcare system will be to move it toward a future that is not bounded by four walls but is digitally enabled, focused on health and wellness, and that is designed, evaluated and managed by a healthcare team competent and capable of fully engaging in a digital health revolution. Nurses, both entry to practice and advanced, comprise the largest component of the healthcare workforce. Nurses are the primary providers of hospital-based care and nurses deliver most of the care in the nation's long-term facilities. Nurses are in a prime position to lead the revolution and evolution of healthcare by becoming innovators of digital health solutions and strategies. However, nurses need a strong foundation in the building blocks of digital health which are the components of informatics and information and communication technologies. Nurses must be competent and capable to engage and lead this digital movement.

Informatics, Technology and Digital Health

To fully appreciate the potential of digital health to revolutionize patient, community and population healthcare, the terms must be defined and described.

The American Medical Informatics Association (AMIA) describes *Informatics* as the science of how to use data, information and knowledge to improve human health and the delivery of healthcare services. Health Information Technology is a part of informatics but the technology and technological considerations are but one component of informatics processes (American Medical Informatics Association [AMIA], 2021).

The National Institute of Standards and Technology (NIST) of the US Department of Commerce describes *Information and Communication Technologies* (ICT) as all categories of ubiquitous technology used for the gathering, storing, transmitting, retrieving or processing of information (e.g., microelectronics, printed circuit boards, computing systems, software, signal processors, mobile telephony, satellite communications and networks). ICT encompasses the capture, storage, retrieval, processing, display, representation, presentation, organization, management, security, transfer and interchange of data and information (US Department of Commerce, 2021). Eye on Tech (2020) has produced a YouTube video that describes Information and Communication Technologies in a very succinct way. You can access this at: https://www.youtube.com/watch?v=5PDQKu2-bAc

Finally, what exactly is digital health? The Health Information Management Systems Society (HIMSS) describes digital health as that which connects and empowers people and populations to manage health and wellness, augmented by accessible and supportive provider teams working within flexible, integrated, interoperable and digitally enabled care environments that strategically leverage digital tools, technologies and services to transform care delivery (Comstock, 2020). The US Food and Drug Administration describes digital health as a broad scope of technology categories such as mobile health (mHealth), health information technology (IT), wearable devices, telehealth and telemedicine, and personalized medicine that use computing platforms, connectivity, software and sensors for healthcare and related uses (US Food and Drug Administration [FDA], 2020).

Digital Health is then the application of information and communication technology to provide digital health interventions to prevent disease and improve quality of life. Digital health includes concepts from technology and healthcare. Digital health applies transformational processes to healthcare incorporating software, hardware and services. Digital health includes mobile health (mHealth) applications, electronic health records (EHRs), wearable devices, telehealth, telemedicine and personalized medicine. Digital health technology and processes support interventions to prevent disease, improve quality of life, address global health concerns related to aging, illness and mortality, epidemics and pandemics by providing digital health platforms, health systems, and related technology and infrastructure (Bernstein, 2021).

For nurses to be full participants, to lead, to innovate and to engage in this evolutionary change in healthcare, they have to demonstrate basic informatics and information technology competencies and capabilities. These competencies and capabilities have been listed and described by several organizations nationally, internationally and interprofessionally. Here are a few:

1. The American Association of Colleges of Nursing (AACN) Essentials: https://www.aacnnursing.org/AACN-Essentials
2. Canadian Association of Schools of Nursing (CASN) Entry to Practice Nursing Informatics Competencies: https://www.casn.ca/2014/12/casn-entry-practice-nursing-informatics-competencies/
3. HIMSS TIGER International Competency Synthesis Project Global Health Informatics Competency Recommendation Frameworks: https://www.himss.org/resources/global-health-informatics-competency-recommendation-frameworks
4. National Nursing and Midwifery Digital Health Capability Framework: https://www.digitalhealth.gov.au/sites/default/files/2020-11/National_Nursing_and_Midwifery_Digital_Health_Capability_Framework_publication.pdf

Reviewing this representative listing of global and interprofessional competencies and capabilities, it becomes apparent that in order to achieve a digital health evolution, the education of healthcare professionals must change to incorporate these competencies and capabilities. The professional development of those who teach, guide and mentor healthcare professionals has to occur and the employing healthcare systems leaders have to be willing to engage, evolve and re-envision.

Nurses Engage with Data and Technology

Nurses are key to this digital health evolution as nurses comprise approximately 30% of the healthcare professional workforce. Nurses are engaged across the spectrum of care from the home to the acute care system, to long-term care, to the community and out to the population. Nurses work in all segments of the healthcare sector and in roles as varied as direct care, advanced practice, education, research and policymaking (Schur, 2020). All nurses who provide care, expertise and compassion to patients, communities or populations do their work using a variety of technologies to (1) enter data collected during assessment, (2) develop information from which to make decisions, and (3) to form knowledge from information and experiences. Most often this is accomplished not with paper and pencil but while using some type of information technology as a matter of routine business. All nurses engage with digital health tools daily. They need to be competent and confident to use these tools to change the system. Nurses use informatics processes and a variety of information technologies during every shift of every workday without considering the complexity of these processes or the ubiquitous nature of the information systems and digital health tools all around them. Nurses use information systems and data to formulate actions based on critical thinking using formed information and a distinct body of evidence. Nurses are often the last point of interaction between a patient and a treatment, and this decisive action often is supported and guided by technology, such as Bar Code Medication Administration systems. Some of the information systems are interacted with in an active way and some passively. The trackers that patients, clinicians and staff wear gather data on location, date and time using radiofrequency readers. Decisions are made from this passively collected data. Some of those decisions are helpful and a few can be harmful or unsafe. During this current COVID-19 pandemic, nurses use an information and communication technology tool, the tablet, to facilitate the last communications between a dying patient and their loved ones. This informatics process was developed to meet a tragic human need to connect and out of a deep concern for safety. All this is to say that nurses use information technology, the data and information contained within their related databases as a matter of course and as part of their routine work often without considering that this is informatics and that they should have a keen role in guiding the development, implementation and use of these systems and processes as we all move toward digital health.

According to Nagle (2016):

> the time has come to stridently move past the misconception of nursing informatics as: *nurses using computers* ... to an age of clinical intelligence (Harrington, 2011); one in which the tools are merely facilitative and practice informs the evidence. Getting there will require some work by our leadership including the development of informatics savvy nurse leaders and educators and the integration of informatics entry to practice competencies into undergraduate nursing education.
>
> **(p. 3)**

The efficient use of information and communication technology and informatics processes is a key competency of all care providers including nurses and will be key to successful digital health evolutionary change.

Nursing: A Long History of Change Using Informatics Processes and Technology

The use of data and information to make significant changes in healthcare is not new for the profession of nursing nor is the use of technology tools news. Selected nurse leaders have always been on the forefront of the digital revolution pushing for systems change as soon as the tools were available for use. Today, to truly evolve healthcare into a digital sphere, we have to engage not just a selected group of nurse leaders but all nurses need to be part of the process.

The art and science of nursing has long required the use of data to create information and knowledge from which to make informed clinical decisions and to create care systems that are efficient and effective for patients, families, consumers, communities, populations and professional care partners. This is not new. Florence Nightingale, in 1863, stated:

In attempting to arrive at the truth, I have applied everywhere for information, but in scarcely an instance have I been able to obtain hospital records fit for any purposes of comparison. If they could be obtained, they would enable us to decide many other questions besides the one alluded to. They would show subscribers how their money was being spent, what amount of good was really being done with it, or whether the money was not doing mischief rather than good; they would tell us the exact sanitary state of every hospital and of every ward in it, where to seek for causes of insalubrity and their nature; and, if wisely used, these improved statistics would tell us more of the relative value of particular operations and modes of treatment than we have any means of ascertaining at present. They would enable us, besides, to ascertain the influence of the hospital with its numerous diseased inmates, its overcrowded and possibly ill-ventilated wards, its bad site, bad drainage, impure water, and want of cleanliness - or the reverse of all these - upon the general course of operations and diseases passing through its wards; and the truth thus ascertained would enable us to save life and suffering, and to improve the treatment and management of the sick and maimed poor.

(Notes on Hospitals, p. 176)

Using information to determine appropriate care has been key to the nursing profession from its inception. Florence Nightingale (1820–1910), who is credited with propelling the practice of nursing into a profession, used data to provide information on the effect of nursing care on morbidity and mortality rates among soldiers during the Crimean War and later went on to use the data to improve hospital care for all patients (Nightingale, 1863; Selanders, 2021). Nightingale made significant contributions to the evolution of healthcare in her era using informatics principles but with manual processes. Her work impacted the healthcare system, the education of nurses and the outcome of patient care through improved quality.

As computers became available in the 1960s, pioneering nurses began to explore ways that computing power could be used to successfully drive care on the clinical side of healthcare. Harriet Helen Werley, PhD, RN, FAAN, FACMI, became the first 'nurse informatician' even before there was an official name for this specialty. In the late 1950s, Dr. Werley was officially designated as the first nurse researcher at Walter Reed Army Institute of Research.

In this role, Werley participated in conferences initiated by IBM to identify data processing needs for healthcare and explored the potential uses for computer applications by clinicians (Werley & Lang, 1987). In the 1970s, as the field of clinical informatics began to grow, Dr. Werley looked for opportunities to use information technology to reuse clinical data for research and management (Ozbolt, 2003).

Today, in a technology rich environment, registered nurses hold over 3.1 million jobs, exceeding the number of physicians by approximately five to one (Smilet et al., 2018). Over 60% of nurses work in hospitals; however, many are providing care to patients in ambulatory settings, nursing and residential care, the government and educational services all of which use information and communication technologies and which should use informatics processes to move data to information to knowledge (Bureau of Labor Statistics, 2021). Nurses' work is as diverse and complex as the patients they serve. Nurses function as part of an interprofessional team and in this role, it is important to consider that nurses often serve as the information hub of the healthcare team in acute, home and long-term settings. They collect vast amounts of data from patients, family members and other members of the healthcare team. They are integral to the data entered into the EHR. They oversee and act on the data and information coming from monitors, wearables, implantables and pumps. They document data, either on paper or electronically, and disseminate it to others either through the patient record, with communication technologies, or face to face. Nurses listen to and record the voice of the patient and the caregivers no matter where they are. Nurses stand at the vanguard of the digital health evolutions if given the tools to do so.

Recognizing the potential of nursing to impact digital health, The National Academy of Medicine, in *The Future of Nursing 2020–2030: Charting a Path to Achieve Health Equity* mandates that all nurses are to practice to the full extent of their education and training, assume leadership positions, improve data collection, create a culture of health, reduce health disparities and improve the health and well-being of the US population in the 21st century, all of which rests on a foundation of competent use of information and communication technologies and informatics processes (National Academy of Medicine [NAM], 2021).

For nurses to successfully function in their role today and to be full participants in the digital health evolution, they must be competent in the use of the technology and informatics processes whether they are basic practitioners, advanced practitioners or faculty in nursing. Moreover, as technology becomes more sophisticated and ubiquitous within all settings, the role of the informatics nurse specialist, those nurses who are prepared to support nursing practice and the changes needed to evolve to digital health through the application of nursing science, computer science and information science to improve the health of populations, communities, families and individuals through information management and communication technologies must evolve (American Nurses Association [ANA], 2014). This educational content is as dynamic as information technology itself today and will only continue to change and grow as information technology, the profession of nursing and the healthcare environment evolve.

The AACN Re-envisioned Essentials—Domain 8: Informatics and Healthcare Technology

Recognizing the need to have a competent and capable nursing workforce who can participate in and lead the evolution of healthcare, the American Association of Colleges of Nursing (AACN) created a new and dynamic set of ten domains for professional nursing practice to meet the needs of healthcare today and beyond (American Association of Colleges of Nursing [AACN], 2021). Each domain has an aligned set of competencies with actionable, observable and measurable subcompetencies for which schools of nursing will be held accountable to educate and mentor students and graduates. Among the domains is domain 8, which will provide a solid foundation of competency for entry to practice and advance nurses to participate in the digital health evolution. The other domains will provide leadership, communication and interprofessional competency to support the informatics side as nurses lead change. (AACN, 2021)

The re-envisioned AACN Essentials offers a new model of academic nursing impacting the two levels of nursing practice, one level clearly building from the other. The levels are Entry to Practice and Advanced Practice. Level 2 includes all nurses being educated at the Master's and Doctor of Nursing Practice levels. Both levels contain ten domains or spheres of knowledge.

The domains are (AACN, 2021):

1. Knowledge for Nursing Practice
2. Person-Centered Care
3. Population Health
4. Scholarship for Nursing Practice
5. Quality and Safety

6. Interprofessional Partnerships
7. Systems-Based Care
8. Informatics and Healthcare Technologies
9. Professionalism
10. Personal, Professional and Leadership Development.

All of the domains are meant to work together which will equip nurses to fully participate as interprofessional partners and leaders in the digital health evolution. For example, the need for nurses to lead informatics implementations in the conversion to digital health platform would be supported by competencies in domains 3, 5–8 and 10. Domain 8, Informatics and Healthcare Technologies, will focus specifically on the use of informatics practices with information and communication technologies to manage and improve the delivery of safe, high-quality and efficient healthcare services in accordance with best practices and following professional and regulatory standards. Within domain 8, there are five competency expectations and within each level (entry to practice and advanced), there are specific sub-competencies appropriate for that level which are singular in focus, actionable and measurable. The five competencies found in both levels encompass the following concepts:

1. Evaluate the various information and communication technology tools used in the care of patients, communities and populations.
2. Demonstrate appropriate use of information and communication technology to gather data, create information, generate knowledge and develop wisdom.
3. Describe how patient care and clinical interactions are supported by information and communication technology and informatics processes.
4. Examine how information and communication technology supports chronicling of care and communication between providers, patients and systems at micro, meso and macro levels.
5. Use information and communication technologies in accordance with legal, professional and regulatory standards and workplace policies in the delivery of care.

The very specific nature of the subcompetencies will drive the education. The subcompetencies encompass observable and measurable concepts that mature over the time a student is in their plan of study. Some of the measurable subcompetencies are:

1. Understanding the full complement of information and communication technologies in use in patient, consumer and population care and best practices for their use.
2. Effectively using communication technology to support team care.
3. Identifying and evaluating the data to information to knowledge process.
4. Applying data models and standardized terminology to individual and population based care.
5. Promoting information literacy in self and others.
6. Analyzing the role of the nurse in the information life cycle.
7. Understanding the concepts of interoperability, information exchange and integration.
8. Assessing risk and benefit to the use of technology.

Preparing Faculty

Faculty Teaching All Nurses

If there is an expectation that all nurses are competent and capable of participating in and leading a digital health evolution, those who teach, mentor and develop these nurses have to also be competent, capable and confident to do so. Despite the long history of informatics as an expected competency of nurses at all levels of practice, there still remains a gap. Some schools of nursing have had moderate success in implementing nursing informatics content into curricula across all levels of practice; however, many have struggled to achieve this goal. Incorporating informatics content, either as a stand-alone course or woven into other courses is now urgent, as the revised AACN Essentials were approved in April 2021 and will impact accreditation with significantly clearer and measurable informatics competency expectations for all nurses. Nonetheless, the major barrier to integrating informatics competencies into nursing school curriculum is the lack of adequately prepared faculty to teach informatics content (Rajalathi et al., 2014). The average age of doctorally prepared nursing faculty is 53.5 years (AACN, 2020). Very few nursing faculty were educated at a time when informatics content and competencies were included in the nursing curriculum. In addition, very few nursing faculty have any informatics background or education and few nurses prepared in informatics pursue an academic role. This leaves fewer faculty who have an understanding of key areas required to train students in informatics across programs, such as the conceptual basis of informatics,

informatics implementation and evaluation and emerging healthcare technologies (Booth, 2006; Risling, 2017). As a result, many new nurses are entering a professional environment rich in informatics without adequate preparation in using it effectively and efficiently. This lack of preparation can negatively impact nurses' patients as well as their own professional evaluations. Calls from the American Nursing Association, HIMSS TIGER and the American Association of Colleges of Nursing to address this lack of preparation have largely been ineffective due to the lack of a mandate on how to integrate informatics content. The new AACN Essentials will present a need for deep and ongoing faculty development to improve the level of understanding of non-informatics focused faculty who will teach this content in revised courses in new programs of study.

Resources to Assist Development

The recognition that resources are needed to assist faculty and educators has been on the forefront of work for several years. A variety of organizations are working toward a coordinated effort to provide the needed assistance and tools to faculty and educators so they can impact nurses with the goal of those nurses participating in digital health. Organizations such as those listed are developing key resources and tools for faculty, educators and systems leaders. They are:

1. AACN Essentials Toolkit (https://www.aacnnursing.org/AACN-Essentials/Implementation-Tool-Kit)
2. HIMSS TIGER Virtual Learning Environment (https://www.himss.org/what-we-do-Initiatives-tiger/virtual-learning-environment)
3. Nursing Knowledge Big Data Science Education Workgroup Repository (http://www.nursingbigdata.org),
4. HIMSS TIGER Informatics Educators Resource Network
5. AMIA's 10x10 program (https://www.amia.org/amia10x10)
6. The Summer Institute in Nursing Informatics (https://www.nursing.umaryland.edu/academics/pe/events/sini/)
7. The American Nursing Informatics Association (ANIA) (https://www.ania.org)

Nurse faculty and educators will need an understanding of the best evidence for and best practice use of social media, mobile applications, telehealth, wearables, implantables, robotics, artificial intelligence, gamification and other technologies that lie outside of the Electronic Health Record and the patient portal.

Digital Health Framework

Practicing nurses at all levels, nurse faculty, professional development educators for nurses in current practice not only need the foundational competencies and capabilities laid out in the AACN The Essentials: Core Competencies for Professional Nursing Education (https://www.aacnnursing.org/Portals/42/AcademicNursing/pdf/Essentials-2021.pdf) and the TIGER International Competency Synthesis Project: Global Health Informatics Competency Recommendation Framework (https://www.himss.org/sites/hde/files/media/file/2021/01/29/tiger-icsp-recommendations.pdf), but they need to understand the basic vision of the digital health evolution. Anne Snowden RN, PhD, FAAN Director of Clinical Research, Analytics at HIMSS lays out a framework and timeline of technological development that moves healthcare toward a digitization. From mainframe computing in the 1950s and 1960s, to nascent health information technology in 1970 to 2000, to eHealth in 2000–2020, to digital health in 2020 and beyond (Snowden, 2020).

Her important work describes a current healthcare system that does not fit what empowered consumers value and what they want to achieve (Snowden, 2020). Digital health could break the boundaries of the disease management focus of systems today and move it toward health and wellness with digital tools. Competent nurses could lead this work.

Snowden (2020) describes a framework and model that will require adaptations in governance and leadership that engages stakeholders, shifts toward national leadership, that makes eHealth knowledge and skills available through capacity building at the national, regional and local levels to empower providers and consumers. Nurses could lead and engage in this work.

The framework highlights the importance of predictive analytics through the use of data from smaller populations, the results of which can be applied to the larger population (Snowden, 2020). Nurses can develop and lead not only the analytics portion but the programs that address the issues that are discovered. Nurses can ensure that the digital health developments include person-enabled healthcare through the use of personal characteristics that include lifestyle, goals, beliefs, resources, support, and informed decision-making. Nurses can participate in and lead the quality work that will improve the individual experience of digital care, improve the health of overall populations through digital tools and reduce the cost of care.

Summary

The current state of healthcare is not addressing the needs of the patients, the consumers and the populations, and this is evident by the poor health data measures among the US population. To address this issue, a digital healthcare evolution is underway changing fundamentally how and to whom we provide care. Nurses at all levels must participate in this important work as they represent the majority of the healthcare workforce in all settings. However, this rapid evolution of healthcare into a digital system requires nurses to have the knowledge, skills, competencies and capabilities to participate in and lead the change. To do this, educators, faculty, mentors and preceptors must also have these skills and that is not always the case. The 2021 AACN Essentials provides a foundation. The HIMSS TIGER Global Interprofessional Competency Synthesis provides additional detail. However, the digital health evolution will require understanding of more complex topics such as artificial intelligence, robotics and genomics and the workflows that are needed to make this work efficiently and effectively for patients, consumers and populations.

Key Take-Away Points

- Technological competency, information literacy and information management are key foundational competencies for successful nursing practice. These are the basic competencies needed by both faculty and students to practice in all environments today.
- The evolution to digital health requires all nurses have the foundational competencies to function in healthcare today but to participate and lead in the digital health evolution more evolved skills are needed.
- International and interprofessional research work points to a significant gap in competency in the use of informatics and information technology in the care setting.
- Courses that only provide an overview of informatics as a field are not sufficient to meet this need. Courses directed at successfully incorporating informatics and information and communication technologies must align these skills and best practices to care provision and best communication processes and operational workflows.
- Faculty professional development in order to teach informatics content is mandatory and the existing informatics speciality organizations should coordinate to provide this development. Faculty who have not

been formally trained in the specialization of informatics must participate in professional development activities and administration must support this if all nurses are to be able to fully participate in the digital healthcare evolution.
- Faculty teaching in nursing informatics graduate specialization programs should be knowledgeable and experienced informaticians with the academic background to cover necessary content to build the digital infrastructure needed to participate in big data analytics, data science and artificial intelligence.
- Graduate-level Informatics Nurse Specialists must have the appropriate tools needed to build usable tools for patients, consumers and populations to use successfully as they navigate the digital platforms.

References

American Association of Colleges of Nursing. (2019). *News and information fact sheets* [online]. Available at: https://www.aacnnursing.org/news-Information/fact-sheets/nursing-fact-sheet (Accessed 4 September 2021).

American Association of Colleges of Nursing. (2020). *Nursing faculty shortage* [online]. Available at: https://www.aacnnursing.org/news-information/fact-sheets/nursing-faculty-shortage (Accessed 5 September 2021).

American Association of Colleges of Nursing. (2021). *Essentials task force* [online]. Available at: https://www.aacnnursing.org/About-AACN/AACN-Governance/Committees-and-Task-Forces/Essentials (Accessed 4 September 2021).

American Medical Informatics Association [AMIA]. (2021). *What is informatics?* [online]. Available at: https://amia.org/about-amia/why-informatics/informatics-research-and-practice (Accessed 3 September 2021).

American Nurses Association. (2014). *Nursing informatics: Scope and standards of practice*. 2nd ed. Silver Spring: American Nurses Association.

Bernstein, C. (2021). *TechTarget digital healthcare* [online]. Available at: https://searchhealthit.techtarget.com/definition/digital-health-digital-healthcare (Accessed 5 September 2021).

Booth, R. (2006). Educating the Future eHealth Professional Nurse. *International Journal of Education Scholarship*, 3(1), pp.1–10.

Bureau of Labor Statistics, U.S. Department of Labor. (2021). *Occupational outlook handbook*. Registered Nurses [online]. Available at: https://www.bls.gov/ooh/healthcare/registered-nurses.htm (Accessed 10 September 2021).

Calixte, R., Rivera, A., Oridota, O., Beauchamp, W., & Camacho-Rivera, M. (2020). Social and demographic patterns of health-related internet use among adults in the United States: A secondary data analysis of the health information national trends survey. *International Journal of Environmental Research and Public Health*, 17(18), p.6856. https://doi.org/10.3390/ijerph17186856

Centers for Disease Control and Prevention. (2019). *Chronic disease in America* [online]. Available at: https://www.cdc.gov/chronicdisease/resources/infographic/chronic-diseases.htm (Accessed 6 September 2021).

Centers for Disease Control and Prevention. (2021). *National center for chronic disease prevention and health promotion. Health and economic costs of chronic disease* [online]. Available at: https://www.cdc.gov/chronicdisease/about/costs/index.htm\ (Accessed 7 September 2021).

Comstock, J. (2020). *HIMSS launches new definition of digital health* [online]. Available at: https://www.mobihealthnews.com/news/himss-launches-new-definition-digital-health (Accessed 8 September 2021).

Harrington, L. (2011). Clinical intelligence. *Journal of Nursing Administration*, 41(12), pp.407–409.

Milani, R., Lavie, C., Bober, R., Milani, A., & Ventura, H. (2017). Improving hypertension control and patient engagement using digital tools. *The American Journal of Medicine*, 130(1), pp.14–20.

Nagle, L. M. (2016). The importance of being informatics savvy. *Nursing Leadership*, 28(4), pp.1–4.

National Academy of Medicine [NAM]. (2021). *The future of nursing 2020–2030: Charting a path to achieve health equity* [online]. Available at: https://www.nationalacademies.org/our-work/the-future-of-nursing-2020-2030 (Accessed 9 September 2021).

Nightingale, F. (1863). *Notes on hospitals*. 3rd ed. London: Longman, Green, Longman, Roberts, and Green.

Ozbolt, J. (2003). Harriet Helen Werley, PhD, RN, FAAN FACMI Lieutenant Colonel, U.S. Army (Ret). *JAMIA*, 10(2), pp.224–225.

Rajalathi, E., Heimonen, J., & Saranto, K. (2014). Developing nurse educator's computer skills towards proficiency in nursing informatics. *Informatics for Health & Social Care*, 39(1), pp.47–66. https://doi.org/10.3109/17538157.2013.834344.

Risling, T. (2017). Educating the nurses of 2025: Technology trends of the next decade. *Nurse Education in Practice*, 22, pp.89–22. https://doi.org/10.1016/j.nepr.2016.12.007.

Schur, M. B. (2020). *Lippincott nursing center. US nurses in 2020: Who we are and where we work* [online]. Available at: https://www.nursingcenter.com/ncblog/may-2020/u-s-nurses-in-2020 (Accessed 10 September 2021).

Selanders, L. (2021). *Florence Nightingale. Encyclopedia Britannica online: Academic edition* [online]. Available at: https://www.britannica.com/biography/Florence-Nightingale (Accessed 14 September 2021).

Smilet, R. A., Lauer, P., Berg, J. G., Shireman, E., Reneau, K. A., & Alexander, M. (2018). The 2017 national nursing workforce survey. *Journal of Nursing Regulation*, 9(3), pp.S1–S54.

Snowden, A. (2020). *Digital health: A framework for healthcare transformation* [online]. Available at: https://www.gs1ca.org/ (Accessed 12 September 2021).

Statista. (2019). *Global digital population as of October 2019* [online]. Available at: https://www.statista.com/statistics/273018/number-of-internet-users-worldwide/ (Accessed 14 September 2021).

U.S. Department of Commerce. National Institute of Standards and Technology [NIST]. (2021). *Information and communication technologies* [online]. Available at: https://csrc.nist.gov/glossary/term/information_and_communications_technology (Accessed 12 September 2021).

U.S. Food and Drug Administration [FDA]. (2020). *What is digital health?* [online]. Available at: https://www.fda.gov/medical-devices/digital-health-center-excellence/what-digital-health (Accessed 11 September 2021).

Werley, H. H., & Lang, N. M. (1987). Preface. In H. H. Werley, & N. M. Lang, eds., *Identification of the nursing minimum data set.* New York: Springer, p.xvii.

Chapter 8

Nursing Informatics Competencies for the Next Decade

Erika Lozada Perezmitre, Samira Ali and Laura-Maria Peltonen

Contents

Introduction 131
Nursing Informatics Competencies from a Global Perspective 133
      Nursing Informatics Education 136
      Nursing Informatics Competencies for Academia and Practice 137
      Nursing Informatics Certification 139
Future Requirements and Recommendations for Nursing Informatics
      Competencies 141
Bibliography 143

Introduction

There is an influx in the implementation of health and communication technologies in nursing practice, which has the potential to support the delivery of high-quality, safe and effective care to improve population health outcomes. However, the integration of technologies into nursing practice and healthcare also poses numerous challenges and risks. This increases the demands on graduating informatics competent and qualified nurses, as well as ensuring continuing education opportunities for nurses to master new skills and adapt to the rapid-paced implementations of various technologies at the bedside and in healthcare management.

The American Nurses Association defines nursing informatics (NI) as 'the specialty that integrates nursing science with multiple information and analytical sciences to identify, define, manage and communicate data, information, knowledge and wisdom in nursing practice' (ANA, 2015, pp. 1–2). Competence can in general be viewed with multiple lenses and perspectives and nursing experts have examined nursing competence as a complex and multifaceted concept internationally. Nursing informatics competence may be seen as an 'integration of knowledge, skills, and attitudes in the performance of various nursing informatics activities within prescribed levels of nursing practice' (Staggers et al., 2001, p. 306). The level of expertise is associated with the varying actors in the field. While an 'informatics nurse' refers to a registered nurse with experience in informatics, the 'informatics nurse specialist' is a term used for those with a graduate or postgraduate degree in informatics or a field close to informatics (ANA, 2015). Currently, nursing informatics is perceived as part of the core competencies in nursing rather than as a detached set of skills (Abdrbo, 2015; Kleib & Nagle, 2018; Sipes et al., 2017).

Informatics education, requirements and competencies for nurses differ globally. To date, there is no systematic approach to how informatics should be implemented in nursing education across settings (Cummings et al., 2015; Egbert et al., 2018). Without compliance to a standardized set of education and practice level competencies, there is a threat that the variability in nursing informatics practices could increase and potentially impair the provision of high quality, safe and effective care.

Previous research has identified several points for action including a need for collaboration to improve infrastructure to guide nursing informatics education (Peltonen et al., 2019b); increased engagement with the introduction, implementation and use of technology in clinical practice (Nes et al., 2021); competence guidelines to better support continuous education in nursing; and increased nursing informatics reach through improved visibility beyond the nursing informatics community, as well as transdisciplinary collaboration with other actors in the field (Ronquillo et al., 2017a). A recent scoping review, which aimed at mapping technological literacy in nursing education, found a further need to develop and implement models focusing on the entire process for the acquisition, measurement and maintenance of technological literacy in nursing education (Nes et al., 2021).

Ensuring nursing informatics competencies on different levels in the healthcare setting is a key strategy in safe care provision, building capacity and development of care. Due to the increased demand in both the number and the competence of nursing informatics professionals in healthcare, it is essential to scrutinize the current state of nursing informatics education and competence requirements. Reflecting contemporary competencies in nursing informatics on projections of future environments and services of healthcare helps to gain insights into areas in need of improvement. This is to ensure knowledge and skills required for nursing informatics competent professionals also in the future. This chapter describes the nursing informatics competencies from different perspectives and the importance of implementing them, and provides recommendations for implications in the future.

Nursing Informatics Competencies from a Global Perspective

Several initiatives have globally been attempted to gain insights into the level of skills required, to guide educators and practitioners, and to recommend ways to incorporate nursing informatics competencies into nursing education as well as prepare competent nursing informatics professionals. Education in nursing informatics is nowadays competency-based rather than focusing on particular topics alone (Hübner et al., 2018). There are several competency frameworks developed for a multidisciplinary perspective (see, e.g., Wholey et al., 2018), this section provides a few examples of initiatives for competence frameworks used in nursing informatics, including the Technology Informatics Guiding Education Reform Initiative (TIGER) based Assessment of Nursing Informatics Competencies (TANIC), the Canadian Association of Nursing Schools (CASN) Entry-to-Practice Nursing Informatics Competencies, and the Quality and Safety Education for Nurses (QSEN) competencies (Table 8.1).

The TIGER nursing informatics competencies model was developed initially in the United States in 2006 to recommend the required skills and competence of nursing students and practicing nurses. The TIGER competencies were summarized under three main domains: basic computer competencies, information literacy and information management (including the use of electronic health records). Currently, TIGER competencies are aligned with the European Computer Driving License (EDCL) (Hübner et al.,

Table 8.1 Nursing informatics competence requirements and recommendations

Source	Country	Competence domain	Expected level competencies
Staggers et al. (2001)	United States	Knowledge Attitudes Computer skills	Application of informatics competencies for nurses at four levels of practice
Staggers et al. (2002)	United States	Computer skills Informatics knowledge In these areas: Research Practice Education	Level 1—Beginner Level 2—Experienced Level 3—Informatics specialist Level 4—Informatics innovator
The TIGER-based assessment of nursing informatics competency (TANIC) 2006–2020 (HIMSS, 2016)	United States	Basic computer information literacy Information management Due care User skills The European Computer Driving License (ECDL)	Demonstrate proficiency in ECDL modules 1, 2 and 7 and categories 3.1 and 4
The Canadian Association of Schools of Nursing (CASN) (2013)	Canada	Information and knowledge management Professional or regulatory accountability Information and communication technology management	Use of relevant information and knowledge for the delivery of evidence-based patient care Use of information and communication technologies consistent with professional and regulatory standards and organizational policies Use of information and communication technologies in care delivery
The Quality and Safety Education for Nurses (QSEN) (2018)	United States	Knowledge Skills Attitudes	Knowledge: explain why information technology skills are essential for safe patient care Skill: understand how information is managed and apply information and technology tools to support safe care processes Attitudes: value the nurses' involvement in the design, implementation or evaluation of information technologies to support patient care

2018, p. e32). The TIGER has been used to develop an international recommendation framework for core competencies in nursing informatics for education, which consists of 24 core competency areas in health informatics, which have been described for five nursing roles, including clinical nursing, quality management, coordination of interprofessional care, nursing management and information technology management in nursing (Hübner et al., 2018, p. e30).

In 2013, the Canadian Association of Nursing Schools (CASN) developed a set of foundational informatics skills that were incorporated in the undergraduate nursing programs. These entry-level informatics skills are grouped under three domains: (1) information and knowledge management, (2) professional and regulatory accountability, and (3) use of information and communication technologies. These are intended to improve information use in the delivery of safe and effective care. These competencies are aligned with a list of indicators that can be observed and measured to evaluate the nurses' level of competence (Canadian Association of Schools of Nursing, 2013).

The Quality and Safety Education (QSEN) initiative focused more broadly on nursing education and building a culture of patient safety. QSEN builds on the Institute of Medicine (IOM) framework and competencies relate to developing patient-centered care, teamwork and collaboration, evidence-based practice, quality improvement, safety and using informatics to prepare future nurses' knowledge, skills and attitudes required to improve quality and safety of the healthcare systems (QSEN, 2021). These core competencies may serve as a guide in the curriculum development while preparing the student for application of the theory into practice.

Based on the informatics competencies reviewed, the common themes among these competencies include basic computer skills, informatics knowledge and attitudes. The outcomes' measures of educational competencies focus on course curriculum that develops nurses' knowledge, skills and use of computers, i.e., information and communication technologies that are used to deliver high quality and safe care. Knowledge competency relates to preparing informatics nurses in the mastery of the health information and communication technologies, and skills in managing them to promote the delivery of quality, safe and effective care. Education targeting attitudes can prepare the student for a lifelong journey of learning and adapting to fast and dynamic healthcare systems, and the implementation of vast amount of information and communication technologies that are used to automate processes, improve safety and patient outcomes.

Nursing Informatics Education

Although the history of informatics in nursing is generally seen to date back to Florence Nightingale (Nightingale 1902, 1861), the informatics education in nursing started receiving more attention when the digitalization of healthcare increased the need for education about the use of computers in nursing at the bachelor's level (Hannah et al., 2006; Tellez, 2010). However, the lack of available education in nursing informatics led to a situation, where the first nurses were mainly self-educated, up until a time when the first programs on master's level emerged for informatics nurse specialists in the end of the 1980s (Hannah et al., 2006). This section describes the informatics nurse specialist education from an international perspective.

There are great differences in the spread and level of education provided in nursing informatics internationally depending on setting and level of technological maturity (Peltonen et al., 2018; Darvish et al., 2014). One survey showed that only about one-third of respondents working with nursing informatics from 44 countries in Asia, Africa, Australia, Europe and North, Central and South America reported having education for a formal degree in nursing informatics available in their environment (Peltonen et al., 2018). However, the development and spread of nursing informatics education is on the increase.

In some countries, informatics is being systematically implemented into the nursing curriculum on undergraduate (bachelor), graduate (master) and postgraduate (doctoral) levels, as well as in continuing education programs for registered nurses. Other countries face challenges in the implementation of nursing informatics education due to a lack of information and communication technologies, skills to use technologies, effective strategies for integration and standardized requirements for competencies (Harerimana et al., 2020). Also, the focus of informatics programs vary, as some focus on health informatics or health technologies, while others target nursing informatics specifically.

Although nursing informatics education has been available for more than four decades in some countries, there is yet no global standardization for this education, regardless of the exponential need for such knowledge and skills in clinical practice and research. Educators play a pivotal role in advancing nursing informatics capacity, and hence building their capacity to develop education on the topic and take advantage of available resources on all levels becomes a key strategy for the future (Nagle et al., 2020). An evidence-based standardized curriculum could provide a framework for both content for learning as well as indicators for measuring targeted results. Such a document to guide global development of nursing informatics education could enhance capacity building to better support the ever-changing needs of practice in this era where advanced information technologies have become an essential part of care provision.

There are general frameworks that could be used for guiding curriculum development. For example, the American Association of Colleges of Nursing (AACN) has established core educational competencies or what is known as the essentials for all levels of nursing education on bachelor's, master's and doctoral levels. These essentials are intended to provide guidance to nursing educators in the development of nursing curriculum overall (AACN, 2021). Hence, they may also function as a roadmap to standardize nursing informatics curriculum and align core competencies and expectations among nursing education, while preparing new graduates for the dynamic and technology-driven healthcare systems. The AACN (2021) essentials or core educational competencies focus on ten main domains. The required competence for each domain is to ensure that educators and students have clear expectations on the required performance. In addition, students are held accountable to demonstrate these expected outcomes. According to AACN (2021), the competencies in the essentials provide a bridge between the current and future nursing practice and aim to support in preparing competent practitioners. The domains include the following: (1) knowledge of nursing practice, (2) person-centered care, (3) population health, (4) scholarship for nursing practice, (5) quality and safety, (6) interprofessional partnership, (7) systems-based practice, (8) information and health technologies, (9) professionalism, and (10) personal, professional and leadership development.

Nursing Informatics Competencies for Academia and Practice

The rapid advancements in the use of technology in nursing practice have created a need to keep pace with developing competencies. Nowadays, nurses are required to expand their roles in mastering technological tools and using information systems (Anderson, 2017). A nurse informatician should at least integrate information management, and analytic skills to identify and communicate data in different settings (Borycki et al., 2017). The role of these nurses in the healthcare system supports several aspects of nursing, such as education, research, management and nursing practice.

Nursing informatics practitioners are required to develop specific knowledge, behavior, skills and capacities to collect, store, retrieve and process the information.

The competency requirements in nursing practice have expanded from just using the computer for electronic records to incorporate knowledge into practice, to improve their abilities, and to state better practices as the environment evolves (Egbert et al., 2019). Competencies are required to ensure the effective use of technologies. The Nursing Informatics Workshop Survey (HIMSS, 2020) demonstrated the importance of the nursing informatics role in the development, implementation and optimization of information systems and applications. There is evidence that shows that nurses need to understand nursing informatics to fulfill their professional responsibilities (Honey et al., 2017). However, it is not sufficient to focus only on developing nursing informatics education for practicing nurses. It is important to develop competencies for nursing leadership (Westra & Delaney, 2008), educators and researchers as well. Examples of tools to evaluate NI competencies are presented in Table 8.2.

Table 8.2 Tools for evaluation of nursing informatics competencies

Nurse's role	Competencies	Name of instrument
Leadership (Rahman, 2015)	Computer literacy (10 items, items 1–10) Informatics literacy (13 items, items 11–23) Information management skills (7 items, items 24–30)	Nursing Informatics Competency Assessment Tool (NICAT)
Pre-licensure nurses (QSEN, 2003)	Three domains: Knowledge (5 items) Skills (8 items) Attitudes (4 items)	Quality and Safety Education for Nurses by the Institute of Medicine (IOM) (6 core)
General Nurses (Yoon et al., 2009)	10 items evaluating basics skills Items for the role of clinical informatics in nursing (factor 1; items 1–5), basic computer knowledge and skills (factor 2; 6–20), applied computer skills (factor 3; 21–24), clinical informatics attitudes (factor 4; 25–28) and wireless device skills (factor 5; 29–30).	Self-Assessment Nursing Informatics Competencies Scale (SANICS)

Nursing Informatics Certification

On the other hand, international and regional organizations have brought on credentialing and accreditation systems for standardization of nursing informatics education and competencies. A certification is considered to be both a self and an external peer assessment process for evaluation of the level of performance mirrored against specific standards (HIMSS, 2014). First, credentialing systems targeted at specific nurses are used on both regional and national levels (Saba et al., 2004). Examples of such credentialing systems include the Informatics Nursing Certification (RN-BC) by the American Nurses Credentialing Center in the United States, the Certified Health Informatician Australasia (CHIA) program by the Australian Institute of Digital Health (AIDH) in Australia, and the Nursing Informatics specialization by the Nurses Association in Finland. Second, institutions are being accredited for their programs in nursing (Monsen et al., 2019) and health informatics education (Commission on Accreditation for Health Informatics and Information Management (CAHIIM)).

Certifications are mainly provided for individuals according to their countries, for example in the United States, the Nursing Informatics Board Certification is given by the board certification in informatics nursing and is offered by the American Nurses Credentialing Center (ANCC) affiliated with the American Nurses Association. Both the American Board of Nursing Specialties and the National Commission for Certifying Agencies accredit ANCC. This certification is the only accredited certification in Nursing Informatics available in the United States and it is open for international applicants. The eligibility depends on the following requirements: a baccalaureate degree in nursing, licensure as a registered nurse (RN), 2 years of experience as a registered nurse and continuing education in informatics. Graduate education in informatics is not required and the examination is tailored to the role of the informatics nurse versus the informatics nurse specialist. The content of the examination includes foundation of practice, system design life cycle, data management and healthcare technology. Similar certifications for nursing informatics were not identified in other countries, including Canada, UK, Europe, Australia, Asia or Latin America (Cummins et al., 2016).

The global competencies of nursing informatics are developed in four levels of practice (Straggers, 2002). In the United States, for the Quality and Safety Education for Nurses, nurse informaticians can identify essential information that must be available in a common database to support patient care.

They can describe examples of how technology and information management are related to the quality and safety of patient care. Recognizing the time, effort and skills required for computers, databases and other technologies to become reliable and effective tools for patient care. Also, applying technology and information management tools to support safe processes of care. Nurses can appreciate the necessity for all health professionals to seek lifelong, continuous learning of information technology skills by valuing technologies that support clinical decision-making, error prevention and care coordination among others.

The situation is similar in Canada, according to the Canadian Association of Schools of Nursing. Canadian nurses informaticians have the skills and acquire competence to describe the processes of data gathering, recording and retrieval, in hybrid or homogenous health records (electronic or paper), and identify informational risks, gaps and inconsistencies across the healthcare system. Also, to identify and report system process and functional issues according to organizational policies and procedures, and recognize the importance of nurses' involvement in the design, selection, implementation and evaluation of applications and systems in healthcare. Nurses can articulate the significance of information standards necessary for interoperable electronic health records (EHRs) across the healthcare system and articulate the importance of standardized nursing data to reflect nursing practice, advance nursing knowledge and contribute to the value and understanding of nursing. Further, they comply with legal and regulatory requirements, ethical standards, and organizational policies and procedures and advocate for the use of current and innovative information and communication technologies (ICTs) that support the delivery of safe, quality care.

In Australia, the competencies, recorded by the Australian Nursing and Midwifery Federation in Nurses Informaticians, include managing information collected or generated, and identifying effectively and efficiently information to support evidence-based practice. They also have the ability to use ICT to promote safe, effective use of information to support nursing and midwifery practice and demonstrate the ability to include research, evidence-based practice and quality improvements, thus supporting the use of ICTs. They can comply with the legal and regulatory requirements and ethical principles for all uses of ICTs in nursing and midwifery practice. These are just some of the competencies that Australian nurses have.

In Asia and India, nursing informatics competencies are still in process of development and standardization. The competencies are related to how to get into practice in nurses who work at hospitals to the health information systems. There is a need to adopt a more comprehensive curriculum on advanced levels. Nurses still need to develop their knowledge, skills and attitudes toward nursing informatics and information management to provide more effective, efficient and safer healthcare in this connected world (Wu & Wang, 2017).

In Europe, the European Qualifications Framework (EQF) defines competencies, skills and knowledge related to all vocational degrees and the directive describes professional minimum competencies for nurses. In Finland, the Finnish Nurses Association organizes the competencies in four levels. On the first level, the novice nurse has basic knowledge and skills in information management and health literacy, as well as the use of various technologies. On the second level, an experienced nurse has expertise in her field and is very skilled in information management. She uses information technology to support her practice and work in collaboration with a nurse specializing in information management to improve various methods. On the third level, the nurse specializing in information management is an information management expert with both nursing and information management training. Nurses participate in the development of information systems in an organization, utilizing their own expertise. Finally, on the fourth level is the information management innovator, an information management developer who researches and develops theories and leads information management practices and research. Achieving Nursing Informatics Certification requires level 3–4 competence (Finnish Nursing Association, 2019).

In Latin America, Brazil and Argentina have the most developed nursing informatics competencies within the postgraduate programs for nurses. However, the rest of the continent still has a long way to go to standardize competencies and to open programs in nursing informatics specifically. There is a need for leaders in nursing informatics and educators with nursing informatics skills to be active to increase awareness in nursing schools to promote nursing informatics (Barbosa, 2017).

Future Requirements and Recommendations for Nursing Informatics Competencies

Currently, and from a global perspective, there is no coherent and systematic methodology for educating nursing informatics to students in nursing and available tools for evaluating competencies in nursing informatics need to be further validated. The role and tasks of nurses are changing with the increase of digital services, an increase in service users' health literacy and access to information, and evolving technologies such as artificial intelligence-based systems (Booth et al., 2021). The challenge with keeping up to date with this rapidly and continuously evolving field has been acknowledged already long ago (Gonçalves et al., 2012.). This challenge has also been noted in curriculum development more broadly in the health informatics community (Sapci & Sapci, 2020; Wholey et al., 2018). Nurses need to be prepared, not only for understanding the technology that they use, but also for taking an active role in development and implementation of technologies, hence nurses need to be prepared with renewable knowledge, skills and attitudes in nursing informatics (Ronquillo et al., 2021). This puts pressure on curriculum development in preparing nurses for practice, education and research, but it also emphasizes the need to advance learning opportunities in nursing informatics in continuing education.

The gap between available education and competency needs in nursing informatics is compounded by a lack of a unified set of required competencies, skill sets and knowledge that a nurse in informatics must possess. Ensuring sufficient preparedness of nursing informatics capacity is key in the future health service delivery, as information management plays a pivotal role in high quality, safe and effective care. In addition, there is a demand for globally standardized educational frameworks to develop nursing informatics curriculum, as well as a renewing framework adjustable to the rapidly evolving environment regarding competencies needed to prepare competent and skilled nursing informatics professionals. A standardized educational framework could serve as a roadmap and guideline to develop educational curriculum for nursing informatics, and competencies could reduce the confusion and enhance the expectation from educators and students globally. An area that could be explored in the future and be recommended is the use of a well-developed comprehensive guideline such as the AACN (2021) and aligning that with a set of practice competencies.

To finalize, there are five main areas the future nursing education and competencies should focus on:

- First, standardizing an educational curriculum for nursing informatics and practice competencies globally, which considers technological maturity and specific needs of the environment of adoption. This would reduce the variability and confusion on the education and competencies required to prepare informatics nurses and would reduce the gap

among developed and underdeveloped countries in nursing informatics education requirements. An important part of this is to educate the educators.
- The second area is aligning the nursing informatics education curriculum, which is based on a well-developed framework, such as the ten core competencies for professional nursing education described by AACN in 2021 with three most common nursing informatics competencies that focus on knowledge, skills and attitudes. This would clearly outline both the education and practice-based competencies required to produce graduates that are knowledgeable, skilled and prepared for dynamic and technology intensive healthcare systems. In addition, the outcome measure for each competence in the three main domains should be linked to curriculum on all levels and have outcome measures
- The third area is bridging the gap in the nursing informatics education between developed and underdeveloped countries. That could be achieved by committing and developing virtual educational conferences for faculty and bringing them up to speed on the current updates and requirements for education and competencies of informatics nurses. Hence, enhancing collaboration between countries that are digitally mature, and those that are still developing and implementing digital technologies. All these taking into consideration local level of technological variation.
- The fourth area to be considered is to re-evaluate and standardize the tools used to assess nursing informatics competencies to meet the needs of the rapidly evolving working environment of nurses both in academia and in practice.
- The final area to focus on is the development of frameworks for leadership competencies in nursing informatics. Preparing nurse informaticians with the appropriate leadership skills may improve nursing involvement in informatics projects from development to implementation across settings and potentially improve outcomes of these.

Bibliography

Abdrbo, A. (2015). Nursing informatics competencies among nursing students and their relationship to patient safety competencies. *Computers, Informatics, Nursing*, 33(11), pp.509–514. https://doi.org/10.1097/CIN.0000000000000197

American Association of Colleges of Nursing (AACN). (2020). *The essentials: Core competencies for professional nursing education* [online]. Available at: https://www.aacnnursing.org/Education-Resources/AACN-Essentials (accessed 24 July 2021).

AACN. (2021). *CCNE accreditation* [online]. Available at: https://www.aacnnursing.org/CCNE (Accessed 05 August 2021).

American Nurses Association. (2015). *Nursing informatics: Scope and standards of practice.* 2nd ed. Silver Spring, MD: American Nurses Association.

Anderson, C. (2011). Improving informatics skills for clinicians, new foundation incorporates. *Computers Informatics Nursing*, 29(10), p.543.

Anderson, C. (2017). Improving informatics skills for clinicians, new foundation incorporates. *Computers, Informatics, Nursing*, 29(10), p.543.

Australian Nursing and Midwifery Federation. (2015). *ANMF national informatics standards for nurses and midwives* [online]. Available at: https://anmf.org.au/documents/National_Informatics_Standards _For_Nurses_And_Midwives.pdf (accessed 25 May 2021).

Barbosa, S. F. (2017). Competencies related to informatics and information management for practicing nurses and nurses leaders in Brazil and South America. *Studies in Health Technology and Informatics*, 232, pp.77–85.

Booth, R., Strudwick, G., McMurray, J., Chan, R., Cotton, K. & Cooke, S. (2021). The Future of nursing informatics in a digitally-enabled world. In P. Hussey & M. A. Kennedy, eds., *Introduction to nursing informatics*. Cham: Springer, pp.395–417.

Borycki, E. M., Cummings, E., Kushniruk, A. W., & Saranto, K. (2017). Integrating health information technology safety into nursing informatics competencies. *Studies in Health Technology and Informatics*, 232, pp.222–228.

Borycki, E. M., & Foster, J. (2014). A comparison of Australian and Canadian informatics competencies for undergraduate nurses. *Studies in Health Technology and Informatics*, 201, pp.349–355.

Burke, K. G., Johnson, T., Sites, C., & Barnsteiner, J. (2017). CE: Original research: Creating an evidence-based progression for clinical advancement programs. *American Journal of Nursing*, 117(5), pp.22–35.

Canadian Association of Schools of Nursing. (2012). *Nursing informatics entry to practice competencies for registered nurses* [online]. Available at: http://www.casn.ca/2014/12/casn-entry-practice-nursing- informatics-competencies/ (Accessed 24 May 2021).

Canadian Association of Schools of Nursing. (2013). *Nursing informatics teaching toolkit: Supporting the integration of the CASN nursing informatics competencies into undergraduate nursing curricula* [online]. Available at: https://www.casn.ca/2014/12/nursing-informatics-teaching-toolkit/ (accessed 23 July 2021).

Chung, S. Y., & Staggers, N. (2014). Measuring nursing informatics competencies of practicing nurses in Korea: Nursing informatics competencies questionnaire. *Computers Informatics Nursing*, 32(12), pp.596–605.

Cummings, E., Borycki, E.M, & Madsen, I. (2015). Teaching nursing informatics in Australia, Canada and Denmark. In E. M. Borycki, A. W. Kushniruk, C. E.

Kuziemsky, & C. Nøhr, eds., *Context sensitive health informatics: many places, many users, many contexts, many uses.* Amsterdam, The Netherlands: IOS Press.

Cummins, M. R., Gundlapalli, A. V., Murray, P., Park, H. A., & Lehmann, C. U. (2016). Nursing informatics certification worldwide: History, pathway, roles, and motivation. *Yearbook of Medical Informatics*, 1, pp.264–271. https://doi.org/10.15265/IY-2016-039

Darvish, A., Bahramnezhad, F., Keyhanian, S., & Navidhamidi, M. (2014). The role of nursing informatics on promoting quality of health care and the need for appropriate education. *Global Journal of Health Science*, 6(6), pp.11–8. https://doi. Org/10.5539/gjhs.v6n6p11

Davies, A., Mueller, J., Hassey, A., & Moulton, G. (2021). Development of a core competency framework for clinical informatics. *BMJ Health and Care Informatics*, 28(1), p.e100356. https://doi.org/10.1136/bmjhci-2021-100356

Egbert, N., Thye, J., Schlte, G., Liebe, J. D., Hackl, W. O., Ammenwerth, E., et al. (2016). An iterative methodology for developing national recommendations for nursing informatics curricula. *Studies in Health and Technology Informatics*, 228, pp.660–664.

Egbert, N., Thye, J., Hackl, W., Müller-Staub, M., Ammenwerth, E., & Hübner, U. (2018). Competencies for nursing in a digital world. Methodology, results, and use of the DACH-recommendations for nursing informatics core competency areas in Austria, Germany, and Switzerland. *Informatics for Health and Social Care*, 44(4), pp.351–375. https://doi.org/10.1080/17538157.2018.1497635

Egbert, N., Thye, J., Hackl, W. O., Müller-Staub, M., Ammenwerth, E., & Hubner, U. (2019). Competencies for nursing in a digital world: methodology, results, and use of the DACH-recommendations for nursing core competency areas in Austria. *Germany and Switzerland. Informatics for Health and Social Care*, 44(4), pp.351–375.

Finnish Nurses Association (FNA). 2019. *Digital social and health services. Nursing certification* [online]. Available at: https://www.nurses.fi/nursing_and_nurse_education_in_f/digital-social-and-health-servic/ (Accessed 03 August 2021).

Gonçalves, L. S., Wolff, L. D., Staggers, N., & Peres, A. M. (2012). Nursing informatics competencies: An analysis of the latest research. In 2012 11th International Congress on Nursing Informatics Proceedings, Montreal, QC, p.127.

Hannah, K. J., Ball, M. J., & Edwards, M. J. (2006). The future for nurses in health informatics. In: *Introduction to nursing informatics. Health informatics (formerly computers in health care).* New York: Springer. https://doi.org/10.1007/978-0-387-32189-9_21

Harerimana, A., Wicking, K., Biedermann, N., & Yates, K. (2020). Integrating nursing informatics into undergraduate nursing education in Africa: A scoping review. *International Nursing Review*, 68(3), pp.1–14.

Healthcare Information and Management Systems Society (HIMSS). (2014). *The evolution of TIGER competencies and informatics resources* [online]. Available at: www.himss.org/library/evolution-tiger-competencies-and-informatics-resources (Accessed 09 August 2021).

HIMSS. (2016). *Workforce development. Global health informatics competency recommendation frameworks.* Available at: https://www.himss.org/resources/global-health-informatics-competency-recommendation-frameworks (Accessed 23 May 2021).

HIMSS. (2020). *Nursing informatics workforce survey* [online]. Available at: https://www.himss.org/resources/himss-nursing-informatics-workforce-survey (Accessed 09 August 2021).

Herath, D., & Mathotaarachchi, Y. L. (2018). Information technology competency of registered nurse under-graduates at the completion of IT preparatory course in BSc nursing degree at a selected private university in Sri Lanka. In 2018 National Information Technology Conference (NITC), Information Technology Conference (NITC) Proceedings, p.1.

Honey, M. L., Skiba, D. J., Procter, P., Foster, J., Kouri, P., & Nagle, L. M. (2017). Nursing informatics competencies for entry to practice: The perspective of six countries. *Studies in Health and Technology Informatics*, 232, pp.51–61.

Hübner, U., Shaw, T., Thye, J., Egbert, N., Marin, H. F., Chang, P., O'Connor, S., Day, K., Honey, M., Blake, R., Hovenga, E., Skiba, D., & Ball, M. J. (2018). Technology informatics guiding education reform – TIGER. *Methods of Information and Medicine*, 57(S 01), pe30–e42. https://doi.org/10.3414/ME17-01-0155

Hussey, P., & Kennedy, M. A. (eds.). (2021). *Introduction to nursing informatics, health informatics.* 5th ed. Cham: Springer, p.427.

Jouparinejad, S., Foroughameri, G., Khajouei, R., & Farokhzadian, J. (2020). Improving the informatics competency of critical care nurses: Results of an interventional study in the southeast of Iran. *BMC Medical Informatics and Decision Making*, 20(1), p.220. https://doi.org/10.1186/s12911-020-01244-5

Kassam, I., Nagle, L., & Strudwick, G. (2017). Informatics competencies for nurse leaders: Protocol for a scoping review. *BMJ Open*, 7(12), pe018855.

Khezri, H., & Abdekhoda, M. (2019). Assessing nurses' informatics competency and identifying its related factors. *Journal of Research in Nursing*, 24(7), pp.529–38.

Kleib, M., & Nagle, L. (2018). Development of the Canadian nurse informatics competency assessment scale and evaluation of Alberta's registered nurses' self-perceived informatics competencies, *Computers, Informatics, Nursing*, 36(7), pp.350–358. https://doi.org/10.1097/CIN.0000000000000435

Kleib, M., Chauvette, A., Furlong, K. E., Nagle, L. M., Slater, L., & McCloskey, R. (2019). Approaches for defining and assessing nursing informatics competencies: A scoping review protocol. *JBI Database of Systematic Reviews and Implementation Reports*, 17(6), pp.1071–1078. https://doi.org/10.11124/JBISRIR-2017-003889

Monsen, K., Bush, R. A., Jones, J., Manos, E., Skiba, DJ., & Johnson, S. (2019). Alignment of American association of colleges of nursing graduate-level nursing informatics competencies with American medical informatics association health informatics core competencies. *Computers, Informatics, Nursing*, 37(8), pp.396–404. https://doi.org/10.1097/CIN.0000000000000537

Nagle, L. M., Crosby, K., Frisch, N., Borycki, E., Donelle, L., Hannah, K. et al. (2014). Developing entry-to-practice nursing informatics competencies for registered nurses. *Studies in Health Technology and Informatics*, 201, pp.356–363.

Nagle, L. M., Kleib, M., & Furlong, K. (2020). Digital health in Canadian schools of nursing part A: Nurse educators' perspectives. *Quality Advancement in Nursing Education: Avancées en formation infirmière*, 6(1), p.4.

Nes, A., Steindal, S., Larsen, M., Heer, H., Lærum-Onsager, E., & Gjevjon, E. (2021). Technological literacy in nursing education: A scoping review. *Journal of Professional Nursing*, 37, pp.320–334.

Nightingale, F. (1861). *Notes on nursing*. New York: Dover Publications.

Nightingale, F. (1902). *Notes on nursing: What it is, and what it is not*. New York: Dover Publications.

O'Connor, S., Hubner, U., Shaw, T., Blake, R., & Ball, M. (2017). Time for TIGER to ROAR! Technology informatics guiding education reform. *Nurse Education Today*, 58, pp.78–81. https://doi.org/10.1016/j.nedt.2017.07.014

Peltonen, L. M., Siirala, E., Junttila, K., Lundgrén-Laine, H., Vahlberg, T., Löyttyniemi, E., Aantaa, R., & Salanterä, S. (2018). Information needs in day-to-day operations management in hospital units: A cross-sectional national survey. *Journal of Nursing Management*, 27, pp.233–244. https://doi.org/10.1111/jonm.12700

Peltonen, L. M., Nibber, R., Lewis, A., Block, L., Pruinelli, L., Topaz, M., Perezmitre, E. L., & Ronquillo, C. (2019a). Emerging professionals' observations of opportunities and challenges in nursing informatics. *Nurse Leadership*, 32(2), pp.8–18. https://doi.org/10.12927/cjnl.2019.25965

Peltonen, L.-M., Pruinelli, L., Ronquillo, C., Nibber, R., Peresmitre, E. L., Block, L., Deforest, H., Lewis, A., Alhuwail, D., Ali, S., Badger, M. K., Eler, G. J., Georgsson, M., Islam, T., Jeon, E., Jung, H., Kuo, C. H., Sarmiento, R. F. R., Sommer, J. A., Tayaben, J., & Topaz, M. (2019b). The current state of nursing informatics: An international cross-sectional survey. *Finnish Journal of EHealth and Ewelfare*, 11(3), pp.220–231. https://doi.org/10.23996/fjhw.77584

Quality and Safety Education for Nurses. (2003). Competencies [online]. Available at: https://qsen.org/competencies/pre-licensure-ksas/ (Accessed 29 December 2021).

Quality and Safety Education for Nurses. (2018). *QSEN informatics* [online]. Available at: https://qsen.org/informatics/ (Accessed 29 December 2021).

Quality and Safety Education for Nurses. (2021). *Quality and safety education for nurses' competencies* [online]. Available at: https://qsen.org/competencies/pre-licensure-ksas/ (accessed 25 May 2021).

Rahman, A. (2015). *Development of a nursing informatics competency assessment tool (NICAT)*. Walden Dissertations and Doctoral Studies [online]. Available at: https://scholarworks.waldenu.edu/dissertations/1745 (accessed 23 August 2021).

Ronquillo, C., Topaz, M., Pruinelli, L., Peltonen, L., & Nibber, R. (2017a). Competency recommendations for advancing nursing informatics in the next decade: International survey results. In J. Murphy et al., eds., *Forecasting informatics competencies for nurses in the future of connected health.* Amsterdam, The Netherlands: IOS Press, pp.119–132.

Ronquillo, C., Topaz, M., Pruinelli, L., Peltonen, L. M., & Nibber, R. (2017b). Competency recommendations for advancing nursing informatics in the next decade: International survey results. *Studies in Health and Technology and Informatics,* 232, pp.119–129.

Ronquillo, C. E., Peltonen, L. M., Pruinelli, L., Chu, C. H., Bakken, S., Beduschi, A., Cato, K., Hardiker, N., Junger, A., Michalowski, M., Nyrup, R., et al. (2021). Artificial intelligence in nursing: Priorities and opportunities from an international invitational think-tank of the Nursing and Artificial Intelligence Leadership Collaborative. *Journal of Advanced Nursing,* 18. https://doi.org/10.1111/jan.14855

Saba, V. K., Skiba, D. J., & Bickford, C. (2004). Competencies and credentialing: nursing informatics. *Studies in Health Technology and Informatics,* 109, pp.75–89.

Sapci, A. H., & Sapci, H. A. (2020). Teaching hands-on informatics skills to future health informaticians: A competency framework proposal and analysis of health care informatics curricula. *JMIR Medical Informatics,* 8(1), p.e15748. https://doi.org/10.2196/15748

Sipes, C., Hunter, K., McGonigle, D., West, K., Hill, T., & Hebda, T. (2017). The health information technology competencies tool. *Computers, Informatics, Nursing,* 35(12), pp.609–614 https://doi.org/10.1097/CIN.0000000000000408

Staggers, N., Gassert, C. A., & Curran, C. (2001). Informatics competencies for nurses at four levels of practice. *Journal of Nursing Educcation,* 40(7), pp.303–316. https://doi.org/10.3928/0148-4834-20011001-05

Staggers, N., Gassert, C., & Curran, C. (2002). A Delphi study to determine informatics competencies for nurses at four levels of practice. *Nursing Research,* 51(6), pp.383–390.

Takase, M., Teraoka, S., Miyakoshi, Y., & Kawada, A. (2011). A concept analysis of nursing competence: A review of international literature. *Nihon Kango Kenkyu Gakkai Zassh,* 34, pp.103–109. https://doi.org/10.15065/jjsnr.20110404011

Tellez, M. (2010). Nursing informatics education: past, present, and future. *Computers, Informatics, Nursing,* 30(5), pp.229–233. https://doi.org/10.1097/NXN.0b013e3182569f42

Westra, B. L., & Delaney, C. W. (2008). Informatics competencies for nursing and healthcare leaders. In AMIA... Annual Symposium Proceedings. AMIA Symposium, pp.804–808.

Wholey, D. R., LaVenture, M., Rajamani, S., Kreiger, R., Hedberg, C., & Kenyon, C. (2018). Developing workforce capacity in public health informatics: Core competencies and curriculum design. *Frontiers in Public Health,* 2(6), p.124. https://doi.org/10.3389/fpubh.2018.00124

Wu, Y., Wang, Y., & Ji, M. (2017). Competencies related to informatics and information management for practicing nurses in select countries in Asia. *Studies in Health Technology and Informatics,* 232, pp.86–96.

Yoon, S., Yen, P., & Bakken, S. (2009). Psychometric properties of the self-assessment of nursing informatics competencies scale. *Studies in Health Technology and Informatics,* 146, pp.546–550.

Chapter 9

Interprofessional Practice and Education: Interrelationship with Knowledge Generation, the IPE Core Data Set and National Information Exchange Infrastructure

Laura Pejsa, Christine Arenson, James T. Pacala, Jennifer Kertz and Barbara Brandt

Contents

Introduction 150
National Center for Interprofessional Practice and Education (National
    Center) 152
The 'New' IPE: Interprofessional Practice and Education 152
The Nexus: Optimal Alignment of Education and Practice 152
Workplace Learning 154
National Partnerships 154
    Knowledge Generation in Action at the Nexus of Practice and
        Education 155
Framework for Generating New Knowledge 157
    Interprofessional Learning Continuum Model 157

IPE Core Data Set 159
Interprofessional Competencies 159
Interprofessional Educational and Clinical Learning Environments 159
Critical Events of IPE 160
Teamness 160
Quadruple Aim Outcomes... 160
National Center Interprofessional Information Exchange 162
Case Example: Minnesota Northstar Geriatric Workforce Enhancement
    Program 163
Conclusions and Outlook 166
    Funding Attribution 166
References.. 167

Introduction

The value of interprofessional education (IPE) was first articulated in the United States over 60 years ago, as a critical success factor to addressing already long-standing issues of poor health and health equity in an increasingly complex healthcare and social environment. However, competing factors including increased specialization of medicine, nursing and other professions and the rise of preferential reimbursement of healthcare technologies over other health and social services prevented interprofessional education from developing sustained traction. The current emphasis on interprofessional education is often dated to the publication of three seminal reports from the Institute of Medicine (now National Academy of Medicine), *To Err Is Human*, *Crossing the Quality Chasm* and finally *Health Professions Education: A Bridge to Quality* (IOM, 2000, 2001, 2003).

These reports were followed by a significant uptick in interprofessional education in pre-licensure health professions programs. International (WHO, 2010) and US (Interprofessional Education Collaborative, 2016) competencies were first published in 2010 and 2011 and have informed curricula in health professions education programs. More recently, a group of 25 health professions accreditors published guidance on developing high-quality IPE (HPAC, 2019). In a largely parallel process, clinical organizations have sought to improve communication and situational awareness among practicing teams. The *TeamSTEPPS* program (Agency for Health Research and Quality [AHRQ], 2012) was an early example. More recent movements to create high-reliability organizations and learning health systems are more comprehensive approaches, which draw on much of the same literature as interprofessional education but have occurred largely in parallel with efforts in accredited education programs.

The movement to reimagine health and healthcare delivery within the context of interprofessional, person-engaged teams has often been challenged by perverse incentives driven by our large fee for service healthcare system and the disconnect between healthcare and social service sectors in the United States. However, since passage of the Affordable Care Act in 2010, the gradual but increasing move to value-based payments in healthcare, along with increased recognition that attention to social determinants of health (US Department of Health and Human Services, 2020) is critical to optimize individual and population-level health outcomes. This has facilitated increased interest in effective IPE.

Since 2020, the twin crises of the COVID-19 pandemic and the social awakening engendered by the murder of George Floyd and the Black Lives Matter movement have made it impossible to ignore the deep-seated inequities driven by systemic racism and poverty. At the same time, the COVID-19 pandemic highlighted the benefits of true interprofessional collaborative practice and the barriers that traditional silos exacerbated. Balsar et al. (2021) have synthesized early pandemic lessons for care settings, including deploying the workforce in new ways across the continuum of care, focusing on health disparities and health inequity and improving data collection and exchange, among others.

Two recent reports from the National Academies of Medicine further highlight these important trends. *The Future of Nursing 2020–2030* (NAM, 2021a) highlights the critical need and opportunity for nursing professionals to expand their roles in addressing social determinants of health and health equity and expanding collaboration across professions, disciplines and sectors. *Implementing High-Quality Primary Care* (NAM, 2021b) calls for paying 'for primary care teams to care for people, not doctors to deliver services' and to 'train primary care teams where people live and work' as two of its five recommendations. Finally, George Thibault, who led the Josiah Macy, Jr. Foundation for over a decade described emerging trends in health professions education as the COVID-19 pandemic was disrupting education and practice across the globe. He predicts interprofessional education, longitudinal clinical education oriented to patients, communities and chronic disease, and increased emphasis on the social determinants of health and the social and humanistic missions of health professions education programs will be critical drivers of retooling health professions education to meet the needs of the nation (Thibault, 2020).

These trends have the potential to accelerate the shift to interprofessional collaborative practice and education. However, the relative lack of high-quality, comparable data on effective strategies to transform healthcare practice and education constitutes a significant barrier to widespread adoption of IPE, particularly in the face of significant culture change that must drive this change.

National Center for Interprofessional Practice and Education (National Center)

Charged by Health Resources and Services Administration (HRSA) and four foundations to advance interprofessional education and collaborative practice in the nation in 2012, the National Center for Interprofessional Practice and Education (National Center) has developed a strong track record of implementing and studying academic–community partnerships, called the *Nexus*, primarily with underserved, high-risk populations. The National Center is committed to resetting the relationship between educational institutions, health systems and communities by creating a deeply connected system that benefits education and healthcare simultaneously while demonstrating outcomes that matter to individuals, populations, organizations and health teams.

The 'New' IPE: Interprofessional Practice and Education

Traditionally, IPE has referred to interprofessional education. From its launch in 2012, the National Center introduced the concept of 'interprofessional practice and education,' or the 'new' IPE, as a conceptual bridge between interprofessional education and collaborative practice, recognizing that learning in practice and education is nonlinear and spans the continuum from classroom to community and practice.

The Nexus: Optimal Alignment of Education and Practice

Since its inception, the National Center has envisioned and committed to the Nexus by aligning interprofessional education with the health systems and communities they serve. By designing curriculum together with communities

Figure 9.1 Our vision for a transformed health system.

within the Nexus, partnerships are able to work together to strive to achieve outcomes that matter most to the individuals and populations served (Figure 9.1). When fully realized, communities become full partners with health education and practice to co-create sustainable, impactful and integrated practice and education to affect the learning and health outcomes that matter most to those being served.

In these partnerships, local data and expertise, coupled with best practices in interprofessional practice and education, support the design, implementation and evaluation of impact. These partnerships foster interprofessional learning in practice (workplace learning) and promote meaningful engagement among all involved. Within the community's context, partners work together to improve quality of care, support innovation in care delivery and drive health equity while learners in these settings provide added value to the clinical environment and the individuals served.

With a solid foundation in a practice–education partnership, transformation toward a Nexus can be accomplished through aspirational principles, including:

- Sharing a compelling vision for the future.
- Partnering with individuals, families, communities and populations as full members of the health team.
- Incorporating learners into the interprofessional team in ways that improve learning and add value to healthcare and the practice setting.
- Creating a closed-loop model between the practice and education partnership for continuous improvement by using data to demonstrate measurable outcomes.
- Encouraging situational leadership across the practice–education partnership continuum.
- Committing to identifying and addressing systems-level issues together that create barriers to achieving goals (e.g., professional culture, institutional culture, workforce policy, financial policy).
- Sharing responsibilities and resources in the partnership to ensure sustainable, effective change across the Nexus.

Workplace Learning

In order to realize the vision of the Nexus of practice and education, it is imperative that new and current members of the health team learn together in authentic practice settings. This must include all members of the team, not only those who are licensed professionals. Workplace learning is increasingly recognized as important in maintaining professional competence and is defined as 'predominantly unstructured, experiential, and non-institutional' occurring in everyday practice. Individuals and interprofessional teams observe from their practice situation to learn from it to improve outcomes (Brandt, 2020; Marsick & Volpe, 1999; Nisbet et al., 2013; Regehr & Mylopoulos, 2008).

National Partnerships

The National Center has worked with over 70 sites implementing over 100 interprofessional education and collaborative practice programs in a wide variety of academic and community-based practice settings to inform the Nexus concept. Deep National Center experience and expertise led to blending traditional and emerging research approaches and using design-thinking principles for interprofessional workforce development, clinical practice and community-engaged practice-based research.

For instance, from 2016 to 2019, the Accelerating Community-based Interprofessional Education and Practice Initiative (National Center, 2019) supported the development of interprofessional teams in diverse community-based settings serving vulnerable, high-risk populations, including low-income housing facilities, a residential addiction treatment center, a skilled nursing facility, a federally qualified health center, a primary care teaching clinic, a public school, and rural and urban primary care clinics. At the outset, sites were charged with (1) committing to a zip code to impact 'upstream' factors of social determinants and health equity beyond the walls of hospitals and clinics; (2) designing an interprofessional education program, 'community as curriculum,' for health professions students, clinicians and other stakeholders to teach teamwork skills while implementing collaborative practice; and (3) demonstrating real patient, population and community health outcomes as a result of the program. A number of these sites worked with community resources such as transportation services, police, government agencies, legal services and housing authority, among others.

In 2019, external evaluators and local researchers documented a number of patient/health, learning and organizational outcomes in individual sites. Most notably, improvements were reported in health (decreased emergency department visits, increased access to care, decreased hospitalizations and decreased diabetic markers-HbA1c levels), organizational measures (increase in staff satisfaction, expansion of services such as two new primary care teaching clinics with development of additional sites and services), expansion of the number of professions involved, and the progression of interprofessional teamness among faculty, staff and students and community members (Harder+Company, 2019).

The external evaluation data led to research design around a proposal process focused first on individuals, families, communities and populations for community-engaged practice-based research using a unique data platform, the National Center Interprofessional Information Exchange (NCIIE) and Interprofessional Core Data Set that is built on the University of Minnesota (UMN) Clinical and Translational Science Institute technology platform (Delaney, AbuSalah et al., 2020). The IPE Core Data Set elements include interprofessional collaborative practice competencies, clinical learning environment, teamness and practice/patient/system outcomes.

Knowledge Generation in Action at the Nexus of Practice and Education

Knowledge Generation can be defined as a process that gathers evidence to promote innovative models of care and learning using real-time tools, standardized, sharable and comparable data, and analytics-based platforms to improve important outcomes. Knowledge Generation envisions advancing best practices for the care of individuals by incorporating the science of big data and big data analytics. By collecting and sharing data together as a field, *IPE Knowledge Generation* supports collaboration at the nexus of practice and education by linking locally generated data on individual programs to additional data across programs. The Knowledge Generation approach represents a significant shift in how data is collected, studied and used. This approach allows a single program to use near real-time data to inform ongoing program improvement to achieve outcomes. At the same time, data becomes a reusable resource across IPE programs over time (Delaney et al., 2015; Delaney & Simpson, 2017).

Developmental Evaluation is a key philosophical underpinning of the Knowledge Generation approach to transformative interprofessional practice and education. Patton (2016) has described Developmental Evaluation as a uniquely valuable approach when evaluating outcomes in settings of rapid change and high innovation, such as is occurring currently in interprofessional practice and education.

> Traditional evaluation approaches advocate clear, specific and measurable outcomes that are to be achieved through processes detailed in a linear logic model. Such traditional evaluation demand for up-front, preordinate specificity doesn't work under conditions of high innovation, exploration, uncertainty, turbulence, rapid change and emergence. Indeed, premature specificity can do harm by constraining exploration, limiting adaptation, reducing experimental options, and forcing premature adoption of a rigid model, not because such a model is appropriate, but because evaluators demand it in order to do what they understand to be good evaluation. [Developmental Evaluation] emerged as a response to the need for an alternative way to engage in evaluation of social innovations and adaptive developmental processes in complex dynamic environments.

Knowledge Generation and Developmental Evaluation provide a synergistic approach to using standardized, comparable data and reporting (Knowledge Generation) in an iterative approach that allows real-time monitoring of processes and outcomes in complex, unpredictable clinical settings (Developmental Evaluation).

The ultimate goal of the National Center Knowledge Generation strategy is to enable simultaneous transformational rapid cycle redesign of practice and education at the local level while providing comparative data to identify trends and best practices that can inform national and international work to expand interprofessional practice and education. Such transformation is beneficial only if it results in improved outcomes that matter most to individuals, families, communities, health organizations and members of the health team (Brandt et al., 2014). This includes understanding the human factors that enable or inhibit collaborative interprofessional work and learning. Originally framed within the context of the Triple Aim (Berwick, 2008), the NCIIE captures structured clinical data documenting the experience of care, health outcomes, and cost or efficiency of care. More recently, the National Center has adopted the Quadruple Aim (Bodenheimer, 2014) and includes outcomes metrics addressing the well-being of members of the health team.

Framework for Generating New Knowledge

Increasingly, decisions about care delivery, public and population health, team-based workforce models and expected outcomes are being informed through big data, machine learning and artificial intelligence. Likewise, educational programs are called to monumental transformation to meet the demands of modern healthcare practice. The goal of the knowledge generation approach is to move beyond transactional data, most often designed to serve payment systems, to understand the human processes and interactions that support teams, the care that is delivered, community-based health solutions and health-based outcomes. Ultimately, healthcare teams are looking at not just evidence or data for quality improvement. Rather they are seeking actionable, real-time data about what matters most for the individuals, families and communities served.

Harnessing the vast healthcare data and information available to improve systems and impact patient outcomes is the challenge for even the most established and advanced research enterprises. As a field with a relatively scant research tradition, interprofessional practice and education is in need of frameworks and systems to guide the generation of new knowledge. Many programs do not have practical experience designing and measuring the interprofessional learning experiences that will impact patient and systems outcomes—nor do they have an informatics infrastructure to harness the data to study and improve program effects. The National Center has established several key frameworks and systems to advance the field in educational design, healthcare transformation, standardized data collection, informatics and big data analytics. One important goal of this structured approach is to allow comparisons and learnings across disparate projects in a variety of clinical and educational environments, supporting the development of a virtual 'network of networks' to study best practices in IPE, supporting the vision of Carney et al. (2018).

Interprofessional Learning Continuum Model

Since its inception, the National Center and its network of sites across the country have researched and disseminated new knowledge about the relationship of interprofessional practice and education to learning, organizational and health/patient outcomes (National Center, 2020). Based on this experience and scholarship, the National Center adapted and expanded the Institute of Medicine Interprofessional Learning Continuum Model

(IOM, 2015) to guide program development and knowledge generation. The Interprofessional Learning Continuum Model adapted the modified Kirkpatrick model for interprofessional educational evaluation (Barr et al., 2005; Kirkpatrick, 1959; Reeves et al., 2011) and draws on the Triple Aim (Berwick et al., 2008) to define health and systems outcomes. The National Center Expanded Interprofessional Learning Continuum Model (EIPLCM) (Figure 9.2) is a framework for designing practice and education programs, measurement and research that link levels of learning (intermediate goal) to organizational, professional well-being and individual, and population-level health outcomes (ultimate goal) for local and national knowledge generation (Delaney et al., 2020). The model makes explicit what IPE practitioners know from experience—that successful interprofessional education, embedded in practice, can improve Quadruple Aim outcomes. By mapping the IPE Core Data to the EIPLCM, an important step is taken in moving from program design to measurement toward impact evaluation and research.

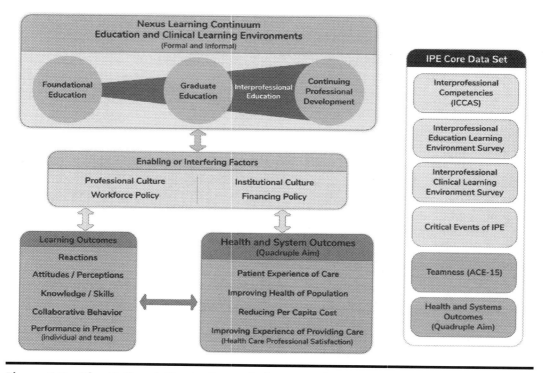

Figure 9.2 The National Center Expanded Interprofessional Learning Continuum Model. The National Academy of Medicine granted permission to use the Interprofessional Learning Continuum Model, which has been adapted by the National Center

IPE Core Data Set

Described in detail by Delaney et al. (2020), the IPE Core Data Set represents the essential, standardized data needed to empower collaborative work and use of shareable, comparable data and big data analytics across micro-, meso- and macro-levels of change to advance the generation of interprofessional practice and education knowledge. The IPE Core Data Set draws from validated tools where available and creates a standardized approach to collecting data across education and practice settings. The usage of existing clinical outcomes and patient satisfaction data is encouraged to facilitate ease of data collection. Standardized tools capture readily available data to ensure comparable data on the clinical and educational environments and local education and practice goals. Created based on extensive review of the literature, experience with partnerships across the United States, and validation by experts in informatics, education, health services, measurement and practice transformation, the IPE Core Data Set includes six categories of essential data: (1) interprofessional competencies, (2) interprofessional educational learning environment, (3) interprofessional clinical learning environment, (4) critical events of IPE, (5) teamness, and (6) health and system outcomes. Each category is briefly described below.

Interprofessional Competencies

Interprofessional Competencies across the learning continuum from foundational education, graduate education and continuing professional development can be assessed using the Interprofessional Collaborative Competency Attainment Survey (ICCAS). The instrument is a self-reported measure of interprofessional care competencies in interprofessional education programs. Using a retrospective pretest/posttest design, the survey invites learners to reflect on their knowledge, skills and attitudes prior to and after an interprofessional educational experience (Archibald et al., 2014). The ICCAS allows comparisons across sites and programs, demonstrates strong validity and has been used across the learning continuum in Canada, New Zealand and the United States (Schmitz et al., 2016).

Interprofessional Educational and Clinical Learning Environments

Two instruments have been developed by the National Center, based on decades of research and scholarship on interprofessional learning, teams, and environments: the Interprofessional Educational Learning Environment Survey (IELES) and the Interprofessional Clinical Learning Environment Survey (ICLES). The two instruments, which are mirror measures of the education and practice learning environments, include six domains of data: (1) organizational structure for IPE, (2) organizational culture for IPE, (3) organizational investment in IPE, (4) Nexus program team and processes, (5) professional development opportunities, and (6) managing the Nexus program. These two instruments are completed at baseline and yearly, providing an ongoing picture of the contexts in which IPE programs are operating.

Critical Events of IPE

The critical events of IPE instrument serves as a record of the challenges and positive forces having an impact on an IPE program, including common factors around leaders, partners, strategy/approach and resources and unforeseen forces. This instrument is completed in real time, when programs encounter events and circumstances that may impact implementation or outcomes and provides a dynamic timeline of critical events that programs can map to outcomes to understand enabling and interfering factors in program success.

Teamness

The National Center selected a rapid assessment instrument to diagnose and document clinical learning environments. The Assessment for Collaborative Environments (ACE-15) gathers clinical team member perceptions of interprofessional clinical teamwork. The purpose of the 15-item instrument is to provide a single measure of 'teamness' that can be used to assess team functioning and compare assessment scores over time. Items address qualities such as team communication, shared goals, roles, trust, measurable processes and outcomes, and organizational support. The ACE-15 is applicable as IPE moves from classrooms to practice to ensure appropriate interprofessional clinical learning environments for learners (Tilden et al., 2016).

Quadruple Aim Outcomes

The approach to Quadruple Aim outcomes demonstrates sensitivity to data collection burden and acknowledges the abundance of existing data in health systems. The IPE Core Data Set adopts widely used and validated instruments already used in health systems for measuring perceived health and health-related quality of life, and the patient experience of care (Nichol et al., 2001). Outcome data is de-identified before submission and facilitated through automatic data feeds when possible. Sources of outcome data include the following.

- Short-Form Health Survey (SF-36 or SF-12). Core data for population health includes measures for general health, recent changes in health and deaths in the past year. The 36-item short-form and 12-item short health surveys (SF-36 and SF-12, respectively), developed by the RAND Health Insurance Experiment, have been extensively tested and been found reliable for measuring functional health (physical and mental) and well-being (Ware et al., 1992).
- Consumer Assessment of HealthCare Providers Surveys (CAHPS). The US Agency for Health Research and Quality (AHRQ) has developed a series of instruments designed to capture patient experiences and satisfaction with their healthcare providers and services. Several different surveys exist for different provider settings (e.g., clinics, home healthcare, dental, adult and child hospital) (AHRQ, 2018). If CAHPS are not appropriate for an IPE setting, or it is difficult to obtain this in a setting, a subset of four questions from CAHPS can be substituted that are readily standardized across diverse populations and are patient-completed and easily understood (Crofton et al., 1999).
- Use of Health Services. This information comprises office visits, home healthcare, emergency room visits, hospitalizations, etc. Service usage constitutes a proxy for cost, as well as disease burden. Usage is best measured through the extraction of patient data using nationally accepted administrative codes in the United States such as the International Statistical Classification of Diseases and Related Health Problems (ICD) and Diagnostic-Related Groups (DRGs). Programs should identify and select only those codes that reflect the Program's IPE intervention.
- Healthcare Professional Satisfaction. The final component of the Quadruple Aim concerns improving the experience of providing care (healthcare professionals including provider, clinician and staff satisfaction). The National Center has adopted healthcare professional satisfaction, measured by site-specific determined standardized instruments, to be the current proxy.

The National Center is recruiting interprofessional programs across the country to adopt the IPE Core Data Set by offering it as a user-friendly toolkit to collect information to inform team processes, attainment of interprofessional competencies and an understanding of the clinical practice and learning environments. The Center has also developed the infrastructure (described in the next section) to capture this data. The promise for local programs is a real-time, 360-degree view of what is working and what needs ongoing enhancement as teams and organizations seek to continuously improve their education and delivery strategies to achieve outcomes that matter most. At the national level, the Center can use its informatics infrastructure and expertise to conduct sophisticated research linking education and practice to outcomes.

National Center Interprofessional Information Exchange

The National Center developed a national infrastructure, the *National Center Interprofessional Information Exchange* (*NCIIE*) for generating new IPE knowledge to operationalize a vision for new knowledge discovery about outcomes of interprofessional practice and education (Delaney et al., 2015). The infrastructure, leveraged by the University of Minnesota's Clinical and Translational Science Institute's informatics infrastructure, captures core and operational data of interprofessional practice and education programs and supports organizations in using that data for program management and new knowledge linking interprofessional practice to individual and population health outcomes. Within the NCIIE, IPE program leaders and researchers complete a proposal that clearly defines the learning, organizational, and health/patient outcomes that they intend to impact through their IPE programs. The programs collect the *IPE Core Data Set* (described above), representing the essential data needed to advance what we know and understand about interprofessional teams and models of care and learning.

The vision and evolution of this infrastructure has been disseminated in numerous publications (Cerra et al., 2015; Pechacek et al., 2015). The NCIIE is designed to (1) facilitate capture, access and exchange of the IPE Core Data Set; (2) capture operational data within an IPE implementation program; (3) support local program management for individual IPE programs to track their own progress and reporting; (4) support use of informatics to catalyze discoveries across the spectrum of IPE; and (5) share contributions and new knowledge nationally. As described in Delaney, AbuSalah et al. (2020):

> The NCIIE is a protected health information (PHI) compliant infrastructure that ensures the implementation of best data practices and

national standards related to 1) secure and encrypted data exchange and storage; 2) role-based user authentication management that supports local control of data access; 3) data de-identification methods that ensure no PHI data are uploaded; 4) regular secure data backups; 5) use of PHI compliant tools for data extraction and delivery; and 6) additional security measures (e.g., firewalls, password requirements, data retention and destruction). The use of data is governed through specific data use agreements between the National Center and the individual programs along with security models and data management policies governed by the University of Minnesota Health Sciences Technology Data Protection Services. Agreements and policies are regularly (at least annually) reviewed by all relevant privacy, compliance, Institutional Review Board (IRB), and Health Insurance Portability and Accountability Act of 1996 (HIPAA) entities. The NCIIE is a secure HIPAA-and Family Educational Rights and Privacy Act (FERPA) compliant state-of-the-art environment that ensures both data privacy and security provisions for safeguarding health information (HIPAA) and protection of the privacy of student education records (FERPA).

In addition to supporting the functions described above, the NCIIE infrastructure advances collaboration and collective understanding of IPE best practices across local practice and education settings, a single system, and national and international environments. The NCIIE contains programmed data dictionaries and can generate standardized reports for each of the IPE Core Data Set instruments (e.g., ICCAS, ACE-15) to enable program leaders to access data on their own programs at any time and can download their own reports that are available at any time. The individual program standard reports provide information about how their results change over time. The National Center can also provide aggregate reports that compare findings across programs. The ultimate goal is advancing the evidence base for IPE learning and organizational and healthcare outcomes.

Case Example: Minnesota Northstar Geriatric Workforce Enhancement Program

The Minnesota Northstar Geriatrics Workforce Enhancement Program (MN GWEP) at the University of Minnesota was an early partner in the IPE Knowledge Generation approach and IPE Core Data Set utilization. The MN

GWEP is a 5-year, US$ 3.74 million program funded by the Health Resources & Services Administration (HRSA) focused on implementing a range of distinct projects under the grant program's umbrella, incorporating eight community partners and faculty and learners from dentistry, family medicine, internal medicine, nursing, pharmacy, physical therapy, public health and social work.

One major aim for MN GWEP is to make significant strides toward closing the gap when it comes to age-friendly care by transforming primary care delivery for older adults through the use of accessible, practical tools that can be incorporated into everyday practice. The ultimate goal is for all Minnesotan geriatric patients to receive treatment that faithfully adheres to the 4M framework: what matters in their lives, their medications, their mobility, and their mentation (Institute for Healthcare Improvement, 2020).

The National Center National Center is a key partner for the MN GWEP Age-Friendly Care initiative. MN GWEP uses the National Center IPE Information Exchange to plan, track and report data on educational and health systems outcomes. This includes HRSA-required data on geriatrics-related interventions and Centers for Medicaid and Medicare Merit-Based Incentive Payment System (MIPS) measures. MN GWEP is contributing data to the NCIIE using the IPE Core Data Set as well, expanding the potential impact of collected data beyond accountability reporting to inform national conversations around effective strategies for interprofessional practice and education transformation efforts.

MN GWEP's clinical transformation intervention is creating tools, training and support for Family Medicine Clinics to provide improved age-friendly care for adults 65 and over. Although the goal of the intervention was clear in MN GWEP's grant proposal, the mechanisms for transforming care were not. Interprofessional clinical teams at two pilot clinics (an Federally Qualified Health Center (FQHC) and community-based university clinic) explored clinic needs, goals and capabilities together before ultimately deciding to develop a 'smartset' or similar clinical tool in the practices' electronic health record (EHR) (Epic) to guide providers through a data-informed geriatric visit based on the four 'Ms' of age-friendly care—What Matters, Mentation, Medication and Mobility. The National Center's framework, infrastructure and expertise provided guidance in developing an intervention that not only addressed key outcomes but incorporated the necessary elements for collecting and extracting usable and shareable data. Throughout the development phase, the grant evaluator documented enabling and interfering factors, and used the critical events of IPE tool to document significant events. Programmatic shifts in the midst of COVID-19 were key contextual factors, as the pandemic impacted clinical intervention timelines, as well as taking a toll on team members.

The MN GWEP will be expanding its clinical intervention to over 50 clinics following initial pilots in 2021. This expansion includes adoption of the final smartset as a Geriatrics Care Package in Epic and training for clinical teams (including physicians, residents, nurse practitioners, certified medical assistants and additional interprofessional learners). As the MN GWEP program moves beyond its pilot phase, it is committed to using the NCIIE and IPE Core Data Set in the following ways:

- Data agreements and key partnerships have been established by the MN GWEP and National Center to guide Epic builds, data extraction and reporting that take maximum advantage of available systems data. The MN GWEP's program-specific outcomes include measures around dementia assessment, depression screening, falls risk assessment, medication review, patient goals and advanced care planning. This data will be shared in the NCIIE, along with patient and provider satisfaction measures identified in the IPE Core Data Set.
- The Interprofessional Collaborative Competency Attainment Survey (ICCAS) will be administered to interprofessional learners following training in participating clinics.
- The Educational Learning Environment and Clinical Learning Environment Surveys will track the students, faculty, clinicians, teams, clinics and institutions involved in the intervention. The program will have a yearly record of key factors such as learner numbers, professions and backgrounds; learning objectives; leadership; funding; team composition; patient population served; and partnerships.
- As mentioned above, the critical events of IPE tool is currently in use to document the timeline and key events in development; this practice will continue through implementation. The critical events of IPE reports have already provided key information for accurate narrative reporting to funders and other stakeholders.
- The ACE-15 has been administered at pilot clinics, assessing the 'teamness' of the environment. As additional clinics are added, their clinical team members will also complete this assessment. Administered at least yearly, the ACE-15 will provide a snapshot of the baseline interprofessional team environment and change over time for each distinct clinic as the intervention proceeds. MN GWEP will analyze this data along with other measures to explore the effects of the clinical environment on project implementation, and vice versa.

The developmental evaluation approach built into the National Center Interprofessional Information Exchange has proved ideally situated for this interprofessional practice and education project. Like all practice transformation work, the MN GWEP Age-Friendly Care initiative involves creating change within a series of complex, unique practice environments that are simultaneously responding to a myriad of influences, even without the added stress of the COVID-19 pandemic. External partners such as the local Epic team are necessary to achieve project aims, but have their own priorities that impact this project. Each member of the team, including patients and families, bring their own experiences, biases and conflicting demands as they engage with new care pathways. However, there are clearly defined benefits to transforming individual primary care practices to meet the goals of Age-Friendly Care, and the NCIIE and Interprofessional Core Data Set provide a novel strategy to facilitate design, data collection and outcomes evaluation across a broad spectrum of practice sites.

Conclusions and Outlook

The National Center Interprofessional Information Exchange and Interprofessional Core Data set represent a unique partnership, firmly rooted in the Nexus of practice and education and fully informed by the latest in informatics and data science. Drawing from knowledge generation and developmental evaluation strategies, the NCIIE represents a new tool that supports local, iterative initiatives to improve outcomes that matter to organizations, health professionals, individuals and populations. At the same time, as more projects populate the NCIIE with Core Data Set measures across diverse practice and education settings, the same data that drive local efforts will inform the critical need to identify common elements of successful, sustainable and impactful interprofessional practice and education efforts. This infrastructure provides a secure, practical and approachable new tool in this long-standing but urgent work.

Funding Attribution

The Minnesota Northstar GWEP is supported by the Health Resources and Services Administration (HRSA) of the US Department of Health and Human Services (HHS) as part of an award totaling US$ 747,581. The contents are those of the author(s) and do not necessarily represent the official views of, nor an endorsement, by HRSA, HHS or the US Government. Additional funding for the Minnesota Northstar GWEP is provided by a gracious gift from the Otto Bremer Trust Foundation. The Minnesota Northstar GWEP is supported by the University of Minnesota Office of Academic Clinical Affairs.

References

Agency for Healthcare Research and Quality. (2012). *TeamSTEPPS 2.0* [online]. Available at: https://www.ahrq.gov/teamstepps/index.html (Accessed 7 August 2021).

Agency for Healthcare Research and Quality. (2018). *CAHPS surveys and guidance* [online]. Available at: http://www.ahrq.gov/cahps/surveys-guidance/index.html (Accessed August 5 2021).

Archibald, D., Trumpower, D., & MacDonald, C. J. (2014). Validation of the interprofessional collaborative competency attainment survey (ICCAS). *Journal of Interprofessional Care*, 28(6), pp.553–558. https://doi.org/10.3109/13561820.2014.917407

Balsar, J., Ryu, J., Hood, M., Kaplan, G., Perlin, J., & Siegel, B. (2021). *Care systems COVID-19 impact assessment: Lessons learned and compelling needs, perspectives: Expert voices in health & health care.* Washington, DC: National Academies of Medicine. April 7, 2021. [online] Available at: https://nam.edu/programs/value-science-driven-health-care/emerging-stronger-after-covid-19-priorities-for-health-system-transformation/ (Accessed 6 August 2021).

Barr, H., Koppel, I., Reeves, S., Hammick, M., & Freeth, D. eds. (2005). *Effective interprofessional education: Argument, assumption and evidence.* Oxford, UK: CAIPE, Blackwell Publishing, Ltd.

Berwick, D. M., Nolan, T. W., & Whittington, J. (2008). The triple aim: Care, health and cost. *Health Affairs*, 27(3), pp.759–769. https://doi.org/10.1377/hlthaff.27.3.759

Bodenheimer, T., & Sinsky, C. (2014). From triple to quadruple aim: Care of the patient requires care of the provider. *Annals of Family Medicine*, 12, pp.573–576. https://doi.org/10.1370/afm.1713

Brandt, B. F., & Barton, A. J. (2020). Getting started with interprofessional practice and education in community-based settings. *Journal of Nursing Education*, 59(5), pp.243–244. https://doi.org/10.3928/01484834-20200422-01

Brandt, B., Lutfiyya, M. N., King, J. A., & Chioreso, C. (2014). A scoping review of interprofessional collaborative practice and education using the lens of the triple aim. *Journal of Interprofessional Care*, 28(5), pp.393–399. https://doi.org/10.3109/13561820.2014.906391

Carney, P. A., Brandt, B., Dekhtyar, M., & Holmboe, E. S. (2018). Advancing health professions education research by creating a network of networks. *Academic Medicine*, 93(8), pp.1110–1112. https://doi.org/10.1097/ACM.0000000000002189

Cerra, F., Pacala, J., Brandt, B. F., & Lutfiyya, M. N. (2015). The application of informatics in delineating the proof of concept for creating knowledge of the value added by interprofessional practice and education. *Healthcare*, 3(4), pp.1158–1173. https://doi.org/10.3390/healthcare3041158

Crofton C, Lubalin J, & Darby C. (1999). Consumer assessment of health plans study foreword. *Medical Care*, 37(3), Supplement, pp.MS1–MS9. https://doi.org/10.1097/00005650-199903001-00001

Delaney, C. W., AbuSalah, A., Yeazel, M., Kertz, J. S., Pejsa, L., & Brandt, B. F. (2020). National center for interprofessional practice and education IPE core data set and information exchange for knowledge generation. *Journal of Interprofessional Care*, Ahead of Print, pp.1–13. https://doi.org/10.1080/13561820.2020.1798897

Delaney, C. W., Kuziemsky, C., & Brandt, B. F. (2015). Integrating informatics and interprofessional education and practice to drive healthcare transformation. *Journal of Interprofessional Care*, 29(6), pp.527–529. https://doi.org/10.3109/13561820.2015.1108735

Delaney, C. W., & Simpson, R. L. (2017). Why big data? Why nursing? In C. W. Delaney, C., Weaver, J. J. Warren, T. R. Clancy, & R. L. Simpson, eds., *Big data-enabled nursing: Education, research, and practice*. New York: Springer International Publishing AG, pp. 3–10. https://doi.org/10.1007/978-3-319-53300-1_23

Harder Company Community Research. (2019). *Accelerating interprofessional community-based education and practice imitative: Final evaluation report*. San Francisco, CA [online]. Available at: https://nexusipe-resource-exchange.s3-us-west-2.amazonaws.com/Harder%2BCo%20Final%20Accelerating%20Report%20FINAL.pdf (Accessed 6 August 2021).

Health Professions Accreditors Collaborative. (2019). *Guidance on developing quality interprofessional education for the health professions*. Chicago, IL: Health Professions Accreditors Collaborative [online]. Available at: https://healthprofessionsaccreditors.org/wp-content/uploads/2019/02/HPACGuidance02-01-19.pdf (Accessed 6 August 2021).

Institute for Healthcare Improvement. (2020). *Age friendly health systems: Guide to using the 4Ms in the care of older adults* [online]. Available at: http://www.ihi.org/Engage/Initiatives/Age-Friendly-Health-Systems/Documents/IHIAgeFriendlyHealthSystems_GuidetoUsing4MsCare.pdf (Accessed 7 August 2021).

Institute of Medicine. (2015). *Measuring the impact of interprofessional education on collaborative practice and patient outcomes*. Washington, DC: The National Academies Press. https://doi.org/10.17226/21726

Institute of Medicine (US) Committee on Quality of Health Care in America. (2000). *To err is human: Building a safer health system*, Kohn, L. T., Corrigan, J. M., & Donaldson, M. S., eds. Washington, DC: National Academies Press. https://doi.org/10.17226/9728

Institute of Medicine (US) Committee on Quality of Health Care in America. (2001). *Crossing the quality chasm: A new health system for the 21st century*. Washington, DC: National Academies Press. https://doi.org/10.17226:10027

Institute of Medicine (US) Committee on the Health Professions Education Summit. (2003). *Health professions education: A bridge to quality*, Greiner, A. C., & Knebel, E., Eds. Washington, DC: National Academies Press. https://doi.org/10.17226/10681

Interprofessional Education Collaborative. (2016). *Core competencies for interprofessional collaborative practice: 2016 update.* Washington, DC: Interprofessional Education Collaborative.

Kirkpatrick, D. L. (1959). Techniques for evaluation training programs. *Journal of the American Society of Training Directors*, 13, pp.21–26.

Marsick, V. J., & Volpe, M. (1999). The nature and need for informal learning. *Advances in Developing Human Resources*, 1(3), pp.1–9. https://doi.org/10.1177/152342239900100302

National Academies of Sciences, Engineering, and Medicine. (2021a). *The future of nursing 2020–2030: Charting a path to achieve health equity.* Washington, DC: The National Academies Press. https://doi.org/10.17226/25982

National Academies of Sciences, Engineering, and Medicine. (2021b). *Implementing high-quality primary care: Rebuilding the foundation of health care.* Washington, DC: The National Academies Press. https://doi.org/10.17226/25983

National Center for Interprofessional Practice and Education. (2019). *Accelerating interprofessional community-based education and practice* [online]. Available at: https://nexusipe.org/advancing/accelerating (Accessed 6 August 2021).

National Center for Interprofessional Practice and Education. (2020). Publications summary [online]. Available at: https://nexusipe.org/advancing/national-center-publications (Accessed 5 August 2021).

Nesbit, G., Lincoln, M., & Dunn, S. (2013). Informal interprofessional learning: An untapped opportunity for learning and change within the workplace. *Journal of Interprofessional Care*, 27(6), pp.469–475. https://doi.org/10.3109/13561820.2013.805735

Nichol, M. B., Sengupta, N., & Globe, D. R. (2001) Evaluating quality-adjusted life years: Estimation of the health utility index (HUI2) from the SF-36. *Medical Decision Making*, 21(2), pp.105–112. https://doi.org/10.1177/0272989X0102100203

Patton, M. Q. (2016). What is essential in developmental evaluation? On integrity, fidelity, adultery, abstinence, importance, long-term commitment, integrity, and sensitivity in implementing evaluation models. *American Journal of Evaluation*, 37(2), pp.250–265. https://doi.org/10.1177/1098214015626295

Pechacek, J., Shanedling, J., Lutfiyya, M. N., Brandt, B. F., Cerra, F. B., & Delaney, C. W. (2015). The National United States center data repository: Core essential interprofessional practice & education data enabling triple aim analytics. *Journal of Interprofessional Care*, 29(6), pp.587–591. https://doi.org/10.3109/13561820.2015.1075474

Reeves, S., Goldman, J., Gilbert, J., Tepper, J., Silver, I., Suter, E., & Zwarenstein, M. (2011). A scoping review to improve conceptual clarity of interprofessional interventions. *Journal of Interprofessional Care*, 25(3), pp.167–174. https://doi.org/10.3109/13561820.2010.529960

Regehr, G., & Mylopoulos, M. (2008). Maintaining competence in the field: Learning about practice through practice, in practice. *Journal of Continuing Education in the Health Professions*, 28(Suppl 1), pp.S19–S32. https://doi.org/10.1002/chp.203

Schmitz, C. C., Radosevich, D. M., Jardine, P., MacDonald, C. J., Trumpower, D., & Archibald, D. (2016). The Interprofessional collaborative competency attainment survey (ICCAS): A replication validation study. *Journal of Interprofessional Care*, 31(1), pp.28–34. https://doi.org/10.1080/13561820.2016.1233096

Thibault, G. E. (2020). The future of health professions education: Emerging trends in the United States. *FASEB BioAdvances*, pp.1–10. https://doi.org/10.1096/fba.2020-00061

Tilden, V. P., Eckstrom, E., & Dieckmann, N. F. (2016). Development of the assessment for collaborative environments (ACE-15): A tool to measure perceptions of interprofessional 'teamness.' *Journal of Interprofessional Care*, 30(3), pp.288–294. https://doi.org/10.3109/13561820.2015.1137891

U.S. Department of Health and Human Services. (2020). *Healthy people 2030: Social determinants of health* [online]. Available at: https://health.gov/healthypeople/objectives-and-data/social-determinants-health (Accessed 6 August 2021).

Ware, J. E., & Sherbourne, C. D. (1992). The MOS 36-item short-form health survey (SF-36) I. Conceptual framework and item selection. *Medical Care*, 30(6), pp.473–483. https://www.jstor.org/stable/3765916%0A

World Health Organization Health Professions Network Nursing and Midwifery Office within the Department of Human Resources for Health. (2010). *Framework for action on interprofessional education & collaborative practice*. Geneva, Switzerland: World Health Organization.

Chapter 10

The use of the IMIA Education Recommendations and the IMIA Knowledge Base as a Foundation for Competencies in Health Informatics in Africa

Graham Wright, Helen J. Betts, Frank Verbeke,
Martin C. Were, Frances B. da-Costa Vroom and Kimutai Some

Contents

Introduction 172
    The IMIA Knowledge Base and Recommendations 172
    Model 1: MSc HI Curriculum Review for the Regional eHealth
        Centre of Excellence in Rwanda 173
    Model 2: Developing Benchmarks for the Master of Health
        Informatics Programmes in East Africa 175
    Model 3: Towards a Harmonized Master's Curriculum for Public
        Health Informatics in Francophone Africa 178
Conclusion 180
References 181

Introduction

This chapter explores the use of the International Medical Informatics Association (IMIA) Strategy Model (Murray et al., 2007), endorsed Knowledge Base (Wright, 2011) and Recommendations on Education in Biomedical and Health Informatics (Mantas et al., 2010) in the development of educational programmes in several Sub-Saharan African countries. These resources are available on the IMIA website (IMIA, 2013). We explore the educational processes in these IMIA documents and their use as frameworks for curriculum and programme development. The first model describes the review of the Master in Health Informatics curriculum for the Regional eHealth Centre of Excellence (REHCE) in Rwanda. The second model illustrates the development of benchmarks for master degree programmes in Health Informatics to be used across the East African Community. The final model explains the conception and ongoing processes of creating a master's curriculum for Public Health Informatics in Francophone Africa.

The IMIA Knowledge Base and Recommendations

At the 2007 IMIA General Congress, it was agreed to adopt the strategic document, 'Towards IMIA 2015' (Murray, 2008). IMIA shows in this strategic plan a conceptual framework with knowledge at the core. This strategic plan thinking underpinned many revisions of earlier work including the mapping to Lorenzi's Scientific Content Map (Lorenzi, 2002). Following conversations between IMIA, the British Computer Society (BCS) and the Centre for Health Informatics Research and Development (CHIRAD), the three organizations supported several research projects that developed the IMIA Knowledge Base which has 28 rows and 245 units (Wright, 2011).

Additionally, IMIA endorsed and adopted the framework and recommendations proposed by Mantas and colleagues for education in biomedical and health informatics (Mantas et al., 2010). Together, these seminal works form the main toolsets and guidelines used over the last decade in developing academic Health Informatics programmes. Since their publication, there has been widespread application of these tools in Health Informatics (HI) curricula worldwide and translations to other languages (IMIA, 2013). The 40 IMIA recommendations (Mantas et al., 2010) have provided a platform for the creation of Health Informatics (HI) programmes at the bachelor, master and doctoral levels of education.

Model 1: MSc HI Curriculum Review for the Regional eHealth Centre of Excellence in Rwanda

The curriculum review started in 2014 against the backdrop of Rwanda's Regional e-Health Centre of Excellence (REHCE) (Wright et al., 2015) already having many digital health implementation projects in process. Most of these projects faced considerable staffing issues causing a high demand in the labour market for advanced health informatics specialists. Therefore, economically justifying the existence of a local or regional MSc in Health Informatics programme was not in question. To respond to the existing human capacity gaps, a programme had to be competence-based with a specific focus on the Rwandan situation.

The Rwandan Ministry of Health (MoH) had shifted its policy from in-house to outsourcing digital health application development. Several elements influenced this decision: (i) software development stopped being considered a core business for the MoH; (ii) retention of software programmers had proven to be problematic due to inadequate public sector salaries; and (iii) digital health implementations had increasingly become a multidisciplinary activity involving other ministries such as Public Sector and Labour, Finance and Education. These policy changes had an important impact on the knowledge and skills that would be needed for the public health IT sector in the next few years. The rapid and uncoordinated growth of new digital health solutions in the country had been responsible for several interoperability issues.

Hence, special attention was paid to capacity building related to systems interoperability. These requirements included the following: (i) Open Health Information Exchange (OpenHIE); (ii) EMR– Health Management Information Systems (HMIS) integration through secondary use of primary source data; (iii) integrated human resource information management; (iv) mobile health application extensions; (v) performance-based financing information systems; and (vi) health insurance information management bridges between the MoH, the Ministry of Finance and health insurance organizations.

Rwanda planned for a large-scale electronic medical record (EMR) deployment in the following few years, which would require a major reinforcement of the available health informatics workforce's knowledge and skills in information systems (IS) and information management (IM). Considering the huge need for health informatics training to cope with these ambitious plans for the Rwandan public sector, education and training were expected to offer valuable employment opportunities. Specific didactic and research skills were also added to the existing demand for information technologies (IT), information systems (IS), information management (IM) and health system (HS) proficiencies.

Stakeholder interviews combined with a need's analysis identified a list of job opportunities in the field of digital health:

- The MoH would be seeking HMIS implementers, EMR deployment managers, information systems evaluators and specialists in information systems cost–benefit analysis.
- Health facilities were expected to offer jobs for district-level Chief Information Officers (CIOs), national reference hospital CIOs, clinical information system managers, as well as pharmacy and laboratory information managers.
- Huge needs were identified for transforming (mainly paper-based) traditional content into electronic learning solutions. Centres, such as REHCE, and many non-governmental organizations (NGOs) and public sector organizations were expected to offer jobs to graduates with combined IS, IM and didactic skills. Furthermore, the important anticipated need for MSc level HI graduates justified building local teaching capacity in digital health.
- Data-driven financial management skills are key for private, for-profit organizations. The creation of jobs for high-level IM/financial specialists who can relate cost reduction and increased financial efficiency to effective healthcare would be needed.

The needs assessment and the labour market analysis made it possible to identify a set of human resource profiles for future MSc HI graduates. These profiles provided important, high-level guidelines for defining the country's competence needs in terms of digital health for the following roles:

- Health information managers, mainly focusing on IM and HS knowledge.
- Clinicians proficient in IT, IS and IM, based in health facilities.
- Information System Implementers and System Integrators (e.g., for EMR–HMIS integration).
- Information system evaluators for health informatics interventions impact measurement and information systems quality evaluation.

- Educational staff (academic staff and information systems training staff as well as functional experts).
- Researchers in the field of digital health.

Based on the results obtained from the needs assessment, the evaluation of the existing curriculum against the international health informatics education standards, and the pressing needs in the labour market, the reviewers developed a reference 'target' curriculum for Rwanda. This target curriculum then needed to be compared to the existing one resulting in a competence and content gap analysis and leading to a series of recommendations to migrate towards the target curriculum (Verbeke et al., 2016).

Through a series of evaluative comparisons between Rwanda's baseline curriculum and IMIA's Knowledge Base units, it was possible to develop a set of curriculum modules with 100% IMIA Knowledge Base coverage whilst avoiding any redundant teaching. One module content was planned so as to produce an equally distributed weight of 10 credits per module. The postgraduate certificate year consisted of six modules, as did the postgraduate diploma year (Verbeke et al., 2016). This design exercise resulted in an MSc in Health Informatics curriculum that was a better match for the Rwandan labour market and covered the full scope of IMIA Recommendations and Knowledge Units in a more balanced way.

Model 2: Developing Benchmarks for the Master of Health Informatics Programmes in East Africa

The East African Community (EAC) is composed of six countries: Burundi, Kenya, Rwanda, South Sudan, Tanzania and Uganda (East African Community, 2019). Ethiopia and Somalia participate in the community as observer countries. The community is a common education zone through the framework of the East African Common Higher Education area that was declared by the 18th Ordinary Summit of the EAC Heads of States in May 2017 (East African Community, 2017). This framework guides over 300 universities in the region to support the mobility of students, faculty and workforce (Trines, 2018). Were et al. (2020) evaluated the IMIA-recommended competency coverage in seven of eight institutions with accredited MSc HI degree programmes across East Africa. These researchers found variabilities in the existing MSc HI programmes competency coverage when compared to the full set of the *IMIA Recommendations in Biomedical and Health Informatics* (Mantas et al., 2010). The authors reported that coverage of the 40 IMIA competencies ranged from 62.5% to 97.5%, with an additional 25 unique competencies present in programmes by the EAC's Higher Education Institutions that were not part of the IMIA Recommendations (Were et al., 2020). Their evaluation suggests that the higher educational institutions (HEI) within the EAC selected the IMIA recommendations to various degrees when designing their MSc HI degree programmes. Further, the additional unique competencies contained in the EAC programmes highlighted a need for region-specific competencies that might not be emphasized in international health informatics competency recommendations.

In a follow-up 2021 study, Were et al. (2021) compared similarities and differences in competencies covered within the curricula of the seven EAC universities. This consisted of a university-to-university comparison of competencies within curricula to evaluate how each of the university-covered competencies compared with each of the other universities. Several observations were made, namely (a) there was a wide variability in the number of courses within the various MSc HI degree programmes, ranging from 8 to 22; (b) there were statistically significant differences in competency coverage across the seven institutions ($p = 0.012$); and (c) only four of the 21 university-pairs (19%) met a cut-off of over 70% similarity in covered competencies (Were et al., 2021). The extensive variability in covered competencies for MSc HI programmes throughout the EAC poses a significant threat to the mobility of students, faculty and labour. Further, it brings into focus the need to formulate benchmarks or standards that would guide MSc HI degree content and quality assurance mechanisms.

Fortunately, the HEIs, employers, Ministries of Health, National Commissions of Education and other stakeholders recognize the threats posed when MSc HI graduates from various institutions present with widely varying skills and capabilities. There is a need to support the academic and employment mobility of students and faculty within the common education zone. In response to this recognized need for greater curriculum standardization, HEIs in the region are working closely with the Inter-University Council of East Africa (IUCEA) to develop the benchmarks for MSc HI for East Africa. The IUCEA Credit Accumulation and Transfer System (CATS) in East Africa is a regional quality assurance project, under the auspices of three regional regulatory agencies: the Commission for University Education, Kenya; the National Council for Higher Education; and the Uganda and the Tanzania Commission for Universities, which aims to harmonize academic programmes for ease of student movement among the East African member states.

The MSc HI benchmarks were developed through a consultative, multistep process that involved reviews of existing curricula, alignment with knowledge bases and IMIA recommendations, and inputs from key stakeholders—all guided by experts from the IUCEA. In May 2019, HEIs in East Africa that had accredited programmes for MSc HI met to set minimum standards for these programmes. The harmonized curriculum was submitted through the Commission of University Education in Kenya to the IUCEA for approval in late December 2019. The comprehensive benchmarks outline the MSc HI degree programme goal, objectives, admission criteria, graduation requirements, and expected learning outcomes (ELOs). From the ELOs, a consensus was reached on courses that covered all identified skills and competencies. Highlights of the benchmarks, derived from the IUCEA document, are as follows:

Programme goal and objectives: to produce graduates capable of using informatics in different health domains for the acquisition of knowledge, research, improved healthcare and decision making.

Expected learning outcomes (ELOs): 12 ELOs were identified that covered knowledge, skills (cognitive, practical, interpersonal) and attitudes expected of graduates.

Admission requirements: candidates could have a bachelor's degree in health or information sciences, with flexibility allowed per university guidelines, such as the incorporation of work in relevant fields.

Programme structure: the benchmarks recommend a programme structure that includes (a) basic/foundation phases—composed of prerequisites and crossover courses/subject areas; (b) core courses/subject areas; and (c) electives. Students are required to meet thesis requirements and to participate in an attachment for practical training.

Once approved, the National Commissions and Councils within the EAC are expected to align their standards for MSc HI with the developed benchmarks. Universities with existing MSc HI programmes should review curricula to align with these benchmarks, while those developing new programmes should use the benchmarks for guidance. However, the benchmarks are not prescriptive, rather they provide a minimum set of common competencies with room for additional competencies determined by each institution and allow universities to decide on additional content, courses and modes of delivery. This standardization and harmonization work is currently in process.

Model 3: Towards a Harmonized Master's Curriculum for Public Health Informatics in Francophone Africa

The World Health Organization (WHO) Regional Office for Africa sites 47 countries in Africa of which 20 speak French, 22 English and 7 Portuguese as a legacy of European colonization. Most of the French-speaking countries are in West and Central Africa (WHO, 2021), 34.8% of the world's 300 million French speakers live in sub-Saharan Africa. Eleven African countries use French as the only official language. French is also the main or only language for schools in 13 African countries (Quartz, 2018).

Over the past decade, several academic training programmes have been created to meet the new challenges linked to the advancement of digital health in sub-Saharan Africa. English-speaking countries have often taken the lead in this area and, in addition to setting up short courses related to applications, have frequently focused on master's programmes in biomedical informatics. Several hundred students have now graduated in this exciting field, but few have succeeded in making the most of their degrees in the workforce. In most sub-Saharan countries, few relevant positions have been foreseen for these profiles in public health administration and healthcare facilities. Skills in pure biomedical informatics often only partially meet the needs of the healthcare systems. Adding knowledge in biomedical informatics to existing training in the health sector may offer a solution to this. At first glance, a master's programme in public health lends itself well for this purpose, and in recent years, there has been a tendency to place existing biomedical informatics programmes in schools of public health.

A similar undertaking to that described in Model 2 is currently in progress across Francophone Africa. In late August 2020, the first colloquium was organized by the Digital Health Campus of the Democratic Republic of Congo (DRC) on the theme of developing a master's curriculum in public health informatics (MPHI). Thirteen academic institutions from nine different countries participated: DRC, Senegal, Guinea, Mali, Ivory Coast, Burkina Faso, Rwanda, Burundi and Madagascar. Their academic context was broad: schools of public health, medical science training institutes, a biomedical computer institute and a centre for biomedical engineering. It was agreed that students graduating with a master's degree in public health informatics (MPHI) were expected, in addition to the basic skills associated with a public health degree, to also acquire relevant knowledge and skills in biomedical informatics that enabled them to use today's key modern digital tools for building the African health systems of tomorrow. It is recognized that the development of such a curriculum, which is specifically aimed at the African context, is an exercise that requires time, experience and professional knowledge in the field of public health and health informatics. In most universities and schools of public health, faculty expertise and teaching capacity are only partially available and it, therefore, seems important to collaborate on a regional level in the creation of this curriculum. In addition, a harmonized curriculum is expected to contribute to mobility for students and teaching staff, as well as content standardization and international collaboration in digital public health.

In 2020, the 13 academic institutions agreed on the following: the thematic accents would be different depending on the country; strengthening the quality of care in rural areas; the digitization of hospitals; the development of biomedical engineering; the implementation of telemedicine solutions; and that educational outcomes must match major national health systems challenges and priorities. This consensus confirmed the broad range of skills that had been summarized in a preparatory note distributed before the conference.

A handicap for the field of digital health in sub-Saharan Africa today is that most professionals working in this sector have either a 'health' or an 'IT' profile. Health informatics or digital health as a profession remains largely underdeveloped.

The content of the programme should focus on the concrete operational needs of countries in sub-Saharan Africa. Graduates of this master's degree should acquire skills that help them solve real problems in African health systems, especially for the benefit of the patient. Hence, the curriculum ought to be aligned with the sustainable development goal of universal health coverage.

The skills acquired through the MPHI must meet the needs of the labour market. It is key to dynamically adapt to current developments in digital health in the public and private health sectors. It is important to capitalize on the existing programmes in terms of content and teaching capacity in digital health training rather than introduce a new competing programme that may weaken already successful similar programmes. Developing and accrediting a new programme is complex and time consuming. It is better to integrate the targeted curriculum into existing public health programmes. (Please refer to Wright et al. (2022) for an insight into the differences in these African countries, as most public health data is collected by nurses.)

Through follow-up meetings after the 2020 Digital Health colloquium, a consensus emerged on the development of a master's in public health informatics in the form of a specialized 2-year programme in public health (120 credits). The first year (60 credits) will offer a common core of public health courses and the second year (60 credits) will focus on specialized courses in digital health. These specialized courses may be offered as a compulsory package supplemented by elective courses. The content of the master programme will be harmonized through the collaborative work of the participating universities and accreditation of the programme will be sought at each university. Admission requirements for the master's degree will be those which are already applicable in the schools of public health. Access to the master's degree should be wide and not limited to the health or IT professions as many public health students already come from other fields.

Most colloquium participants have expressed a commitment to continue the work started and agreed that priority should be given to developing the list of skills and competencies for the master's degree. This list is expected to be finalized in late 2021. The content of the curriculum will be derived from this list, considering the resulting teaching capacity needs. A working group, in which the participating institutions are represented, has been established for this purpose. At the time of writing, the first concrete academic MPHI programmes are scheduled to start in 2022 at the Digital Health Campus of DRC (Schools of Public Health of Kinshasa, Lubumbashi and Bukavu), the National Public Health Institute of Burundi and the University of Conakry (UGANC) in Guinea.

Conclusion

The chapter highlights the need for tools that resonate with thinking in Africa. The three models demonstrate the strength of cooperation between African nations that share a common purpose of improving health and healthcare to all African people whilst situating that healthcare within the unique contexts that compose Africa and her people. It also shows the willingness of the African nations to be guided by international (IMIA) endorsed, health informatics curriculum standards. All with the goal of building quality health informatics programmes that enable graduates to cross country borders with their academic qualifications knowing that their academic achievements will be acknowledged by other African countries. This work is ongoing and is an example to other continents on how collaboration, commitment and determination can improve the healthcare of populations through the education of its healthcare staff in biomedical informatics. The pan-African region of IMIA, Health Informatics in Africa (HELINA), has supported and encouraged academics to develop meaningful education that is transferable within African countries. The HELINA Education Working Group has supported academic discourse on the development of health informatics and in partnership with the University of Vanderbilt has developed 'HELINA eLearn,' a Moodle- and Zoom-based website (Tchuitcheu et al., 2020). HELINA eLearn has many innovative features including automatic translations to French, English and Portuguese, and repositories of literature and the ability to support formal education programmes with its management functions.

References

East African Community. (2017). *Jointcommuniqué: 18th ordinary summit of heads of state of the East African Community* [online]. Available at: https://www.eac.int/communique/847-jointcommuniqué-18th-ordinary-summit-of-heads-of-state-of-the-east-african-community (Accessed 29 May 2021).

East African Community. (2019). *The common higher education area. Content of higher education (CHEA) of the East African community* [online]. Available at: https://wenr.wes.org/2018/12/common-higher-education-area-chea-of-the-east-african-community (Accessed 29 May 2021).

IMIA. (2013). *IMIA endorsed documents* [online]. Available at: https://imia-medinfo.org/wp/imia-endorsed-documents/ (Accessed 27 August 2021).

Kouematchoua Tchuitcheu, G. B., Oluoch, T., Wanyee, S., da-Costa Vroom, F. B., Nguefack-Tsague, G., Were, M., Verbeke, F., & Wright, G. (2020). Pan African Health Informatics Association (HELINA). *Yearbook of Medical Informatics*, 29(1), pp.291–292. https://doi.org/10.1055/s-0040-1701967

Lorenzi, N. M. (2002). *Scientific content map* [online]. Available at: https://imia-medinfo.org/wp/wp-content/uploads/2017/12/Scientific-Map8-September-2001.pdf (Accessed 10 September 2021).

Mantas, J., Ammenwerth, E., Demiris, G., Hasman, A., Haux, R., Hersh, W., Hovenga, E., Lun, K. C., Marin, H., Martin-Sanchez, F., & Wright, G. (2010). Recommendations of the international medical informatics association (IMIA) on education in biomedical and health informatics-1st revision. *Methods of Information in Medicine*, 49, pp.105–120.

Murray, P. J. (2008). The IMIA strategic plan: Towards IMIA 2015. *Yearbook of Medical Informatics*, pp. 7–15.

Murray, P. J., Wright, G., & Lorenzi, N. M. (2007). Developing the knowledge base for health informatics: From the Otley Think-Tank to the IMIA strategic plan. In Medinfo 2007: Proceedings of the 12th World Congress on Health (Medical) Informatics; Building Sustainable Health Systems, August, Brisbane, Australia, 2263.

Quartz. (2018). *French speaking*. Quartz Africa [online]. Available at: https://qz.com/africa/1428637/french-is-worlds-fifth-spoken-language-thanks-to-africans (Accessed 10 September 2021).

Trines, S. (2018). Bologna-type harmonization of higher education in the East African community: The East African community common higher education area [online]. Available at: https://web.archive.org/web/20200218140805/http://iucea.org:80/eahea1/harmonization-higher-education-east-african-community/ (Accessed 29 May 2021).

Verbeke, F., Wright, G., & Nyssén, M. (2016). A competence based MSc in health informatics for Rwanda. In Proceedings of the International Conference on eHealth, EH 2016: Part of the Multi Conference on Computer Science and Information Systems, July, Madeira, Portugal, 2016.

Were, M. C., Gong, W., Balirwa, P., Balugaba, B. E., Yeung, A., Pierce, L., Ingles, D., Kim, Y., Lee, H. J., & Shepherd, B. E. (2021). Comparative analysis of competency coverage within accredited master's in health informatics programs in the East African Region. *JAMIA*, 28(9), pp.1843–1848. https://doi.org/10.1093/jamia/ocab075

Were, M. C., Gong, W., Balirwa, P., Balugaba, B. E., Yeung, A., Pierce, L., Ingles, D., Kim, Y., & Shepherd, B. E. (2020). Coverage of IMIA-recommended competencies by masters in health informatics degree programs in East Africa. *International Journal of Medical Informatics*, 143, p.104265. https://doi.org/10.1016/j.ijmedinf.2020.104265.

WHO. (2021). *Africa* [online]. Available at: https://www.afro.who.int/countries (Accessed 27 August 2021).

Wright, G. (2011). The development of the IMIA knowledge base. *SA Journal of Information Management*, 13(1), pp.1–5.

Wright, G., Betts, H. J., Kabuya, C., & Adams, H. (2022). South Africa's healthcare systems, technology and nursing. In: C. W. Delaney, C. A. Weaver, J. Sensmeier, L. Pruinelli, & P. Weber, eds., *Nursing and Informatics for the 21st Century— Embracing a Digital World, 3rd Edition—Book 1: Realizing Digital Health—Bold Challenges and Opportunities for Nursing*. Boca Raton, FL: CRC Press, pp. 169–186.

Wright, G., Verbeke, F., Nyssen, M., & Betts, H. (2015). Health informatics: Developing a masters programme in Rwanda based on the IMIA educational recommendations and the IMIA knowledge base. *Studies in Health Technology and Informatics*, 216, pp.525–528.

Chapter 11

Simulation-Based Learning from across the Globe

Juan Antonio Muro Sans, Laura Gonzalez and Virginia La Rosa-Salas

Contents

Simulation-Based Learning	184
Simulation in Healthcare	184
Simulation in Nursing	185
Types of Simulation	186
Simulation Based on Needs Assessments	186
Simulation Based on Learning Objectives	187
Simulation Based on the KSA Model	188
Simulation Based on Non-technical Skills	189
Preparing a Simulation Session in Nursing	190
Pre-briefing/Learner Preparation	190
Briefing	191
Simulation Session/Activity	192
Debriefing	193
Evaluation	194
The Future of Simulation for Nursing	195
References	196

DOI: 10.4324/9781003281009-11

Simulation-Based Learning

Education of healthcare professionals has been evolving throughout the last few decades. Safety concerns related to healthcare practice and the use of patients by students to learn new skills led to the development of new teaching methodologies that would reduce risks to patients and increase patients' safety from working healthcare professionals. One of these new teaching methodologies is known as simulation-based learning (SBL).

SBL is a pedagogical technique that aims at replacing and/or amplifying real experiences in a fully interactive manner. Based on the experiential learning model described by Kolb (1984), this method allows learners to practice skills and attitudes, through previously designed and prepared sessions by educators, in a safe environment for both the patient and the learner. Then, the student may review those experiences through guided reflection and finally, allowing for repetition of the same, so that it can finally be applied in the real clinical environment. These sessions are usually guided by facilitators (International Nursing Association for Clinical Simulation and Learning (INACSL), 2016), who require a set of specific education and skills necessary to ensure that learners achieve their learning objectives.

Learning through simulation can be done through different methods, using partial task trainers to practice technical skills, or using high-fidelity mannequins to engage immersive in previously prepared scenarios. Finally, the use of computer-based programs also allows students to develop skills such as clinical reasoning. All these different methods have in common that in order to be effective for a transformational learning they need to be guided by a facilitator who is competent in using this pedagogical method. It has been found that guided reflective sessions through debriefing after the simulation experiences enhance the achievement of the learning objectives in order to become safer healthcare professionals (Kardong-Edgren et al., 2011; O'Donnell et al., 2011; Pinar, 2015; Teteris et al., 2012).

Simulation in Healthcare

Fatalities secondary to healthcare professional errors, together with the increased dilemma of having students practice skills on patients, have led to the introduction of SBL (Gaba, 2004; Galloway, 2009). Additionally, there is less time in clinical practice to devote to learners, the setting in which learning occurs today is far broader and more complex (Famiglio et al., 2013).

Additionally, there is evidence about more efficient ways of learning (Gomez Fleitas et al., 2011) that have all led to a change in instructional/teaching methods among healthcare professions.

Within the healthcare professional education community, there is an understanding that SBL's needs to be based on experience in order to acquire knowledge, skills and attitudes. Adult experiential learning theories attributed to Dewey (1916) and Kolb (1984) offer that learning is a lifelong process and involves feeling, perceiving, thinking and behaving. In this way, simulation is a learning method where participants need to be actively involved in an activity and where they have the opportunity to play a role and experience not only concrete events in a cognitive fashion but also transactional events in an emotional fashion. SBL has proven to assist learners in accomplishing learning objectives that are directly linked to their clinical practice (Steadman et al., 2006).

Simulation in Nursing

Learning to practice basic skills in nursing has been practiced now for a long time, either using partial task trainers or the use of full-body mannequins. The development of new knowledge, skills, attitudes, duties and responsibilities within nursing worldwide has required an evolution of these simulation methods that have taken a step forward with regard to different types of simulation practices and different types of resources utilized.

Different learning theories and standards have been developed in order to ensure safe and effective educational practices in nursing education when using simulation as a learning methodology. Some of these learning theories are linked to different debriefing models used in nursing education, such as Debriefing for Meaningful Learning© (Dreifuerst, 2010), PEARLS (Promoting Excellence and Reflective Learning in Simulation; Eppich et al., 2015), Debriefing with good judgment (Rudolph et al., 2006) and some other models. Likewise, the INACSL developed simulation standards for simulation education of healthcare professionals, standards that include a guide on how to prepare a simulation session, how to debrief the session, what are the duties and responsibilities of the facilitator, etc. (INACSL, 2016).

Overall, nowadays, SBL forms part of current nursing education programs at both undergraduate and postgraduate levels, sometimes led by governmental regulations such as the Nursing and Midwifery Council in the United Kingdom (2018) and the WHO (2018).

Types of Simulation

It is important to note that simulation is a teaching technique that is based on sound educational pedagogy. The decision to use simulation to achieve certain outcomes is based on a needs assessment, specific learning objectives and KSA (knowledge, skills and attitudes). Simulation is also a viable technique to teach non-technical skills (NTS). In this chapter, we will explore each concept as it relates to simulation.

Simulation Based on Needs Assessments

Integral to any simulation program is a robust needs assessment program. In other words, you do not know what you need until you query your stakeholders. Your stakeholders can be your learners, faculty, staff development team or the community at large. Utilizing a formal assessment garners significant data that, in turn, can be the basis of any simulation program. The first step to developing a simulation-training program should be problem identification and general needs assessment to ensure that the outcomes are aligned with learner needs. Problem identification and general needs assessment are defined as identifying and characterizing the healthcare problem that a curriculum will address. Exploring the gap between how the problem is currently being addressed and how it should ideally be addressed constitutes the general needs assessment (Nayahangan et al., 2018). The needs assessment may include analysis of underlying causes for concern (root cause analysis), organizational analysis such as SWOT (strengths, weaknesses, opportunities, threats), outcome data and professional credentialing bodies (INACSL, 2016). Simulation-based experiences (SBEs) are born out of needs assessment. At a higher-level, emergent conditions, such as a pandemic, may reveal healthcare providers' need for immediate training for a given condition.

In this instance, needs assessment, planning and implementation may run parallel and may change rapidly as the circumstances unfold (Contreras et al., 2021). One example of a needs assessment is focus groups with stakeholders using open-ended questions. Questions can range from perceived training gaps and skills acquisition. Analyzing the data can lead to identification of themes that emerge from the focus groups (Wehbi et al., 2018). Gonzalez and Allred (2017) conducted focus groups with community professional nurse development staff to identify new graduate shortcomings. Using the data, concepts were identified, which in turn were used to develop SBE.

From the focus groups, it was evident that new graduates had no experience with protocols (diabetic management, chest pain). This information led to the development of senior nursing student SBE with a learning outcome of greater confidence using established protocols for care (Gonzalez & Allred, 2017). Another popular approach to needs assessment is the Delphi process. The Delphi process relies on a panel of experts to gather information and achieve consensus. This typically requires multiple iterations (Nayahangan et al., 2018). The Society for Simulation in Healthcare (SSH Accreditation, n.d.) Teaching-Education Standards and Criteria for accreditation requires that all simulation programs implement a needs assessment program to identify simulation activities. Likewise, the Standards of Best Practice (INACSL, 2016) criterion 1 requires a needs assessment to provide the foundational evidence of the need for a well-designed simulation experience (p. S6). Lack of an unstructured approach can be costly and result in a misalignment of learner outcomes and curriculum development.

Simulation Based on Learning Objectives

After a comprehensive needs assessment, the next step is the development of objectives. One of the core skills of the nurse educator is the ability to write SMART (Specific, Measurable, Achievable, Realistic and Time) objectives (Doran, 1981). Once these objectives are developed, the nurse educator identifies the best strategy, technique, activity or content that will help meet the learning outcomes for the objectives. SBEs are frequently used to meet objectives. Simulation is but one component of the nursing curriculum and should be used to complement the didactic and clinical space. Simulation is not a panacea. The nurse educator needs to consider if the outcomes identified could be better elicited using simulation compared to other strategies (Armijo- Rivera, 2015). The inclusion of an SBE is dependent on the resources and qualified facilitators available. According to the Standards of Best Practice: simulation design, it is at this time the identification of the format of the simulation based on the purpose, theory and modality for the simulation (INACSL, 2016). To take it one step further, it also needs to consider the micro-objectives that can be accomplished with the SBE.

Emerging evidence suggests effectively implemented simulation experiences results in comparable outcomes to those achieved in the clinical setting (Bowen-Withington et al., 2020). The National League for Nursing (NLN) Jeffries Simulation Framework (Jeffries, 2016) was developed to explain for the user or facilitator how the six core elements: context, background, design, educational practices, simulation experience, and outcomes work in tandem to create a meaningful experience for the learner.

By developing SMART objectives, the learner can better meet and measure them. There are numerous simulation modalities or typologies from low technology to high technology, previously referred to as low fidelity or high fidelity, respectively. If the learner's outcome is to understand the psychomotor skills of wound care, a simple task trainer may meet the need. Likewise, if the objective is to auscultate and identify heart sounds, a cardiac task trainer may be the best piece of equipment. It is not necessary to use a high-fidelity mannequin to practice intravenous insertion. Most nurse educators are comfortable with developing objectives in general. However, by using the NLN Jeffries Simulation Framework (Jeffries, 2016) the educator can better align the objectives using a simulation context. To achieve successful learning outcomes, the quality of the learning experience is important and closely associated with the competence of the educator (Karacay & Kaya, 2020).

Regardless of the learning outcomes, nursing educators need specific training in simulation education (Boese et al., 2015). High-fidelity simulation is a popular strategy; however, it is resource-intensive and costly. Sherwood & Francis (2018) found that high-fidelity mannequins exhibited only modest advantages when testing closely followed training. Massoth et al. (2019) found high-fidelity simulation to be an adverse learning tool when compared to low-fidelity simulation and resulted in learner overconfidence. This suggests that higher-end expensive simulators may not confer an added advantage in certain instances. The role simulator fidelity plays on learning outcomes is still under investigation. In fact, there is little evidence that simulators classified as low and high are better assessment and training instruments. Educators must identify what features of a simulator are critical to their learning objectives (Schoenherr et al., 2017). Lastly, a high-fidelity task trainer may seem attractive, however, with a lens to cognitive load theory; it may hinder the early learning process (Gonzalez & Bourgault, 2018). Once the objectives have been developed, it is time to ascribe what KSAs the learner will need to achieve to be successful and the best way to meet them.

Simulation Based on the KSA Model

Learning outcomes focus on the essential, transferable learning that can be observed and assessed in any course or program. The KSA framework is very useful for thinking about and describing learning. Not all disciplines map well to the KSA framework. Nursing education happens to be well suited for this framework because nursing education is reliant on competency assessment. KSA is an acronym for the *Knowledge* you want your learners to acquire. The *Skills* the learner should be able to perform. This is likened to psychomotor skill attainment, i.e., insertion of a Foley catheter and the *Attitudes* or the values and motivation you want to impress upon your student to appreciate. Simulation allows the facilitator to intentionally create opportunities for the learner to understand a particular disorder such as congestive heart failure and require the learner to make clinical decisions such as whether to give a particular medication or may be required to insert a Foley catheter. This is an opportunity to demonstrate skill mastery, and lastly, the debrief is an opportunity to help the learner reflect on their performance, placing a value upon it. Rubrics have been developed with KSA in mind. There are numerous rubrics available for use in simulation, such as the Lasater Clinical Judgment Rubric (LCJR) (Lasater, 2007) and Creighton Simulation Evaluation Instrument (C-SEI) (Todd et al., 2008). Likewise, a practical way to assess KSA is using a dichotomous rubric (yes/no). This has fewer implications for inter-rater reliability.

Simulation Based on Non-technical Skills

Simulation has garnered attention for training NTS, such as communication and teamwork. NTS have been defined as cognitive, social and personal resource skills that complement technical skills and contribute to safe and efficient task performance (Flin et al., 2017). These skills are necessary to prevent injury and harm during healthcare delivery (Garden et al., 2015). Pires et al. (2017) found that high-fidelity simulation could aid in the acquisition of non-technical skills. However, Garden et al. (2015) cautioned educators not to infuse both technical skills and non-technical skills in each simulation as this can result in confusion for the learners during the debrief. Oftentimes, the opportunity to hone these skills is inherent in the quality of the debrief. Learners can reflect on their performance, perhaps view the experience and identify areas for improvement. Recent technological advances in simulation have resulted in virtual platforms with conversation engines™ (Shadowhealth, n.d.) that allows the learner to engage in meaningful and authentic encounters. Peddle et al. (2019) found that interactions with virtual patients aided in the acquisition of NTS. Virtual patients are interactive computer-generated agents that can dialogue with the learner because of sophisticated algorithms and natural language recognition. Virtual simulations were found to positively impact student learning outcomes, specifically critical thinking and self-confidence (Foronda et al., 2020; Verkuyl et al., 2017).

Preparing a Simulation Session in Nursing

In health science education, there are myriad opinions on the best way to prepare an SBE to ensure learners meet their learning objectives. In light of this, the Standards of Best Practice℠ (INACSL, 2016) were developed. This work is the first to offer recommendations based on current evidence and best practice to use simulation as an effective educational tool. Subsequently, the Association for Simulated Practice in Healthcare (ASPiH, 2016) standardized how simulation education with simulated patients should be practiced within healthcare education (Sando et al., 2011). Both associations emphasize the role of debriefing as an essential component of the simulation methodology (Mcdermott, 2017).

As stated by the above-mentioned standards and current best practices, in order to prepare a simulation-based learning experience, there are a series of events that need to take place, from the preparation of the learner for the simulation event, throughout the facilitation and evaluation of the same at the end. Below, all the necessary steps to prepare and facilitate a simulation session will be described in detail.

Even though in the literature both pre-briefing and briefing are used interchangeably, for temporality purposes, a differentiation has been made between pre-briefing (preparatory phase before the simulation-based learning experience) and briefing (the preparatory phase right before the simulation-based learning experience).

Pre-briefing/Learner Preparation

The main goal of the pre-briefing is to get the learner ready for clinical practice through simulation activities (Page-Cutrara et al., 2017). Pre-briefing can be performed months or weeks before the simulation activity. This preparation will start with the acquisition of knowledge. This step usually happens either in the classroom or online. There needs to be a link between the learning objectives to be acquired with the new knowledge and the learning objectives to be acquired during the simulation experience. This acquired knowledge needs to be learned before attending the simulation experience.

Some facilitators will introduce an exam before the learning experience in order to ensure the preparedness of learners for the simulation experience. The objective is that during the simulation activity, learners will be able to put into practice their newly acquired knowledge by giving its meaning in a safe manner.

Another important part of preparing the learners is the introduction to the environment and technology that will be used during the simulation experience. Depending on the time available the day of the simulation experience, this introduction could be done the same day. This is done through an orientation to the simulated clinical scenario, including an introduction to the medical equipment as well as the simulation equipment, so that neither of them becomes an obstacle in the acquisition of the learning objectives (McDermott, 2016).

It is important that learners and facilitators share the same mental model, as part of this, and before the simulation experience. Bibliography, preparatory questions for reflection and exercises might be shared in order to ensure that all discuss the same information during the simulation experience.

A document can be produced with information for the learner with the purpose of the simulation experience, the learning objectives to be achieved, supporting bibliography and/or evidence that will be treated in the simulation experience, links to videos, case studies, pre-test exercises, preparatory questions for reflective exercises, some information about the scenarios that will be facilitated and finally the agenda of the day. This document will support learners in being ready for the day of the simulation experience. This will be followed by the on-site and same-day briefing.

Briefing

Briefing is the phase used in simulation education with the goal of decreasing student anxiety, positively learner's performance, improve confidence, engage learners and consequently assure psychological safety of all the involved (McDermott, 2016). All will impact a more fruitful and efficient debriefing session. Through the use of a written document that is part of the SBL experience document, it can be ensured all the above goals are achieved in a consistent manner.

A time slot needs to be included in the agenda to facilitate the briefing session. This will depend on the number of students, total time allocated for the simulation experience, learner's previous experience with simulation, and the information and/or activities shared during the pre-briefing sessions. Ideally, these briefing sessions should be facilitated in the room used for the debriefing sessions.

With the main goal in mind of preparing the learner for the simulation experience, briefing should include the following, but not be limited to: (1) welcome and presentations of all the involved, (2) purpose of the simulation experience, (3) learning objectives, (4) roles and (5) responsibilities of all the involved (both learners and facilitators), (6) identification of emotional status from learners and defusing if necessary, (7) detailed agenda of the day (this should include starting time, time allocated for briefing, scenario, debriefing and evaluation, if applicable), (8) ground rules related to expected behaviors throughout the whole activity, (9) transmission of basic data for the development of the case, (10) make reference to the work done in the simulation room versus the work done in real clinical practice, (11) evaluation documentation, (12) familiarization with environment, (13) evaluation questionnaires, and (14) certificates (if applicable) (Tyerman et al., 2016). Once the briefing has been completed, we move onto the simulation experience activity.

Simulation Session/Activity

Simulation session is an activity where the goal is to demonstrate knowledge, skills and attitudes (competencies) through an immersive simulation with the use of high-fidelity mannequins or standardized patients or a hybrid solution, or it could be an activity where the learning objective is purely technical, and it is achieved through a procedural simulation activity.

The preparation of the simulation experience will require a clearly defined broad and specific learning objectives, and it is through these, that the simulation activity will be designed (INACSL, 2016). The set of objectives will define both, the modality of simulation best suited to achieve the above and the resources needed in order to facilitate the activity.

When the learning objectives are aiming at knowledge and skills, we are looking at a procedural simulation. This will require a preparation of the learner by the use of demonstration videos or a return demonstration from the facilitator. We will need to decide which one is the best-suited equipment to be used in order for learners to be able to learn, practice and demonstrate mastery with this practice. Here we have different levels of fidelity of simulators that might impact differently on learners' achievements of learning objectives.

When the learning objectives are aiming at knowledge, skills and attitudes, this requires a more thorough preparation as we need to prepare a scenario that should resemble as much as possible in real life. The type of resources to be used needs to be decided based on the learning objectives to be achieved. Sometimes a high-fidelity simulator will be the preferred method, and others, it will be a standardized patient.

As part of the simulation, different levels of fidelity need to be taken into account to ensure learners feel safe and be able to achieve all the set learning objectives in the simulation activity. The different levels of fidelity include the physical (or environmental) aspect, where we need to ensure that the simulation scenario resembles physically the real context; this includes, but is not limited to, the chosen form of patient, environment and equipment. Another aspect will be the conceptual fidelity (Tun et al., 2015), where we ensure that all elements of the scenario will make sense to the learners, this means that the actions witnessed and physiological changes are real and make sense. It is important that this aspect is validated by a subject matter expert (Dieckmann et al., 2007). Finally, psychological fidelity will mimic all those distractions that exist in real environments, such as the presence of family members, noises and time pressure (Kozlowski et al., 2004).

All simulation experiences should be followed by a debriefing session in order to reflect on all the knowledge, skills and attitudes embedded within the simulation experience to ensure learning has happened and that participants can take away what they have learned to the real clinical setting (Galloway, 2009).

Debriefing

Debriefing is the 'formal, collaborative, reflective process within the simulation learning activity. It is an activity that follows a simulation experience and is led by a facilitator' (Lopreiato et al., 2016, p. S41). A facilitator is defined as an individual who is involved in the implementation and/or delivery of the simulation activities, particularly having an important role as a debriefer (Lopreiato et al., 2020). It is said to be the best method to connect theory and practice (Jeffries, 2010). For debriefing to be effective, a series of conditions must be met; some of these conditions are related to the *facilitator's skills* (Krogh et al., 2016), others are related to *elements of the debriefing process* (Ahmed et al., 2012; Arora et al., 2012; Association for Simulated Practice in Healthcare, 2016; Cheng et al., 2017; Gururaja et al., 2008; Hall &

Tori, 2017; INACSL, 2016; Levett-Jones & Lapkin, 2014) and some to *cultural differences* (Chung et al., 2013; Ulmer et al., 2018).

The main objective of the debriefing session is to gather all the actions from the simulation experience, analyze these through open-ended questions to assure reflection and finally summarize through taking home key messages.

There are different styles to practice debriefing, and there is no consensus in the literature about which one is the best method of debriefing. Due to the many variables within healthcare education, such as learner's type, learner's performance, facilitator skills, learning objectives, level of a stake of the simulation activity and learner's emotional status, it is expected from the facilitators to guide these sessions in an adaptive manner. This means that facilitators must know different types of debriefing, must have pedagogical skills to identify both the educational level and emotional status of the learner's group, and then decide on a specific type of debriefing method or a combination of some.

Therefore, the skills of the facilitator are crucial to ensure that learning happens in a safe environment for both the learners and facilitators. These skills can be developed through educational courses, through coaching, through co-debriefing and reflective sessions with others about their own practices.

As part of continuing improvement, an evaluation of the whole simulation experience needs to be performed.

Evaluation

There are two aspects to look at with regard to evaluation. The first one is the evaluation tool for the facilitators and learners to guide their reflective sessions through debriefing, and the second one is the evaluation of the simulation experience from different perspectives that will allow continuous improvement of the learning experiences of the participants.

As part of the preparation of the simulation experience, the evaluation method of the same needs to be clearly identified beforehand—as a formative assessment, summative assessment or high-stake assessment. The different methods of assessment will be used with varied aims and objectives, such as the Lasater Clinical Judgment Rubric (Ashcraft et al., 2013).

With regard to the continuous improvement process, an evaluation from all the involved needs to be performed. This evaluation tool will need to look at both the operational and pedagogical aspects of the simulation experience. The evaluation method is not standardized, and the interreliability comes into question when being used. The goal is to quantify the impact on learners' achievement of learning objectives by looking at an increased level of knowledge and/or understanding, skill performance, learner satisfaction, development of critical thinking abilities and increased self-confidence (Jeffries, 2007, p. 23).

In order to assess learner's achievement, the following pedagogical aspects of the simulation experience need to be looked at: pre-briefing content resources appropriateness and usefulness (bibliography, videos, simulation experience's pre-test, open-ended questions for reflection), evaluation/assessment method and tool, involvement of all participants in the debriefing session, production of a reflective session during debriefing, safety feeling during the whole simulation experience, congruence of a scenario for the achievement of learning objectives set, appropriate time allocated for the simulation experience and its specific activities, facilitator's preparedness, simulation scenario flow, clarity of roles and responsibilities, learner's satisfaction with the chosen pedagogical method, and finally, free text space to ensure feedback given.

With regard to the operational aspects, audiovisual resources used, resources supporting the simulation experience, typology of the patient, classroom layout, clinical environment room, debriefing resources, debriefing room, structural confidentiality assurance, medical and simulation equipment used, refreshments and computing software need to be considered.

Each institution and simulation modality will require a different type of evaluation tool and content, this should be defined based on objectives, resources and teaching methodology, and most importantly, reliability and validity should be taken into account (Considine et al., 2005; Navas-Ferrer et al., 2017).

The Future of Simulation for Nursing

Within the last year, nursing faculty realized they were too reliant on face-to-face, traditional mannequin-based simulation. The need to pivot to remote simulation was a challenge. However, it became evident there were many commercially available products that allowed for continued learning and were suitable clinical replacements. The pandemic has shown a spotlight on digital interactive resources and virtual solutions that could be deployed in a remote asynchronous environment. Products such as Sentinel U (Sentinel U, n.d.), vSim (Wolters Kluwer, n.d.) and (ATI) (Assessment Technologies

Institute) simulation proved to be effective solutions that kept the learner engaged. There is evidence to support the use of virtual solutions, but adoption has been slow (Verkuyl, 2017). Now, these solutions are getting a second look and considered viable options. Moving forward, we may see the inclusion of virtual simulations as an adjunct to traditional simulation.

References

Ahmed, M., Sevdalis, N., Paige, J., Paragi-Gururaja, R., Nestel, D., & Arora, S. (2012). Identifying best practice guidelines for debriefing in surgery: A tri-continental study. *American Journal of Surgery*, 203(4), pp.523–529.

Armijo, S. (2015). Consider this: How to integrate simulation into prelicensure curriculum. In J. C. Palaganas, J. C. Maxworthy, C. A. Epps, & M. E. Mancini, eds., *Defining excellence in simulation programs*. New York: Lippincott Williams & Wilkins, pp.492–493.

Arora, S., Ahmed, M., Paige, J., Nestel, D., Runnacles, J., Hull, L., & Sevdalis, N. (2012). Objective structured assessment of debriefing: Bringing science to the art of debriefing in surgery. *Annals of Surgery*, 256(6), pp.982–988.

Ashcraft, A., Opton, L., Bridges, R., Caballero, S., Veesart, A., & Weaver, C. (2013). Simulation evaluation using a modified Lasater clinical judgment rubric. *Nursing Education Perspectives*, 34(2), pp.122–126.

Association for Simulated Practice in Healthcare. (2016). *2016 consultation report* [online]. Available at: http://aspih.org.uk/wp-content/uploads/2017/07/aspih-standards-framework-consultation-report.pdf (Accessed 28 December 2021).

ATI Simulation. (n.d.) [online]. Available at: https://www.atitesting.com/educator/solutions/consulting/areas/simulation (Accessed 23 July 2021).

Boese, T., Cato, M., Gonzalez, L., Jones, A., Kennedy, K., Reese, C., Decker, S., Franklin, A. E., Gloe, D., Lioce, L., Meakim, C., Sando, C. R., & Borum, J. C. (2015). Standards of best practice: Simulation standard V: Facilitator. *Clinical Simulation in Nursing*, 9(6), pp.S22–S25.

Bowen-Withington, J., Zambas, S., Macdiarmid, R., Cook, C., & Neville, S. (2020). Integration of high-fidelity simulation into undergraduate nursing education in Aotearoa New Zealand and Australia: An integrative literature review. *Nursing Praxis in Aotearoa New Zealand*, 36(3), pp.37–50. https://doi.org/10.36951/27034542.2020.013

Cheng, A., Grant, V., Huffman, J., Burgess, G., Szyld, D., Robinson, T., & Eppich, W. (2017). Coaching the debriefer. *Simulation in Healthcare*, 12(5), pp.319–325.

Chung, H. S., Dieckmann, P., & Issenberg, S. B. (2013). It is time to consider cultural differences in debriefing. *Simulation in Healthcare*, 8(3), pp.166–170.

Considine, J., Botti, M., & Thomas, S. (2005). Design, format, validity and reliability of multiple choice questions for use in nursing research and education. *Collegian*, 12(1), pp.19–24. https://doi.org/10.1016/s1322-7696(08)60478-3

Contreras, M., Curran, E., Ross, M., Moran, P., Sheehan, A., Brennan, A. M., Cosgrave, D., McElwain, J., Lavelle, C., & Lynch, B. (2021). Rapid development of interprofessional in situ simulation-based training in response to the COVID-19 outbreak in a tertiary-level hospital in Ireland: Initial response and lessons for future disaster preparation. *BMJ Simulation & Technology Enhanced Learning*, 7(3), pp.159–162.

Dewey, J. (1916). *Democracy and education: An introduction to the philosophy of education.* New York: The Free Press, p.223.

Dieckmann, P., Gaba, D., & Rall, D. (2007). Deepening the theoretical foundations of patient simulation as social practice. *Simulation in Healthcare*, 2(3), pp.183–193.

Dreifuerst, K. T. (2010). *Debriefing for meaningful learning: Fostering development of clinical reasoning through simulation.* Indiana University. ProQuest Dissertations and Theses, 212 [online]. Available at: https://scholarworks.iupui.edu/bitstream/handle/1805/2459/KTD%20%20Final%20Dissertation.pdf?sequence=1 (Accessed 8 September 2021).

Doran, G. T. (1981). There's a SMART way to write management's goals and objectives. *Management Review*, 70(11), pp.35–36.

Eppich, W., & Cheng, A. (2015). Promoting excellence and reflective learning in simulation (PEARLS): Development and rationale for a blended approach to healthcare simulation debriefing. *Simulation in Healthcare*, 10(2), pp.106–115.

Famiglio, L. M., Thompson, M. A., & Kupas, D. F. (2013). Considering the clinical context of medical education. *Academic Medicine*, 88(9), pp.1202–1205.

Flin, R., & O'Connor, P. (2017). *Safety at the sharp end: A guide to non-technical skills.* Boca Raton, FL: CRC Press, p.330.

Foronda, C. L., et al. (2020). Virtual simulation in nursing education: A systematic review spanning 1996–2018. *Simulation in Healthcare*, 15, pp.46–54.

Gaba, D. (2004). The future of simulation in health care. *Quality & Safety in Health Care*, 13, pp.2–10.

Galloway, S. (2009). Simulation techniques to bridge the gap between novice and competent healthcare professionals. *Online Journal of Issues in Nursing*, 14(2), pp.1–9.

Galloway, S. J. (2009). Simulation techniques to bridge the gap between novice and competent healthcare professionals. *The Online Journal of Issues in Nursing*, 14(3), Manuscript 3. http://doi.org/10.3912/OJIN.Vol14No02Man03

Garden, A. L., et al. (2015). Debriefing after simulation-based non-technical skill training in healthcare: A systematic review of effective practice. *Anaesthesia and Intensive Care*, 43(3), pp.300–308.

Gómez Fleitas, M., & Manuel Palazuelos, J. C. (2011). La simulación clínica en la formación quirúrgica en el siglo XXI. *Cirugía Española*, 89(3), pp.133–135.

Gonzalez, L., & Allred, K. (2017). A collaborative approach to simulation development. *BMJ Simulation and Technology Enhanced Learning*, 3, pp.159–162.

González, L., Bourgault, A. M., & Aguirre, L. (2018). Varying levels of fidelity on psychomotor skill attainment: A CORTRAK product assessment. *BMJ Simulation & Technology Enhanced Learning*, 4, pp.141–145.

Gururaja, R. P., Yang, T., Paige, J. T., & Chauvin, S. W. (2008). Examining the effectiveness of debriefing at the point of care in simulation-based operating room team training. In *Advances in patient safety: New directions and alternative approaches, 3: Performance and tools*, pp.1–18 [online]. Available at: http://www.ncbi.nlm.nih.gov/pubmed/21249934 (Accessed July 23 2021).

Hall, K., & Tori, K. (2017). Best practice recommendations for debriefing in simulation-based education for Australian undergraduate nursing students: An integrative review. *Clinical Simulation in Nursing*, 13(1), pp.39–50.

INACSL Standards Committee. (2016). INACSL standards of best practice: Simulation SM simulation design. *Clinical Simulation in Nursing*, 12(S), pp.S5–S12.

Jeffries, P. (2007). *Simulation in nursing education*. New York: National League for Nursing, p.23.

Jeffries, P. (2010). *The art of debriefing: How to conduct a guided reflection and its importance*. Presented at the National League of Nursing Conference, Las Vegas, NV.

Jeffries, P. (2016). *The NLN jeffries simulation theory*. Philadelphia, PA: Wolters Kluwer.

Karacay, P., & Kaya, H. (2020). Effects of a simulation education program on faculty members' and students' learning outcomes. *International Journal of Caring Sciences*, 13(1), pp.555–562.

Kardong-Edgren, S., Gaba, D., Dieckmann, P., & Cook, D. A. (2011). Reporting inquiry in simulation. *Simulation in Healthcare*, 6(7 SUPPL.), pp.63–66.

Kolb, D. (1984). *Experiential learning: Experience in the source of learning and development*. Englewood Cliffs, NJ: Prentice-Hall.

Kozlowski, S. J., & DeShon, R. P. (2004). A psychological fidelity approach to simulation-based training: Theory, research, and principles. In E. Salas, L. R. Elliott, S. G. Schflett, & M. D. Coovert, eds., *Scaled worlds: Development, validation, and applications*. Burlington, VT: Ashgate Publishing, pp.75–99.

Krogh, K., Bearman, M., & Nestel, D. (2016). "Thinking on your feet": A qualitative study of debriefing practice. *Advances in Simulation*, 1(1), pp.1–11.

Lasater, K. (2007). Clinical judgment using simulation to create an assessment rubric. *Journal of Nursing Education*, 46(11), pp.496–503.

Levett-Jones, T., & Lapkin, S. (2014). A systematic review of the effectiveness of simulation debriefing in health professional education. *Nurse Education Today*, 34(6), pp.e58–e63.

Lopreiato, J. O., Downing, D., Gammon, W., Lioce, L., Sittner, B., Slot, V., & Spain, A. E. (2016). *Healthcare simulation dictionary* [online]. Available at: https://www.hsdl.org/?view&did=797654 (Accessed 9 September 2021).

Lopreiato, J. O., Downing, D., Gammon, W., Lioce, L., Sittner, B., Slot, V., & Spain, A. E. (2020). *Healthcare simulation dictionary*, pp.1–50. [online]. Available at: https://www.ahrq.gov/sites/default/files/wysiwyg/patient-safety/resources/simulation/sim-dictionary-2nd.pdf (Accessed 9 September 2021).

Massoth, C., Röder, H., Ohlenburg, H., Hessler, M., Zarbock, A., Pöpping, D. M., & Wenk, M. (2019). High-fidelity is not superior to low-fidelity simulation but leads to overconfidence in medical students. *BMC Medical Education*, 19(1), pp.1–8.

McDermott, D. S. (2016). The prebriefing concept: A Delphi study of CHSE experts. *Clinical Simulation in Nursing*, 12(6), pp.219–227.

McDermott, M. (2017). Debriefing with reflection: Best practice for learning in simulation in pre-licensure nursing education. *Seton Hall University DNP Final Projects*, 20. [online] Available at: https://scholarship.shu.edu/final-projects/20 (Accessed 9 September 2021).

Navas-Ferrer, C., Urcola_Pardo, F., Subiron-Valera, A. B., & German-Bes, C. (2017). Validity and reliability of objective structured clinical evaluation in nursing. *Clinical Simulation in Nursing*, 13(11), pp.531–543.

Nayahangan, L. J., Stefanidis, D., Kern, D. E., & Konge, L. (2018). How to identify and prioritize procedures suitable for simulation-based training: Experiences from general needs assessments using a modified Delphi method and a needs assessment formula. *Medical Teacher*, 40(7), pp.676–683.

Nursing and Midwifery Council. (2018). [online]. Available at: https://www.nmc.org.uk/globalassets/sitedocuments/education-standards/programme-standards-nursing.pdf (Accessed 28 August 2021).

O'Donnell, J. M., Goode, J. S., Henker, R., Kelsey, S., Bircher, N. G., Peele, P., & Sutton-Tyrrell, K. (2011). Effect of a simulation educational intervention on knowledge, attitude, and patient transfer skills. *Simulation in Healthcare*, 6(2), pp.84–93.

Page-Cutrara, K., & Turk, M. (2017). Impact of prebriefing on competency performance, clinical judgment and experience in simulation: An experimental study. *Nurse Education Today*, 48, pp.78–83.

Peddle, M., Mckenna, L., Bearman, M., & Nestel, D. (2019). Development of non-technical skills through virtual patients for undergraduate nursing students: An exploratory study. *Nurse Education Today*, 73, pp.94–101.

Pinar, G. (2015). Simulation-enhanced interprofessional education in health care. *Creative Education*, 6(17), pp.1852–1859.

Pires, S., Monteiro, S., Pereira, A., Chaló, D., Melo, E., & Rodrigues, A. (2017). Non-technical skills assessment for prelicensure nursing students: An integrative review. *Nurse Education Today*, 58, pp.19–24.

Rudolph, J., Simon, R., Dufresne, R., & Raemer, D. (2006). There's no such thing as "nonjudgmental" debriefing: a theory and method for debriefing with good judgment. *Simulation in Healthcare*, 1(1), pp.49–55.

Sando, C., Faragher, J., Boese, T., & Decker, S. (2011). Simulation standards development: An idea inspires. *Clinical Simulation in Nursing*, 7, pp.e73–e74.

Schoenherr, J., & Hamstra, S. (2017). Beyond fidelity. *Simulation in Healthcare*, 12(2), pp.117–123.

Sentinel U®. (n.d.). [online]. Available at: https://www.sentinelu.com/ (Accessed 23 August 2021).

Shadow Health®. (n.d.). [online]. Available at: https://www.shadowhealth.com/ (Accessed 22 August 2021).

Sherwood, R. J., & Francis, G. (2018). The effect of mannequin fidelity on the achievement of learning outcomes for nursing, midwifery and allied healthcare practitioners: Systematic review and meta-analysis. *Nurse Education Today*, 69, pp.81–94.

Steadman, R. H., Coates, W. C., Ming Huang, Y., Matevosian, R., Larmon, B. R., McCullough, L., & Ariel, D. (2006). Simulation-based training is superior to problem-based learning for the acquisition of critical assessment and management skills. *Critical Care Medicine*, 34(1), pp.151–157.

Teteris, E., Fraser, K., Wright, B., & McLaughlin, K. (2012). Does training learners on simulators benefit real patients? *Advances in Health Sciences Education*, 17(1), pp.137–144.

Todd, M., Manz, J. A., Hawkins, K. S., Parsons, M. E., & Hercinger, M. (2008). The development of a quantitative evaluation tool for simulation in nursing education. *International Journal of Nurse Education and Scholarship*, 5(1), Article 41.

Tun, J. K., Alinier, G., Tang, J., & Kneebone, R. L. (2015). Redefining simulation fidelity for healthcare education. *Simulation & Gaming*, 46, pp.159–174.

Tyerman, J., Luctkar-flude, M., Graham, L., Coffey, S., & Olsen-lynch, E. (2016). Pre-simulation preparation and briefing practices for healthcare professionals and students: A systematic review protocol. *JBI Database of Systematic Reviews and Implementation Reports*, 14(8), pp.80–89.

Ulmer, F. F., Sharara-Chami, R., Lakissian, Z., Stocker, M., Scott, E., & Dieckmann, P. (2018). Cultural prototypes and differences in simulation debriefing. *Simulation in Healthcare*, 13(4), pp.239–246.

Verkuyl, M., et al. (2017). Virtual gaming simulation in nursing education: A focus group study. *Journal of Nurse Education*, 56(5), pp.274–280.

vSim ®. (n.d.). [online]. Available at: https://www.wolterskluwer.com/en/know/lippincott-product-training-support/nursing-students/vsim-for-nursing (Accessed 23 July 2021).

Wehbi, N. K., et al. (2018). A needs assessment for simulation-based training of emergency medical providers in Nebraska, USA. *Advances in Simulation*, 3, p.22.

World Health Organization. (2018). *Accreditation*. Society for Simulation in Healthcare [online]. Available at: https://www.euro.who.int/__data/assets/pdf_file/0011/383807/snme-report-eng.pdf (Accessed 7 May 2021).

Index

A

AACN, *see* American Association of Colleges of Nursing
AACN (2021) essentials, 137
Academia and practice, nursing informatics, 137–138
Academic and practice partnership (APP), 102–103
Accreditation implementation
   assessment process, 36
   EFMI AC2 Committee, 37
   site-visit panel, 36
      satisfactory, 37
      unsatisfactory, 37
Advance education and scholarship, clients/patients learning, 89–90
   digital learning needs of, families/communities
      challenges, 88–89
      communication, 86
      COVID vaccines, 86–87
      electronic health records, 87
      in-person appointments, 86
      National Institute on Aging (NIA) guidelines, 87–88
      patient advocacy organizations, 85
      portals, 89
      resources, 88
      social platforms, 85–86
      telehealth, 85
   eHealth literacy evolution
      digital health literacy, 84
      health technology tools, 83–84
      Lily Model, 85
      overview, 83
      skills, 84
      US Department of Health and Human Services (HHS), 84
   nursing professional development (NPD)
      description, 81–82
      and nursing education, 82–83
   synopsis, 90–91
Advancing nursing education and scholarship, 89–90
American Association of Colleges of Nursing (AACN), 48–51, 97, 137
   re-envisioned essentials
      competencies, 122
      domains, 121–122
      subcompetencies, 122–123
American Nurses Association, 27, 132
American Nurses Association Code of Ethics for Nurses (ANA, 2015), 58
APP, *see* Academic and practice partnership
Applicant preparatory work, 40–41
Artificial intelligence (AI), xviii, 53
Assessment for Collaborative Environments (ACE-15), 160

C

CAHPS, *see* Consumer Assessment of HealthCare Providers Surveys
Canadian Association of Schools of Nursing (CASN), 9–10, 135
CDS, *see* Center for Data Science
Center for Data Science (CDS), 106

Certification, nursing informatics
    Asia and India, 140–141
    Australia, 140
    Canada, 140
    Europe, 141
    Latin America, Brazil and Argentina, 141
    United States, 139
China's Hospital Information System (HIS), 24
Code gray: Ethical dilemmas in nursing, 58
Code of conduct
    independence and confidentiality, 38
    panel attitude, 39
    preparation and procedure, 37–38
    professional attitude, 38–39
Communicator online, 69–70
Community, 77–78
Consumer Assessment of HealthCare Providers Surveys (CAHPS), 161
COVID-19 pandemic, 86–87, 151
COVID vaccines, 86–87
Credentialing systems, 139

D

Data collection, 64–65
Debriefing models, 185
Delphi process, 187
Development of nursing informatics, Mainland China
    computer courses, 26
    domains, 26
    evaluation standards, 26
    first stage, 24
    Information and Communication Technologies (ICT), 26
    second stage, 24–25
    third stage, 25
    TTM workshop, 27
Digital dilemma, 65–66
Digital health, xv–xvii
    evolutions, 120–121
    framework, 125
    literacy, 84
Digital learning, patients/families/ communities
    challenges, 88–89
    communication, 86
    COVID vaccines, 86–87
    electronic health records, 87
    in-person appointments, 86
    National Institute on Aging (NIA) guidelines, 87–88
    patient advocacy organizations, 85
    portals, 89
    resources, 88
    social platforms, 85–86
    telehealth, 85
Digital psychology, 66–67
Digital tool of, technology giants
    about you, 74
    best practices
        hard target, 75–76
        mindful, ransomware and phishing, 76–77
        multi-factor authentication (MFA), 76
        protective tokens, 76
        security community, 77
    caring, digital you and security, 74
    cyber–health outcomes, 75
    digital psychology, 66–67
    digital wellness, 65–66
    family media agreements, 72
    and people skills, 69–70
    personal digital brand, 73
    personal processes, 67
        focus and distraction, 67–68
        processing, 68–69
        time management, 67
        weekly reviews, 69
    phubbing, 72
    profile photo, identification and first impression, 73–74
    social media and relationships, 72–73
    synopsis, 77–78
    trust factor, 74
    upgrades
        data and attention, 64
        devices and software, 65
        smartphone, 65
        social networks, 65
    and wellness, 70–71
        family, friends and coworkers, 71
Digital wellness, 65–66

personal stress threshold, 70
screen time, 71
self-care, 71
state of mind, 71
steps, 71

E

East African Community (EAC), 175–176
Education, nursing informatics, 136–137
EFMI AC2 Accreditation, 36
eHealth literacy evolution
    digital health literacy, 84
    health technology tools, 83–84
    Lily Model, 85
    overview, 83
    skills, 84
    US Department of Health and Human Services (HHS), 84
Electronic health record (EHR), xv, 52–53
Embracing a Digital World, xvi
Emory Nursing, 97–98
Emory Nursing Experience (ENE), 107
Emory Nursing Learning Center (ENLC), 103–105
Enabling digital technologies, xviii
ENE, *see* Emory Nursing Experience
ENLC, *see* Emory Nursing Learning Center
EQF, *see* European Qualifications Framework
The Essentials, 52
European Qualifications Framework (EQF), 141
Evaluation of based criteria, 41

F

Families/communities, digital learning
    challenges, 88–89
    communication, 86
    COVID vaccines, 86–87
    electronic health records, 87
    in-person appointments, 86
    National Institute on Aging (NIA) guidelines, 87–88
    patient advocacy organizations, 85
    portals, 89
    resources, 88
    social platforms, 85–86
    telehealth, 85
First nation-initiated TTM training workshop, 28
The Future of Nursing 2020–2030, 151
The Future of Nursing: Leading Change, Advancing Health (2011), 47

G

Graduate education, 1–2

H

Health and healthcare education
    current state
    intangibles attention
        ethical decision-making, 57–58
        leadership, 58–59
        philosophical ethics, 58
    overview, 47–48
    professional nursing education, leading dimensions
        AACN, 51
        baccalaureate and graduate programs, 50
        diversifying, 49
        The Essentials, 50
        graduate expansion, 51
        nursing programs, 49–50
        Registered Nurse to Master of Science in Nursing (RN-to-MSN), 50
        RN-to-BSN and RN-to-master's programs, 50
        Sullivan Commission, 49
        UMSON, 50
    re-envisioning nursing education roadmap
        academic–practice partnerships, 49
        community-based care, 48
        The Future of Nursing 2020–2030, 48
    synopsis, 59
    technology and practice innovation
        artificial intelligence (AI), 53
        clinical and virtual clinical simulation, 53–54

clinical practice preparation, 53
distance education challenges, 55
DNP program, 52
electronic health records (EHR), 52
The Essentials, 52
information systems, 52
learning management systems, 55
mobile healthcare (mHealth), 52
new challenges and opportunities, 53
standardized patients, 54
UMSON program, 52
web-enhanced course, 54
Healthcare education
affordability of, 57
health professions education, 55–56
Interprofessional Education Collaborative (IPEC), 56
practice and field application, 57
six health professions organizations, 56
workforce shortages, 57
Healthcare Information and Management Systems Society (HIMSS), 9
Healthcare Professional Satisfaction, 161
Healthcare systems, xv–xvi
Health information technology, 2–3
Health IT Curriculum Resources, 9
Health Services use, 161
HELINA Education Working Group, 181
HIMSS, *see* Healthcare Information and Management Systems Society
The HIMSS TIGER Global Interprofessional Competency Synthesis, 126
Hospital information system, 23

I

ICCAS, *see* Interprofessional Collaborative Competency Attainment Survey
ICTs, *see* Information and communication technologies
IMIA knowledge base and recommendations, 172
master of health informatics programmes, East Africa
higher educational institutions (HEI), 176
IUCEA document, 177
MSc HI degree programme, 177
master's curriculum, Francophone Africa
2020 Digital Health colloquium, 180
academic training programmes, 178
digital health, 179
WHO, 178
MSc HI curriculum review, Rwanda
digital health, job opportunities, 174
digital health, roles, 174–175
interoperability issues, 173
planning, 173–174
synopsis, 180–181
IMIA Recommendations in Biomedical and Health Informatics, 175–176
Implementing High-Quality Primary Care, 151
Informatics, technology and digital health
AACN re-envisioned essentials
competencies, 122
domains, 121–122
subcompetencies, 122–123
American Medical Informatics Association (AMIA), 115
assist development resources, 124–125
digital health framework, 125
faculty teaching, nurses, 123–124
The Healthcare Information Management Systems Society (HIMSS), 115
information and communication technologies (ICT), 115
nationally, internationally and interprofessionally, 116
nurses engagement, data and technology
communication technology, 117–118
information technology, 117–118
technology variety, 117
and nursing
digital health evolutions, 120–121
The National Academy of Medicine, 120
Nightingale, F. definition, 118–119
technology rich environment, 120
Werley, H.H., 119–120
synopsis, 126
The US Food and Drug Administration, 116
Informatics competency development model, China and Taiwan, 20–21
Informatics educational programs

Index

academia delivery
  international nursing informatics education, 10–12
challenges, 13
existing curricula, 9–10
faculty informatics competency, 12
need of
  development, 3
  health information technology, 2–3
  online DNP programs, 4
  Technology Informatics Guiding Education Reform (TIGER), 3
skills and competencies
  categories, 4, 8
  conceptual approach, 8
  international evolution and alignment, 8–9
  sources of, 9
standards and competencies, 5–8
synopsis, 13–14
Informatics nurse specialist (INS), 1
Informatics standards and competencies, 5–8
Information and communication technologies (ICTs), 140
INS, see Informatics nurse specialist
Institute of Medicine (IOM) report, 3
Intangibles attention
  ethical decision-making, 57–58
  leadership, 58–59
  philosophical ethics, 58
International Congress in Nursing Informatics (NI2006), 21
International health and healthcare education current state synopsis, 41–42
International Medical Informatics Association (IMIA), 172
International nursing informatics education
  Africa, 12
  Asia, 11–12
  Australia, 11
  Brazil and Canada, 10
  European nations, 11
  Korea, 12
  Netherlands and New Zealand, 11
  North America, 10
  South America, 10–11
  United States, 10
Interprofessional Collaborative Competency Attainment Survey (ICCAS), 159
Interprofessional education (IPE), 150
Interprofessional practice and education
  clinical learning environments, 159–160
  critical events of IPE, 160
  funding attribution, 166–167
  interprofessional competencies, 159
  interprofessional learning continuum model, 157–158
  IPE Core Data Set, 159
  knowledge generation, 155–157
    generating framework, 157
  Minnesota Northstar Geriatrics Workforce Enhancement Program (MN GWEP), 163–166
  national center, 152
  national center interprofessional information exchange, 162–163
  national partnerships, 154–155
  new IPE, 152
  Nexus, 152–153
  overview, 166
  Quadruple Aim outcomes, 160–162
  teamness, 160
  workplace learning, 154
IPE Core Data Set, 159–162

K

Knowledge, skills and attitudes (KSA), 188–189
Knowledge Generation, 155
  Developmental Evaluation, 155–156
  framework generation
    interprofessional learning continuum model, 157–159
    IPE Core Data Set, 159
KSA, see Knowledge, skills and attitudes

L

Learning objectives, simulation, 187–188
Lily Model, 85

M

Machine learning (ML), xviii
Master of health informatics programmes, East Africa
   higher educational institutions (HEI), 176
   IUCEA document, 177
   MSc HI degree programme, 177
Master's curriculum, Francophone Africa
   2020 Digital Health colloquium, 180
   academic training programmes, 178
   digital health, 179
   WHO, 178
Military Health No 1, 25
Minnesota Northstar Geriatrics Workforce Enhancement Program (MN GWEP)
   aim of, 164
   clinical transformation intervention, 164
   developmental evaluation approach, 166
   National Center, 164
   NCIIE and IPE Core Data Set, 165
Mobile nursing information technologies, 25
MSc HI curriculum review, Rwanda
   digital health, job opportunities, 174
   digital health, roles, 174–175
   interoperability issues, 173
   planning, 173–174

N

National Academies of Science, Engineering and Medicine (NASEM), 102
National Center, 154
National Center Expanded Interprofessional Learning Continuum Model (EIPLCM), 158
National center for interprofessional practice and education, 152
National Center Interprofessional Information Exchange (NCIIE)
   collaboration and collective understanding, 163
   description, 162
   protected health information (PHI), 162–163
   vision and evolution, 162
National Center Knowledge Generation strategy, 156
National League for Nursing (NLN), 187–188
National partnerships, 154–155
   Accelerating Community-based Interprofessional Education and Practice Initiative, 154
   external evaluation data, 155
   external evaluators and local researchers, 155
   interprofessional education and collaborative practice programs, 154
   Knowledge Generation, 155
      Developmental Evaluation, 155–156
      framework generation, 157–159
Needs assessments, 186–187
Nell Hodgson Woodruff School of Nursing (NHWSN), 97–98
New IPE, 152
Nexus, 152
   Knowledge Generation, 155
      Developmental Evaluation, 155–156
      framework generation, 157–159
   partnerships, 153
   principles, 153
NHWSN, see Nell Hodgson Woodruff School of Nursing
NI competency vs. management model, 27
NLN, see National League for Nursing
Non-technical skills (NTS), 189–190
NPD, see Nursing professional development
Nurse educator, 187–188
Nurses, own applications
   pediatric medication dosage calculator, 32
   the quality management application for discharge summaries, 32
Nurses engagement, data and technology
   communication technology, 117–118
   information technology, 117–118
   technology variety, 117
Nursing education, xvii
   and digital health strategies
      Centers for Disease Control and Prevention (CDC), 114

consumers, 114–115
informatics, technology and digital health (*see* Informatics, technology and digital health)
key elements, 126–127
nursing professional development (NPD), 82–83
Nursing informatics competencies; *see also individual entries*
future requirements and recommendations, 141–143
global perspective, 133–136
academia and practice, 137–138
certification, 139–141
education, 136–137
evaluation tools, 138
requirements and recommendations, 134
overview, 131–133
Nursing informatics education programs, Taiwan
clinical nurses, 22
educational goal, 23
hospital information system, 23–24
Master's/PhD Degree Examination Committee, 22
teaching units, 22
Nursing professional development (NPD)
description, 81–82
and nursing education, 82–83
experiences, 82–83
information technology, 82
Nursing simulation, 185
preparation session, 190
activity, 192–193
briefing, 191–192
debriefing, 193–194
evaluation, 194–195
pre-briefing/learner preparation, 190–191
types of, 186
knowledge, skills and attitudes (KSA) model, 188–189
learning objectives, 187–188
needs assessments, 186–187
non-technical skills (NTS), 189–190

P

Patient portals, 89
Pediatric medication dosage calculator, 32
Professional nursing education, leading dimensions
AACN, 51
baccalaureate and graduate programs, 50
diversifying, 49
The Essentials, 50
graduate expansion, 51
nursing programs, 49–50
Registered Nurse to Master of Science in Nursing (RN-to-MSN), 50
RN-to-BSN and RN-to-master's programs, 50
Sullivan Commission, 49
UMSON, 50
Project NeLL, 106–107
Protected health information (PHI), 162–163

Q

QSEN, *see* Quality and Safety Education
Quadruple Aim outcomes
National Center, 161–162
overview, 160–161
sources of, 161
Quality and Safety Education (QSEN), 135
Quality Assurance Education, Biomedical and Health Informatics (Europe EFMI)
accreditation, 34
certification, 35
strengths, weaknesses, opportunities and threats (SWOT) analysis, 36
Quality management application, discharge summaries, 32

R

Re-envisioning nursing education roadmap
academic–practice partnerships, 49
community-based care, 48
The Future of Nursing 2020–2030, 48
Regional e-Health Centre of Excellence (REHCE), 173

Registered Nurse to Bachelor of Science in Nursing (RN-to-BSN), 48
REHCE, *see* Regional e-Health Centre of Excellence
Reversing biases innovation
    data based *vs.* evidence based, 101
    people power, 100
    resources, 100–101
    time, 100
RN-to-BSN, *see* Registered Nurse to Bachelor of Science in Nursing
Rwandan Ministry of Health (MoH), 173
Rwanda's baseline curriculum *vs.* IMIA's Knowledge Base units, 175

S

SBEs, *see* Simulation-based experiences
SBL, *see* Simulation-based learning
Scholarship of teaching and learning (SoTL), 89
School of Nursing, 22–23
Self-assessment report template, 39
Shared vision, innovation hub
    academic practice partnership (APP), 97
    American Association of Colleges of Nursing's (AACN), 97
    Emory Healthcare (EHC), 97–98
    Joint Leadership Council (JLC), 98
    mission and vision, 97
Short-Form Health Survey (SF-36/SF-12), 161
Silicon Valley, 64
Simulation-based experiences (SBEs), 186–187
Simulation-based learning (SBL)
    description, 184
    future of, 195–196
    healthcare, 184–185
    nursing, 185
    simulation preparation session, nursing, 190
        activity, 192–193
        briefing, 191–192
        debriefing, 193–194
        evaluation, 194–195
        pre-briefing/learner preparation, 190–191
    types of, 186
        knowledge, skills and attitudes (KSA) model, 188–189
        learning objectives, 187–188
        needs assessments, 186–187
        non-technical skills (NTS), 189–190
Simulation-training program, 186
SMART objectives, 188
SoTL, *see* Scholarship of teaching and learning
State of mind, digital wellness, 71

T

Taiwan nursing informatics (NI), 20
Taiwan Nursing Informatics Association (TNIA), 20
    nurse certificate, 21
    training courses objectives, 20
    training courses topics, 21
Taiwan Training Model (TTM), 20
Teamness, 160
TeamSTEPPS program, 150
Technology and practice innovation
    artificial intelligence (AI), 53
    clinical practice preparation, 53
    clinical simulation and virtual clinical simulation, 53–54
    distance education challenges, 55
    DNP program, 52
    electronic health records (EHR), 52
    The Essentials, 52
    information systems, 52
    learning management systems, 55
    mobile healthcare (mHealth), 52
    new challenges and opportunities, 53
    standardized patients, 54
    UMSON program, 52
    web-enhanced course, 54
Technology changes and new applications, xv
Technology Informatics Guiding Education Reform (TIGER), 10, 133–135
    competency model, Mainland China
        BMI nursing assessment and care supports, 30
        concept transferring, 29

first nation-initiated TTM training workshop, 28
first proficient nursing informatics competency training program, 28
HIMSS TIGER certificates, 31
2nd Chinese National Nursing Informatics Conference, 31
workshop ideas, 28–29
Technology training, 88
Telehealth, 85–87
TIGER, *see* Technology Informatics Guiding Education Reform
TIGER Virtual Learning Environment (VLE), 9
TNIA, *see* Taiwan Nursing Informatics Association
Transformed health system, 153
TTM, *see* Taiwan Training Model
2020 HIMSS Nursing Informatics Workforce Survey, 102
2021 *AACN Essentials* and *2021 Future of Nursing Report*, 98

U

University of Maryland School of Nursing (UMSON), 48–49

W

Wellness of, digital platform
  about you, 74
  best practices, 75–77
  brand, 73
  caring and security, 74
  community, 77–78
  cyber–health outcomes, 75
  family, friends and coworkers, 71
  family media agreements, 72
  phubbing, 72
  profile photo, 73–74
  sleep, 71
  social media and relationships, 72–73
  trust factor, 74
Workforce cultivating disruptors, innovation hub
  big debts, bad data and bureaucratic messes, 99
  Center for Data Science (CDS), 106
  curious nurses welcome, 104–105
  Emory nursing learning center, 103–104
  future recommendations, 108
  great needs, waiting jobs, 101–102
  implications for academia and practice, 108
  long-standing challenge, 96
  Magnet® certification, 96
  National Continuing Education, 107
  nurses innovate, 102–103
  Project NeLL, 106–107
  reversing biases, innovation
    data based *vs.* evidence based, 101
    people power, 100
    resources, 100–101
    time, 100
  shared vision
    academic practice partnership (APP), 97
    American Association of Colleges of Nursing's (AACN), 97
    Emory Healthcare (EHC), 97–98
    Joint Leadership Council (JLC), 98
    mission and vision, 97
Workplace learning, 154

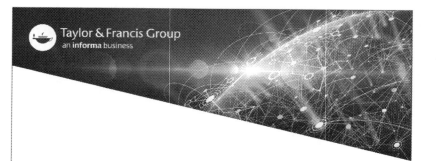

Printed in the United States
by Baker & Taylor Publisher Services